Helion & Company Limited
Unit 8 Amherst Business Centre
Budbrooke Road
Warwick
CV34 5WE
England
Tel. 01926 499 619
Email: info@helion.co.uk
Website: www.helion.co.uk
Twitter: @helionbooks
Visit our blog http://blog.helion.co.uk/

Front cover artwork: At 19,400 tonnes displacement when submerged, nuclear-powered cruise-missile submarines of the Project 949 Granit and Project 949A Antey classes were the largest vessel of this kind in the world, and the pinnacle of the Soviet development of submarines built to carry powerful anti-ship and cruise missiles. A total of 20 units (two Project 949 and 18 Project 949A) were planned, of which 14 were completed. Their primary armament included the P-700 Granit weapons system (ASCC/NATO-codename 'SS-N-19 Shipwreck'): each submarine carried 24 P-700 missiles in a row of 12 launchers on either side of the hull. Each P-700 was 10 metres long, weighted 7,000kg at launch, carried a warhead of 750kg, and had an operational range of 337 nautical miles (625km). (Artwork by Pablo Particio Albornoz © Helion & Company)

Designed and typeset by Farr out Publications, Wokingham, Berkshire
Cover design Paul Hewitt, Battlefield Design (www.battlefield-design.co.uk)

ISBN 978-1-915070-68-5

British Library Cataloguing-in-Publication Data
A catalogue record for this book is available from the British Library

We always welcome receiving book proposals from prospective authors.

CONTENTS

MAP OF EUROPE 1945–1992

Note: In order to simplify the use of this book, all names, locations and geographic designations are as provided in *The Times World Atlas*, or other traditionally accepted major sources of reference, as of the time of described events.

ABBREVIATIONS

ACW	anti-carrier warfare
ASW	anti-submarine warfare
CIWS	close-in weapons system (short-range, self-defence system for surface vessels)
CVBG	aircraft carrier battle group (USN)
GenStab	General Staff of the Soviet Armed Forces
HEN	Hotel, Echo, November (the first three classes of Soviet nuclear submarines)
INS	inertial navigation system (guidance system)
INS	Indian Navy Ship
LMC	liquid medal cooled reactor
MAD	magnetic anomaly detector
NII	Higher Naval Institute (USSR)
nm	nautical mile (2,000 yards or 1,852m)
OTH	Over the Horizon
PWR	pressurised-water reactor
RVSN	Soviet Strategic Missile Forces
Sail	The tower on the upper/dorsal surface of a submarine, also known as the 'fin' or previously, the 'conning tower'
SAM	surface-to-air missile
skipper	from the Dutch 'schipper' (literally 'shipper'), person who commands a boat
SLBM	submarine-launched ballistic missile
SLCM	submarine-launched cruise-missile
SSB	submarine equipped with ballistic missiles
SSBN	nuclear-powered submarine equipped with ballistic missiles
SSG	submarine equipped with guided missiles
SSGN	nuclear-powered submarine equipped with guided missiles
SSM	surface-to-surface missile
SSN	nuclear-powered attack submarine
TERCOM	terrain contour matching (guidance system)
TLAM	Tomahawk Land-Attack Missile
TsKB	design bureau
TTZ	tactical-technical requirement
USA	United States of America
USN	United States Navy
USS	United States Ship
USSR	Union of Soviet Socialist Republics
VLF	very low frequency

INTRODUCTION

This book is the result of study and research of a very special facet of naval warfare: the development of a specific naval weapon system in the Union of Soviet Socialist Republics (USSR, colloquially 'Soviet Union') that had no comparison in the West.

Devastated by the Second World War, and having no modern naval industry to start with, during the Cold War – a period of geopolitical tensions between ideological blocks centred on the USSR in the East and the United States in the West, lasting from 1947 until 1991 – the Soviet Union faced three major sea powers with centuries of tradition: the USA, Great Britain and France. During the Second World War, aircraft carriers replaced battleships as the main source of power of these three navies. Moreover, over the following years their naval aviation forces became capable of projecting power well away not only from their shores, but from their fleets too: indeed, they threatened the major cities of the USSR with nuclear holocaust. With land-based intercontinental missiles still undergoing research and development, Moscow had no option but to fall back upon its large system of design bureaus and shipyards, which if nothing else, were experienced in designing and manufacturing submarines. While complex to maintain and operate, submarines proved cheaper to design and build, and presented a credible threat against the enemy's major surface vessels. Consequently, it is unsurprising that the submarine became the tool Moscow decided to use to confront its primary opponents.

When studying its options, the only armament procurement authority in the USSR, the General Staff of the Soviet Armed Forces (GenStab), quickly concluded that the available submarine classes were rather limited in their capacity. Most were designed for use in proximity to the coast; they were diesel- and electric-powered, and thus slow; and their torpedoes had a rather limited range. The enemy thus had to literally run into one of them for the submarine to actually become a serious threat. Moreover, after having faced the best submarine forces that Germany, Italy and Japan were able to press into service, the United States Navy (USN) and Britain's Royal Navy possessed extensive experience in anti-submarine warfare and immense capacities in this field. After carefully studying its opponents' advantages and combat experiences from the Second World War, the GenStab concluded that it had to massively increase the firepower of its submarines: it needed to increase the range over which they could engage the enemy, and then equip them with weapons capable of at least disabling, if not outright sinking enemy surface vessels with a single blow. This led to the development of the concept of what in the West became known as the 'SSG' – and, later on, when nuclear power was introduced to service, the 'SSGN': conventional-powered and nuclear-powered submarines equipped with guided missiles.

Right from the start, both the SSG and the SSGN were purely Soviet-developed concepts, without precedent in the West. It was only decades later that Western navies began equipping their submarines with guided missiles: even then, these were mainly equipped with weapons for long-range land-attack, which provided them with a strategic role. On the contrary, from the start through to the end, the Soviet concept of the SSG and the SSGN was tactical by nature, limited to developing capability to combat surface warships.

Developing this concept – from an idea, via a paper design to a weapon system that not only worked but represented a serious threat to the enemy – was a painful, expensive and protracted process. Ultimately, while major SSGN classes of Soviet submarines became a matter of great national pride and prestige, they proved so expensive that they proved a heavy burden to the national defence budget; indeed, they played a role in eventually bankrupting the USSR. However, through developing such submarines, the Soviet Navy not only introduced a new variable to naval warfare, deeply impressing its opponents and causing them to invest heavily in the means of countering its new weapons systems but left its stamp on naval history.

1
WHISKEY CLASS

Soon after the onset of the Cold War, in 1947, the GenStab developed two clear strategic theses:

a) A major, all-out war with the West was unavoidable, and
b) The deployment of nuclear weapons was expected to be as common as the deployment of any other available weapons.

Although already organising, equipping and training the most powerful conventional ground forces in the world at the time, the GenStab was seeking ways to increase these forces' firepower. To its leading minds, usually famed as 'Soviet military theoreticians', it appeared that guided missiles offered the best solution – especially in conjunction with nuclear warheads that were already under development (the USSR conducted its first nuclear test in 1949). Furthermore, guided missiles promised to offer the option of delivering a decisive blow with a single stroke. When studying options for increasing the firepower of their submarines, the Soviets also concluded that equipping these with guided missiles would greatly expand their capabilities to combat enemy warships – to the degree where a relatively small submarine could deliver a similar amount of firepower to that of an aircraft carrier.

The Soviet Shipbuilding System

However, the realisation of the idea to deploy guided missiles proved anything but easy, as installing missiles on submarines was by no means a simple task. Indeed, even installing missiles on surface vessels was complex enough, having an impact upon their stability and buoyancy, and ships' hulls offered only limited space for the necessary installations. All of this was even more valid for submarines – especially when one adds the fact that guided-missile technology was still in its infancy, and thus the Soviets had to overcome massive obstacles in the process. Nevertheless, the stakes were considered high enough to be worth trying, even though the necessary technology was far from being researched, and even more so from being tested.

Moreover, the organisation of the necessary processes was not simple. In the USSR at the time, new ideas usually began with the Naval Staff issuing a set of desired capabilities. The Higher Naval Institute (NII) and the main design bureaus would then prepare a set of sketch plans to test the feasibility of the idea, on the basis of which the GenStab would prepare a set of tactical-technical requirements (TTZs). The results were fed back to the Naval Staff, which used them to prepare the TTZ, on the basis of which the ship was actually developed. The TTZ was usually developed in close cooperation with the design bureaus (TsKBs), which developed the sketch design and then the technical design on the basis of which the submarine was built. Contrary to the situation in the aviation industry, where design bureaus were heavily influential in procurement decisions of the GenStab, with few exceptions, it was the NII and the Naval Staff that developed the basic designs, with the TsKBs' influence remaining limited.

The TTZ had to be authorised by the Council of Ministers in Moscow before construction could be initiated. Once this was done, the Ministry of Shipbuilding became involved by planning and issuing orders for related materials, systems and subsystems, which were frequently made yet more complex by the requirement for these to come from all parts of the Soviet Union.

Stalin's 10-Year Plan

It is little known that in 1939 the Soviet Navy operated the world's largest submarine fleet. During the Second World War, however, most of Soviet industry suffered immense damage, including the major shipyards in the Black Sea and Leningrad (modern St. Petersburg) area. Nevertheless, in 1946, Soviet leader Joseph Stalin set up a special naval commission to study the lessons of the Second World War and to develop a 10-year plan for rebuilding the Soviet Navy. Within the first years of the resulting programme, this envisaged the completion of upgraded designs of warships suspended during the war, mainly minesweepers necessary to clear wartime minefields, but also for cruisers and destroyers. The second half of the plan, intended for realisation in the period from 1951–56, included the construction of new types of ships developed in the meantime.

Very early during their studies, the Soviets concluded that the main probable enemies of their navy would be the naval services of the USA, Great Britain and France. The fleets of all three were centred on more than 150 aircraft carriers of all classes. Unsurprisingly, such vessels became the primary concern for the GenStab and the Soviet Navy, even more so as new developments in nuclear weapons and naval aviation would enable them to deliver heavy blows against the USSR.[1]

As well as aircraft carriers, another danger was seen to be an amphibious landing on any of the coasts of the USSR behind the front line, forcing the Red Army and Soviet Navy land units to hold positions to repel such an invasion, causing a major disruption to Soviet war planning. In both of the above situations, the perceived threat came from the sea, and this was seen as a weakness of the Soviet armed forces. The Soviet Navy did not have the capacity to stop the US Navy from reaching its coasts: it possessed no carriers, and its surface fleet was old and obsolete, its weapons badly outdated. Indeed, the mass of its surface ships consisted of minor units, and most of its submarines were coastal, diesel-powered types: very few submarines could reach out to the Atlantic or Pacific Oceans. Soviet naval aviation also operated land-based aircraft with very limited range and was not in possession of air bases outside its national borders that could expand that range. With this fleet and with these threats, Moscow started to develop what in the following decades would become the 'Soviet Naval Strategy'.

A Soviet Whiskey-class attack submarine, seen on 10 March 1987. (US DoD)

The only quick, cheap and effective solution for the Soviets was to develop as soon as possible a massive submarine fleet able to match the 'carrier menace' far away from Soviet coasts. At that point in time, the naval commission had been able to work its way through the latest technology developed by the German Navy, captured in 1945 and brought to the USSR, and the Naval Staff decided to opt for a variety of specialised submarines. Intensive work was initiated on multiple designs, including medium submarines under Project 608, large vessels under Project 611, small submarines (Project 612) and two experimental designs, Projects 615 and 617, aiming to result in the production of 168 large, 204 medium and 123 small vessels. However, Stalin rejected such a plan on the grounds that it would overload the design bureaus. Instead, he insisted on focusing on only three classes: the mass of these were to be based on the medium-sized Project 608, with relatively few on the larger Project 611 and smaller Project 615.

Project 613

Perhaps the most influential of all the weapons systems captured in Germany was the Type XXI diesel-electric attack submarine: the first ever designed for protracted underwater operations in conjunction with guided torpedoes.[2] The Type XXI proved superior to the contemporary Soviet designs, to the extent that the Project 608 design was abandoned and the GenStab initiated work on an adapted version of the German design. The result was Project 613, which in the West became known under the name given to it by the Air Standardisation Coordination Committee (ASCC), the Whiskey-class submarine.[3]

The design of the Project 613 was developed by Design Bureau TsKB-18, directed by Chief Designer V.N. Peregrudov, and officially approved on 15 August 1948. The resulting submarine was 76 metres long, had a beam of 6.3 metres and a draught of 4.6 metres. It had a double hull, with seven watertight compartments, and a surfaced displacement of 1,080 tons, with a submerged displacement of 1,350 tons. The type's maximum operational depth was 200 metres, and its range was estimated at 8,580 nautical miles (nm) on the surface and 252 nautical miles when submerged.[4]

2
TOOLS OF THE TRADE

The principal result of Soviet studies of combat experience in naval warfare during the Second World War was that finding and then actually attacking an aircraft carrier was a major problem: carriers were fast-moving and heavily protected vessels, surrounded by multi-layered defences. At the time, the principal armament of Soviet submarines was the torpedo, a relatively short-range weapon. For a submarine to successfully deploy its torpedoes, it had to first find the enemy fleet and then penetrate a formation of escort vessels specialised in anti-submarine warfare, supported by aircraft with a similar function. If successful, the submarine then had to engage the carrier from a distance of only a few miles for its torpedoes to have a serious chance of a hit. This was a complex process, during which the submarine was very likely to be outrun by the enemy formation, or it had to risk running at high speed in order to bring itself into a position suitable for attack – and thus expose itself to early detection. The question was thus one of how to make a submarine capable of attacking from a stand-off distance. If it could do so, it had a chance of damaging or sinking either escort warships or even the aircraft carrier itself, thereby reducing the speed and manoeuvrability of the enemy formation, which in turn would enable it – or other submarines – to attack with torpedoes from short range.

Another Soviet conclusion was that the most effective weapon deployed against aircraft carriers during the Second World War was the heavy bomb. Actually hitting a ship with one had proved extremely costly until the Japanese developed their Yokosuka MXY-7 Ohka, a rocket-powered, human-guided, suicide attack aircraft. As the Soviets were not interested in pursuing a suicide mission, their solution was to replace the human in the bomb with a guidance system, and then propel everything to high speed: in essence, to develop a guided missile. These were the basic ideas that drove the GenStab and the Soviet Navy into a race to develop submarines equipped with guided missiles.

Change of Fortunes

Joseph Stalin's death on 5 March 1953 enabled a series of profound economic and political reforms in the USSR – including a dramatic

An MXY-7 Ohka flying bomb made by Japan, seen after the capitulation of 2 September 1945. (US Navy)

change in the 10-Year Naval Development Plan. While Stalin had emphasised the construction of big surface units, his successor, Nikita Khrushchev, had different ideas. Searching for solutions to reduce the immense spending on defence, he emphasised a major decrease in conventional elements of the armed forces and their replacement by nuclear weapons, primarily delivered by missiles. The Soviet Navy was to have its submarine fleet reduced from nearly 1,200 small coastal units to about 300 ocean-going vessels, armed with guided missiles and nuclear warheads. Three years later, Khrushchev's reforms were followed by the assignment of a new Commander-in-Chief of the Navy, Admiral Sergey G. Gorshkov. At 41, he was young for a flag officer, but he was already perfectly aware of the potential offered by missiles and nuclear weapons, while conscious of the fact that Soviet industry would take time to research, design and construct all the necessary technology, and that the Navy would need further time to absorb these. Correspondingly, Gorshkov pushed for the Navy and industry to work closely together in order to bring into service all the new ideas.

Project Volna

On 26 January 1954, the Council of Ministers approved a plan for Project Volna: the development of long-range ballistic and cruise missiles deployable from submarines. With several designs undergoing development, the project yielded almost immediate fruit, even if with rather poor results. Lavochkin's P-40 was cancelled, together with the related submarine design, Project 624 – because the missile was too big. For similar reasons, the same fate soon befell fellow engineer Sergey Ilyushin's P-20. The sheer size of the missile forced the Navy to select one of the nuclear-powered Project 627-class submarines as a carrier (ASCC/NATO codename 'November'): they were the only vessels that provided a suitable beam of at least 9.2 metres and enough space for other modifications. The result was Project 653, a submarine with a beam of 12.2 metres, providing enough space for two P-20s. The technical study and set of drawings were completed by 1958, and the Council of Ministers authorised the construction of the first two of a planned 18 units at the shipyard in Severodvinsk. At that time, a comparison between the P-20 and the R-11FM resulted in the decision to cancel the P-20 in favour of the latter SLBM (submarine-launched ballistic missile) offering the option of easier installation. Therefore, the P-20 was cancelled without replacement.[1] However, the R-11FM proved a disappointment, and was cancelled as well. Meanwhile, Georgy Beriev's P-10 was adapted to the Project 611P-class submarine (ASCC/NATO codename 'Zulu'), modified through the addition of a hangar astern of the sail, necessary to roll-out the missile and erect it into the firing position – towards the front of the boat. The submarine was ready by 1957 and is known to have undertaken at least four test-launches, apparently concluded successfully.

Project Volna

In October 1955, Khrushchev held a meeting with members of the GenStab and the Naval Staff to discuss the future composition of the Soviet Navy. Despite the failures of the above-mentioned projects, the Soviet leader was deeply impressed by demonstrations of new anti-ship missiles and expressed doubts about the future of surface fleets: indeed, he wanted to focus entirely on the development of bombers and submarines equipped with anti-ship missiles. With his Minister of Defence, Marshal Georgy Zhukov, supporting this conclusion, work on the majority of major surface warships was stopped by December 1955. In August 1956, the Council of Ministers not only approved a new seven-year plan for development of new submarine weapons but ordered the rapid construction of two new classes of submarines armed with nuclear strategic ballistic and cruise missiles, while Khrushchev rubber-stamped proposals for an expansion of the submarine missile programme. The latter was to be pursued along two lines: priority was given to SLBMs – such as the R-13/D-2 (ASCC/NATO codename 'SS-N-4 Sark') – while a parallel programme for development of long-range/strategic cruise missiles was also conducted.

Project Volna, as the resulting plan for further development of the Soviet Navy became known, resulted in intensive activity by several design bureaus from the aviation and naval sectors. This resulted in missile designs such as the Raduga KS-1 Komet (ASCC/NATO codename 'AS-1 Kennel', and in its shore-launched version, 'SS-C-2B Samlet'), the 4K32 Shchuka ('SS-N-1 Scrubber'), the turbojet-powered Shtorm and the V-2-based R-11FM SLBM. Eventually, the

KS-1 was adapted for aircraft and coastal defence; while the Shtorm was abandoned but its aerodynamic design served as a template for the subsequent ship-launched Raduga P-15 Termit ('SS-N-2 Styx'). The Shchuka, meanwhile, was developed into a primary weapon for a new destroyer class. The primary problem in all cases – but especially regarding the R-11FM – was the missiles' primitive inertial navigation system (INS), which resulted in poor precision. While this was not as important if they were equipped with nuclear warheads, neither the Navy nor the GenStab were satisfied, for what they wanted was a missile capable of causing catastrophic damage to a surface target while armed with a conventional warhead, and a missile compatible with submarines. The bureaus and designs that entered this competition included the Beriev P-10 (with range of 600km), the Ilyushin P-20 (a big missile with a near-strategic range) and the Lavochkin P-40 (with range of about 300km).

The intensity of all these developments reached such a pace that Krushchev eventually reactivated the OKB-52 design bureau, led by Vladimir Nikolayev Chelomy, who had fallen into disfavour during the last years of Stalin's rule, with his bureau disbanded and all his academic accolades removed.[2] However, recognising Chelomy as one of the best missile designers in the USSR, Khrushchev not only reinstated him into his position (the latter quickly returned the favour by contracting Khrushchev's son to work for him as an engineer), but also ordered him to revive his project for a submarine-launched cruise-missile that could threaten the US coast. Originally based on a mix of the German V-1 and the British-made Rolls-Royce Nene turbojet engine, Chelomy's design was named KhN and aimed to deliver a missile with a range of 500km. While Chelomy insisted on using his own designs, the Navy began introducing its own, including, a weapon launched from a container or a silo which received the designation starting with 'P'. The new missile thus received the designation 4K95, and the entire weapons system P-5: the ASCC/NATO assigned it the codename 'SS-N-3 Shaddock'.

As mentioned above, the P-5 was originally meant to serve as a strategic land-attack weapon, and its warhead was expected to be nuclear. However, soon after the project was relaunched, in 1956 the OKB-52 bureau was advised to develop a conventional, 900kg high-explosive warhead. The next problem was the fact that the missile was to be carried and launched from a submarine. Considering the constraints of contemporary submarine hulls, Chelomy and his team decided to pack it into a transportation container which would also serve as a launcher. To limit the size of the container, he designed foldable wings. However, the primary problem was the act of launching the missile from the container, and thus from the submarine. Contemporary technology prohibited an under-surface launch: the boat had to surface, power-up the electrics and hydraulics of the container, erect it into the launching position, open it, establish its position relative to the target and programme the flight parameters into the guidance system of the missile. All of this had to be done within 20 minutes of the submarine's surfacing.

While his team focused on developing the watertight container that could serve as a launcher, and making sure the force of the boosters and the automatic process of unfolding the wings upon launch would not impede the missile's performance, Chelomy – understanding that the submarine-launched missile could not be launched successfully with its own turbojet engine alone – decided to adapt two external, expendable solid fuel boosters: these were to be used to accelerate the missile to the speed necessary to power-up the turbojet. Even once all these issues were solved to a satisfactory level, there remained the problem that the complete process of surfacing, powering-up the launch container, aligning the missile and launching it had to be carried out within 20 minutes: this proved impossible to fix, only to shorten to less than 30 minutes.

Ultimately, although not entirely satisfactory, the P-5 proved superior to all other competitors and was selected to serve on board the future SSGs and SSGNs of the Soviet Navy. The operational range was estimated at 300 nautical miles: well outside the visual range of their potential targets, but also outside that of the submarine. Therefore, OKB-52, TsKB-18 and the Navy were forced to find a solution for target acquisition and guidance. The result was the P-35 Reduit weapons system, which included a fire-control radar installed on the submarine (ASCC/NATO codename 'Front Door/ Front Piece') and a datalink with which targeting information could be provided by another submarine. It was precisely this flexibility that was to convert the P-5 into a highly versatile weapons system, adaptable not only to submarines, but a number of surface vessels too – despite the fact that the big missile was rapidly becoming obsolete even before entering service. Indeed, ultimately, the P-5 not only became a tool of learning for the first generation of the Soviet Navy's missile men, but also greatly influenced further development of electronic warfare and electronic countermeasures.

From Project 613 to Project 644

Meanwhile, a large number of Project 613-class submarines were constructed, introducing a host of new capabilities to the Soviet Navy. Thanks to the addition of a new oxygen generator in 1951, the submarine proved capable of 200 hours of submerged navigation, while – following the introduction of elastic foundations for the engines – it had much reduced acoustic emissions. Unsurprisingly, construction of no fewer than 350 such vessels was ordered. Zhukov and the GenStab largely agreed with this demand but, keeping in mind the pending introduction to service of nuclear powerplants, they reduced the programme to a total of 215 units. These were constructed between 1951 and 1958 in four different shipyards.[3]

The large fleet of common design provided the Soviet Navy with a great pool of units for further research and development. Project 613 vessels were consequently modified for lots of different purposes. Following successful flight testing of the P-5 at the Kapustin Yar range in 1956, the decision was taken to adapt it to the 37th submarine of the Project 613 class. Because Project 644 was to serve for experimentation and training purposes only, TsKB-18 and the Navy decided to keep the installation simple, with the missile container installed astern of the sail, on the deck. Designated S-146, and commissioned to service on 30 June 1953, this submarine was converted to the configuration designated Project 644 by a team from TsKB-18 led by Pavel P. Pustintsev at the Severodvinsk shipyard between November 1956 and November 1957. Upon its appearance, it promptly earned itself an appropriate ASCC/NATO codename: 'Whiskey Single Cylinder'.

Experimentation

Between 1957 and 1959, the S-146 ran a total of 21 test-firings of P-5s in the White Sea. The first, attempted on 1 and 2 November 1957, failed due to a malfunction of the electrical system of the missile container. The first test-launch thus took place on 22 November – and even then, it was only partially successful. Instead of flying over 350km, as expected, the missile crashed into the sea after travelling for only 35–50km. Nevertheless, the test proved that the crew and the hull were well-enough protected, with no damage caused by the missile launch. Following the successful conclusion of further testing, the Soviet Navy officially accepted the P-5 into operational service on 19 June 1959. That said, S-146 continued testing the

S-146, the sole Project 644 submarine (ASCC/NATO codename 'Whiskey Single Cylinder'), seen on the surface with its launch container in firing position. (US DoD)

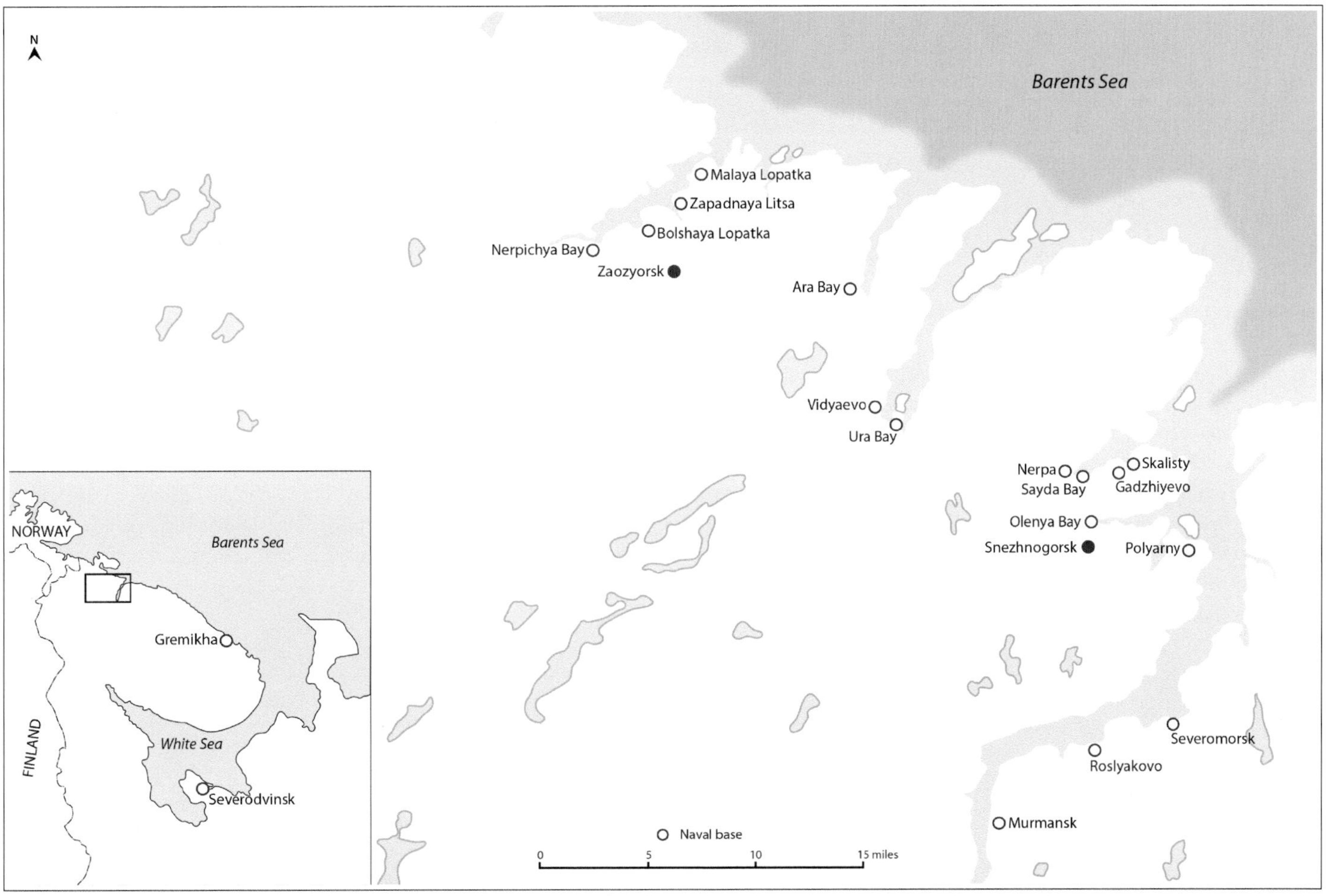

Soviet naval bases on the Kola Peninsula. (Map by George Anderson)

system – especially between May and June of the same year, in the Kola Bay area, resulting in several modifications to the missile's and submarine's electronics, and improved subvariants of the weapon, designated P-5D and P-6. Gradually, the weapon was repurposed away from the land-attack role to that of an anti-ship missile.

Lessons Learned

The testing of the P-5 from the S-146 never proved satisfactory. Indeed, the combination of this missile with the submarine never reached expected specifications, and it was obvious that the submarine would experience major problems just trying to bypass NATO anti-submarine warfare barriers in order to reach designated patrol stations off the most likely targets in the Atlantic Ocean: by the sheer nature of its diesel-electric power plant, the submarine would have to surface several times in order to recharge its batteries. The limited endurance of the Project 644-class submarine meant that even then it could remain on patrol station for only a few days. All of this meant that the Navy would need many weeks' forewarning before it could bring its boats into a position to open hostilities. Furthermore, just like the entire Project 613 class, the S-146 lacked proper means of communication with the General Staff of the Navy, both during the transit to the patrol station and once on station. The means of radio communication in service at the time were extremely unreliable and the GenStab was not keen to risk loss of contact with any platforms carrying nuclear weapons and deployed far away from the USSR. As a result, even standard Project 613-class submarines were always deployed relatively close to their home ports in the Baltic Sea, the Black Sea and the Pacific. Unsurprisingly, the S-146 never carried out any operational deployments. Indeed, it seems to have suffered significant damage during testing in the White Sea during May and June 1959 and required extensive repairs. How far the latter were successful remains unclear, but what is known is that the submarine was decommissioned in 1965.

A poor, but authentic photograph of P-80, one of only six Project 644-class units ('Whiskey Twin Cylinder'). Both launchers for P-5 missiles are clearly visible in their stored position. (US DoD)

Increasing Capacity

Although only partially satisfied with the testing of the P-5, the GenStab and the Soviet Navy decided to continue modifying additional Project 613 vessels to the Project 644-standard. The logical next step was to expand the number of missiles per submarine. In this regards, major issues were the installation of two instead of just a single missile container, and the fact that the overpressure caused by the blast from the missile's boosters during the launch would cause damage to underwater parts of the hull. Prepared by the same team of the TsKB-18 bureau led by Pustintsev in 1956 and 1957, the new modification retained the designation Project 644 but received a new ASCC/NATO codename: 'Whiskey Twin Cylinder'. It included the installation of two containers for P-5 missiles, both pointing towards the rear: one on either side of the hull, behind the sail. The launch procedure could be undertaken only when the submarine was on the surface, and after launch containers were pointed 16 degrees upwards. This was a big handicap, for the submarine depended on its invisibility – below the sea surface – for survival. However, the range of the P-5 was expected to keep it away from harm during time of a war. Related modifications were undertaken by the Gorkiy shipyard on six submarines – S-44, S-46, S-69, S-80, S-158 and S-162 – all assigned to the Northern and Pacific Fleets.

During their service with the Soviet fleet, these six units received many decorations and much praise. They also became the primary tool of training the first generation of crews in this new method of naval warfare. However, they rarely conducted operational deployments, usually undertaking only relatively short cruises along the Soviet coast. The furthest any went was in 1968, when S-46 was deployed – together with two standard Project 613 vessels, S-74 and S-243 – to the western Black Sea during the military intervention by Warsaw Pact forces in Czechoslovakia. Nevertheless, they pioneered the concept of joint operations with other submarines, and thus began the development of suitable tactics and doctrine.

S-80 was lost in the White Sea on 27 January 1961 during an exercise – probably due to a leak in its equipment that caused catastrophic damage. This accident heavily impacted the Main Staff of the Soviet Navy because it was a new submarine with new technologies. Moreover, 68 crew were on board, surpassing its normal complement of 56: they became the first casualties of this unsung war. The Main Staff of the Soviet Navy created a special unit to locate the sunken submarine. When this was done in 1968, a secret operation was undertaken to raise and salvage the wreck from its watery tomb at a depth of 196 metres. The submarine was raised from the bottom of the sea a year later, and after inspection was

A rear view of a Project 644-class submarine in the process of leaving the Balaklava submarine base on the Crimean Peninsula. (Soviet Navy)

A front view of a Project 644-class submarine during Warsaw Pact exercises in the 1960s. (Soviet Navy)

sent to scrap due to the heavy damage suffered and the obsolescence of its technology. Kept secret in the USSR, this operation remained unknown in the West, even though it was the first time in history that a sunken submarine was raised from the bottom of the sea without assistance from divers.[4]

Expansion of the Fleet

Other projects and technologies were improving in parallel in the USSR as the Project 644-class developed, namely nuclear propulsion and new missiles that were more accurate and had better performance. For these reasons, the class was cut to six units, with the remaining two units modernised for other uses. S-158 was converted to the Project 644 standard between 14 October 1958 and 31 August 1960 and assigned to the Northern Fleet. In 1962, it underwent conversion to a new subclass denominated Project 644-7. During this modification, a new system was installed allowing the submarine to use different missiles without any major change. The missiles available were the the P-5, P-5D and P-7, which are discussed in the following chapter. This vessel, after firing more than 40 missiles in tests and training during it operational life, was assigned to the Black Sea Fleet, where it fulfilled a patrol of 201 days. The S-162 was the last unit of the class after being modernised to Project 644 standard, between 1958 and 1961. It was altered to the sub-version designated 644D and served as the test platform of the P-5D missile. In 1964, it was assigned to the Black Sea Fleet, where it received many mentions and recommendations for its level of training and efficiency in conducting missile-firing exercises. The S-162 thus enjoyed a long and distinguished service before being decommissioned in 1982.

Project 665

While still working on the first two experimental missile-carrying submarines, the GenStab, Soviet Navy and industry refocused their attention to the elimination of various flaws in the design and an increase in the military efficiency of modified submarines and their missiles through reducing the time on the surface and minimising damage caused by firing the weapons. In April 1957, the Council of Ministers authorised the Ministry of Shipbuilding to task TsKB-112, under Chief Designer B.A. Lyeontyev, with modifying additional Project 613-class submarines to the standard designated Project 665 (ASCC/NATO codename 'Whiskey Long-Bin').

A Project 665-class submarine inside the port of Sevastopol. Note the dramatic change in the design of the sail, with two pairs of missile launchers atop each other. (Author's collection)

Table 1: Project 613, Project 644 and Project 665-Class Submarines				
	P-613 ('Whiskey')	P-613 ('Whiskey Single Cylinder')	P-644 ('Whiskey Twin Cylinder')	P-665 ('Whiskey Long-Bin')
Propulsion	2 diesel engines, 37-D, 4,000hp 2 electric engines, PG-101, 1,350hp			
Length (m)	76			85
Beam (m)	6.3			6.7
Draught (m)	4.6			5.8
Displacement (surfaced/ submerged, tons)	1,080/1,350			1,490/1,660
Operational Depth (m)	170–200			
Speed (surfaced/ submerged, knots)	18.2/13			15.4/11
Crew	52			
Endurance	5,000nm at 10 knots surfaced 260nm in economical submerged 30 days			8,500nm at 10 knots surfaced. 400nm in economical submerged 45 days
Weapons Systems	6 x 533mm (4 forward, 2 stern) 12 torpedoes or 24 AMD-1000 mines	1 x P-5 6 x 533mm (4 forward, 2 stern) 6 torpedoes	2 x P-5 6 x 533mm (4 forward, 2 stern) 6 torpedoes	4 x P-5 4 x 533mm (4 forward)

An early photograph of a 'Whiskey Long-Bin', as the Project 665-class submarines were codenamed by NATO. (Author's collection)

The submarine still had to surface to launch its missiles, but it could fire a salvo of four weapons – increasing the probability of saturating the enemy defences – and the launch containers and related installations were far better protected than before. The result was an operational weapons system.[5]

The modifications applied by TsKB-112 during the conversion of Project 613-class submarines to the Project 665 standard had significant effects upon their performance. Their length was increased from 76 to 85 metres, the beam widened from 6.3 to 6.7 metres and the average draught from 4.6 to 6.8 metres, while displacement increased from 1,080 to 1,350 tons on the surface, and from 1,490 to 1,660 tons when submerged.[6] In turn, the greater length provided more space for other equipment – mainly for batteries and on the Project 665, there were now enough of these to extend the submerged range from the original 260 to 400 nautical miles.

The effects of the main changes in structural dimensions implied a change in the overall hydrodynamics, with a loss of performance and efficiency. In this particular case, the speed on the surface fell from 18.2 to 15.4 knots and when submerged from 13 to 11 knots – an unavoidable situation when the submarine retained its propulsion plant. That said, the range of the vessel increased from 5,000 to 8,500 nautical miles, providing a more flexible strategic capacity. The aspect impacted most negatively was acoustic by nature. The large sail of the Project 665 heavily disturbed the flow of water, creating turbulence. As a result, these submarines were very noisy, which made them easy to detect by sonar – especially during transit into the combat zone. Nevertheless, the Whiskey Long-Bin-class vessels were rushed into production and then into service, and they undoubtedly represented the first generation of operational SSGs, capable of seriously menacing enemy surface warships. That was the class's major historic and military value.

Lyeontyev and his team produced a rather unusual design: they integrated four missile containers into the structure of the sail, all already inclined at 14 degrees and thus in a position that enabled them to launch as soon as opened, while greatly reducing the weight by making unnecessary all the hydraulics previously needed to bring the launch containers into the firing position. In this fashion, the TsKB-112 bureau managed to save much time during the launch procedure, even if the overall result might appear rather ungainly to many: the submarines modified in this way had a giant bulge around their sail hence their ASCC/NATO codename.

Between 1961 and 1963, six Project 613-class submarines were converted to the P-665 standard: S-61, S-64, S-142, S-152, S-155

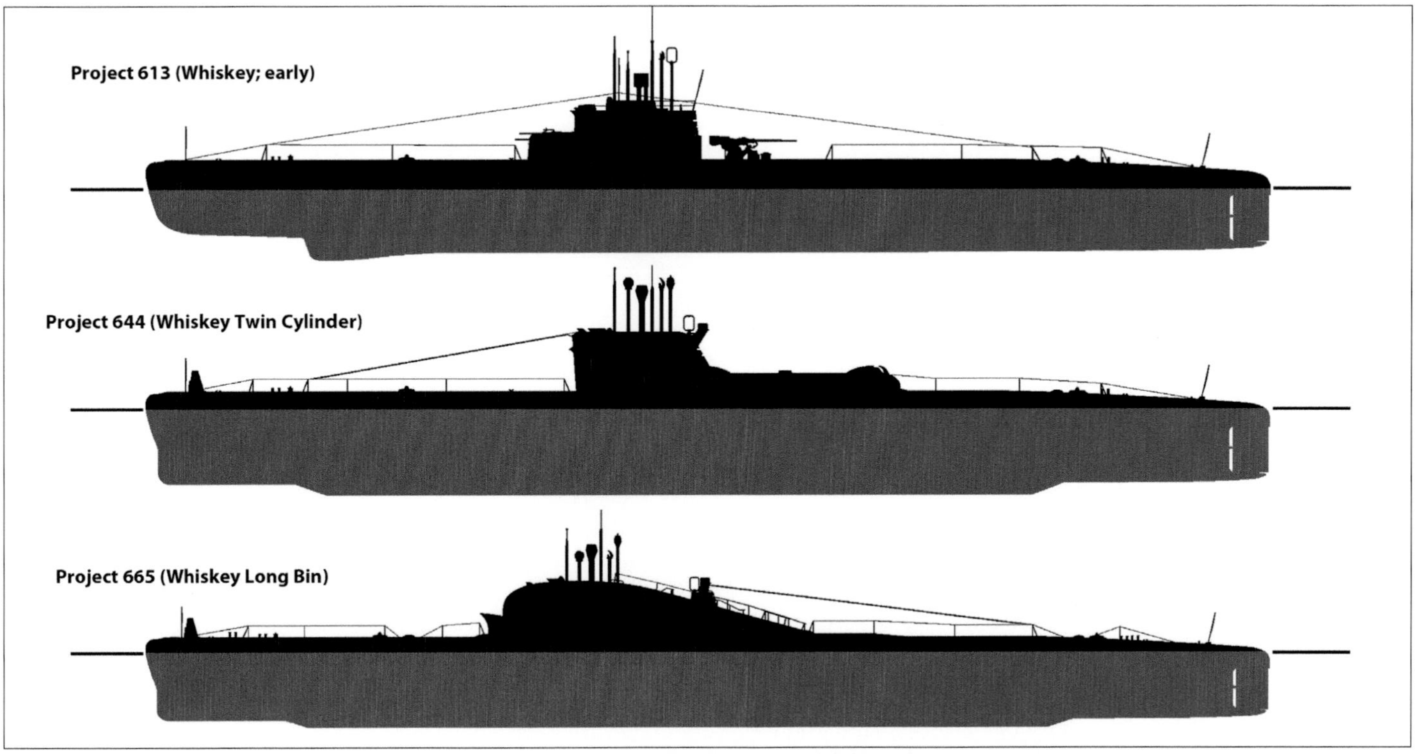

A simplified comparison of the designs of the Project 613, Project 644 and Project 665-class submarines. (Diagram by Tom Cooper)

Three submarines of the Project 665 class tied up at a pier at a Pacific base. (Author's collection)

and S-164. After their conversion in northern shipyards, they spent several years in training and testing before being transferred to other fleets (while the Northern Fleet received more modern and better submarines) as follows:

- S-61, S-64: 12th Squadron, 124th Brigade, Pacific Fleet
- S-142, S-152, S-155: 13th Squadron, 40th Brigade, Baltic Fleet
- S-146: Northern Fleet, Baltic Fleet and, from 1967, Black Sea Fleet

While some have claimed that the GenStab intended to order 76 units of the Project 665 class, the availability of new designs prevented this from happening. That said, all the boats of this class enjoyed a long and successful career and were withdrawn from service only in 1978–1982.

A beautiful study of a Project 665-class submarine. Of particular interest is the design of the top of the sail, around the rear pair of P-5-launchers. (Soviet Navy)

3
JULIETTS, THE SAFE SOLUTION

Long before obtaining evidence for the feasibility of operating guided missiles from submarines, the GenStab had already initiated work on the first custom-tailored design. The result was designated the Project 651-class (ASCC/NATO codename 'Juliett').

Project 651

The initial technical design for the diesel-electric-powered Project 651-class submarines was prepared by Design Bureau OKB-18 (Chief Designer Abram S. Kassatsiyer) by May 1958. It was approved in early 1959, promptly followed by an official order for the Severodvinsk shipyard to start construction. The configuration included two double launchers – both inside the hull, one installed forward and the other aft of the sail – and the installation of a search radar inside the front section of the sail, covered by two hydraulically powered doors. Project 651-class vessels were designed to be particularly strong: their internal bulkheads were made of steel capable of resisting pressure of 60kg/mm^2, enabling diving depths over 100 metres deeper than earlier Soviet submarines. The hull of the first five submarines of this class was made of low-magnetic steel, which reduced their magnetic signature (important in the face of magnetic anomaly detectors – MADs – in widespread service with NATO): due to its susceptibility to corrosion, this material was replaced by 'normal submarine steel' from the sixth boat onwards. Moreover, because it was expected to remain on station for dozens of days, the Project 651-class provided better comfort for the crew, and included machinery installed on elastic foundations to reduce engine noise.

The propulsion included two D-43 main diesel engines (each of 4,000hp), with two PG-141 electric motors (each of 3,000hp), and two PG-140 electric motors for creeping (each of 200hp). Four banks each of 152 cells of batteries – the first in the Soviet Navy to include silver-zinc elements – were charged by the 2D-42 system (1,750hp). These were the first submarine batteries in the Soviet Navy to include silver-zinc elements, and this caused maintenance issues, starting with the fifth boat, but more reliable lead-acid cells were installed instead.[1]

The hull design and batteries provided a good underwater speed of 18 knots for 90 minutes, or three knots over a distance of 810 nautical miles in silent mode. The crew had enough oxygen to remain submerged for 800 hours.

Originally, the Project 651-class vessel was to operate two different missile systems: the P-5 and the P-6. Because of this, every boat was equipped with two different fire-control systems and, before each patrol, it took the crew two days to configure the hardware to the necessary specification. This practice ended only once the P-5 was withdrawn from service in 1966. The P-6 – which included the 4K48 missile (the weapons system and the missile received the ASCC/NATO codename 'SS-N-3c Shaddock') – had a range of 310 nautical miles against surface targets, and could be launched while the submarine was underway at a speed of up to eight knots, and at Sea State 4 (moderate to rough). The longer range of the P-6s required the installation of the new Success-U fire-control system, which enabled the submarine to receive targeting information from aircraft via a datalink. However, there remained problems related to the act of actually launching several missiles in quick succession: the turbojet engine of the following weapon tended to seize when ingesting the smoke from the previous missile, requiring the vessel to first clear the area filled by smoke before launching the next one. Around the same time the P-5 was withdrawn from service, all the Juliett-class SSGNs were equipped with anechoic foam tiles along the entire

The Project 651-class submarine K-68 with its front launcher for P-5 or P-6 missiles in the erected position. (Voeno Tehnichky Zbornik)

hull, which helped decrease the level of noise emitted into the sea, reducing the distance from which they could be detected by sonar. The Project 651-class became the first of the Soviet Navy to be modified this way. The only problem was that the glue used frequently failed, resulting in the loss of tiles during operations.

A view into one of the two launchers of P-5 or P-6 missiles of the Project 651-class, while under construction. (Author's collection)

The remainder of the weapons system included six 533mm torpedo tubes forward and four 406mm tubes aft, but the space inside the submarine was limited to the degree that there were no reloads: all the torpedoes had to be loaded into their tubes before the submarine left port.[2]

The Project 651-class submarines, however, had three main handicaps in their design. The first was the structural deflectors installed in the rear area of the launchers, designed to avoid damage from the blast of the missiles. They produced a lot of flow noise when the submarine was submerged, making them easy to detect – and identify – by NATO sonars from long range.[3]

A close-up view of the fire-control radar (here in folded condition) of the Success-U system, seen on the submarine K-68. Note that the radar was installed in the front section of the sail. (Voeno Tehnichky Zbornik)

Another problem was the necessity to surface before deploying the fire-control radar and launching missiles. During this stage of action, the boat remained extremely vulnerable and, if detected, had minimal ability to survive a counterattack. The last weakness in the original design was the submerged speed. The primary targets of Project 651-class submarines were carrier battle groups, which frequently sailed at speeds of 25 knots or more. The Julietts were unable to reach this speed, which meant that they had no ability to actively pursue their targets, something even silver-zinc cells were unable to improve.

The Nuclear Mess

The staff of the Soviet Navy originally requested the construction of 72 Project 651 submarines, but this number was reduced to 36,

Major Soviet naval bases in the Baltic Sea. (Map by George Anderson)

and then to 16. The reason was political by nature: during the late 1950s, the Khrushchev administration assigned priority to nuclear-powered submarines, three classes of which entered production by 1961. Although two of these were based on the Project 651-class's design, they offered vastly improved performance and endurance and proved capable of carrying twice as many missiles. The question was thus not why the Soviet Navy constructed only 16 boats of the Project 651 class, but why it constructed them at all.

The answer was the capacity of the Soviet nuclear industry, which was unable to deliver the necessary number of nuclear reactors – known under the designation HEN14 – for all the nuclear-powered submarines under construction between 1957 and 1962. With two VM-A reactors (each with an output of 70MW) being necessary for every single vessel, the Navy needed 112 new reactors within only five years. Indeed, even the decision to introduce three new types of nuclear-powered submarines around the same time was dictated by Soviet industrial capacity: while two of these – Projects 651 and 675 – were powered by the same powerplant, the other was propelled by a different system, making things at least a bit easier for the industry. Even then, the rushed introduction to service of nuclear power caused so many problems and resulted in such severe accidents that much of the early Soviet nuclear submarine fleet spent the first years of its service moored to piers, waiting for shipyards to fix problems. This, in turn, was the reason why the Project 651 type was pursued, although still conventionally powered: submarines of the Juliett-class proved highly reliable and popular in service.

Overburdened Shipyards

Despite all the submarines' many problems, the availability of a large number of SSGs and SSGNs prompted the GenStab into outright megalomania, with the idea being born to counter every one of the USN's carrier battle groups (CVBGs) with at least one missile-equipped submarine. This went so far that the Council of Ministers was persuaded to authorise construction of new boats at two shipyards, thus duplicating not only the expense, but also the requirement for necessary manning and materials. In the light of such circumstances, the Project 651 class appeared unimportant, and the number of new submarines constructed to this design continued decreasing: from the original requirement for 72, to seven units for each of five regiments (for a total of 35 boats), then to one regiment with six units with the Northern Fleet, one with four units in the Pacific Fleet and the balance split between the Baltic and Black Sea Fleets.[4]

The next problem was that of finding shipyards suitable for construction of the Project 651 class. The two major submarine-constructors – Shipyard 402 in Severodvinsk and Shipyard 109 in Komsomolsk-na-Amur – were already overburdened with construction of nuclear-powered vessels. Shipyard 112 – the famous Krasnoe Sormovo Works in Gorkiy (nowadays Nizhny Novgorod), one of the oldest submarine constructors in the USSR – was still busy constructing the last conventionally powered Project 633-class submarines (ASCC/NATO codename 'Romeo'). Therefore, the decision was taken to construct the first two in Shipyard 189 (also known as the 'Baltic Shipyard') in Leningrad (present-day St Petersburg), and the remaining 14 in Shipyard 112.

Project 651-class submarines were constructed between 1960 and 1968, and on average it took the Soviets 989 days to construct each one, of which 567 days were on the slipway and 419 while moored to piers for final outfitting or undergoing sea trials.[5] One of the boats of this class spent no fewer than 943 days on the slipway, but another was constructed within only 261 days. Similarly, work on boats already in the water varied between 155 and 1,052 days, while the total time for construction of a single boat was 550 days in the best case and 1,471 days in the worst.

With Julietts becoming the first SSGs to conduct regular patrols far away from shores of the Soviet Union, the story of their operational service will be covered in a separate chapter.

Sub-Classes

As was very common in the Soviet naval industry, when the technology advanced in some aspect, an old platform was selected and modified to be the test bed of the new technology, as happened with

A Project 651-class (ASCC/NATO codename 'Juliett') submarine on the surface in the Mediterranean Sea on 11 August 1986. (US Navy)

Another Project 651/Juliett-class SSG, tied to an Oskol-class repair ship in the Mediterranean on 11 August 1986. The availability of such support platforms was of immense importance in extending the on-station times of Soviet attack submarines in areas far away from home bases. (US Navy)

A Juliett-class SSG underway with its rear P-6-launcher in the process of being erected. (US Navy)

WHAT WAS A CVBG?

USS *Ticonderoga* (CVA-14) – an Essex-class aircraft carrier that saw intensive service during the Second World War – with aircraft of her wing on the deck, while conducing underway replenishment from the oiler USS *Ashtabula* (AO-51), in the South Pacific during 1966. (USN Photo)

In the US Navy of the 1950s to 1980s, a CVBG consisted of one or two aircraft carriers – each typically carrying 86–90 aircraft – protected by other surface ships with a particular role. The doctrine stipulated two types of CVBGs: attack, or anti-submarine warfare (ASW). For much of the 1950s, and well into the 1960s, the attack carrier fleet comprised a mix of significantly modernised ships constructed during the Second World War, and newly built 'supercarriers'. The former included two types: the smaller, but more numerous Essex-class (27 vessels) and the bigger Midway-class (three ships). The latter comprised the Forrestal-class (four ships), Kitty Hawk-class (three ships), and the sole nuclear-powered USS *Enterprise* (CVAN-65). Each CVBG usually included one or two guided-missile cruisers of the Albany or Leahy-class (equipped with surface-to-air missiles) and several destroyers and frigates – mostly constructed during the Second World War – equipped for ASW. The sole exception was 'Task Force 1', centred on USS *Enterprise*: formed during the first half of the 1960s, this was usually protected by the nuclear-powered guided-missile cruisers USS *Long Beach* (CGN-9), and USS *Bainbridge* (CGN-25), both of which were exclusively equipped with surface-to-air missiles.

Regardless of their size, every attack aircraft carrier of this period usually embarked an air wing of two interceptor squadrons (equipped either with McDonnell Douglas F-4 Phantom II or Ling-Temco-Vought F-8 Corsair), two squadrons of Douglas A-4 Skyhawk light fighter-bombers, one of Douglas A-1 Skyraider or A-6 Intruder medium bombers, one of Douglas A-3 Skywarrior or Rockwell A-5 Vigilante strategic bombers, and one flight each of Grumman E-1 Tracer airborne early warning (AEW) aircraft and search and rescue helicopters.

Through the late 1960s and early 1970s, as the USN relaunched construction of nuclear-powered aircraft carriers in form of the Nimitz-class (hull numbers CVN-68, CVN-69 and CVN-70), it also ordered two classes of nuclear-powered guided-missile cruisers for their protection: the California- and Virginia-classes, both primarily armed with surface-to-air missiles (SAMs), but with an important, secondary ASW-capability. The complement of CVBGs at the time was completed by one of the Leahy- or Belknap-class guided-missile cruisers, one or two Charles F Adams-class guided-missile destroyers (equipped both for air defence and ASW), and two Knox-class frigates (specialised for ASW purposes).

Starting in the late 1970s, the escorts of an average CVBG consisted of one Ticonderoga-class guided-missile cruiser equipped with the Aegis air defence system (centred on SPY-1A phased array radars); while one or two Spruance-class guided-

the Whiskey. This also occurred with the Project 651-class, creating a new designation and new platform, usually for special purposes or training.

Project 651K, K-81

Due to the limitations of the Success-U fire-control system, it was decided to install a new system, based on satellite infrastructure and information from the Kasatka-B system, which used targeting information provided by satellites. The modifications were carried out in the Severodvinsk shipyard in 1972 and 1973.

Project 651E, B-86 (BS-86)

The Soviet Navy, looking to improve the performance of its numerous diesel submarines, started a study to fit auxiliary nuclear reactors in this platform, allowing it the capacity to voyage submerged for longer. The project was developed by the Design Bureau Lazurit, with Chief Designer N.I. Kvashi in charge. A VAU-6 600kW nuclear reactor was to be installed, with minimum modifications to the ship's structure. The work was carried out in the Gorkiy shipyard between September 1976 and December 1985. This project was a revolutionary Soviet idea, which was looking for a relatively cheap way to boost the capability of the conventional submarine fleet. From 1986 it was assigned to the 7th Division of Submarines of the Northern Fleet, and in July 1992 to the 346th Brigade for disposal. Apparently, the idea worked well, with only the fall of the Soviet Union and subsequent economic crises in the Russian Federation halting additional research and development of the project.[6]

missile destroyers and one or two Oliver Hazard Perry-class guided-missile frigates were equipped for ASW. For ASW purposes, each carrier had a squadron of Lockheed S-3 Viking ASW aircraft embarked. Each ship of the three escort classes was equipped with one or two Sikorsky SH-60B Seahawk helicopters, responsible for throwing a screen around the CVBG using dipping (or 'dunking') sonar on the end of a cable below the surface of the sea. Such a group of ships included powerful air defences, too – each better balanced than most of the air forces around the globe. These included one squadron of four Grumman E-2C Hawkeye AEW aircraft; two squadrons with a total of 20–24 Grumman F-14A Tomcat interceptors; while recently overhauled carriers were equipped with up to two units of 20–24 McDonnell Douglas F/A-18A/C Hornet fighter-bombers, which were replacing A-7E Corsair IIs in light attack squadrons. Both Hawkeyes and Tomcats were backed by the Aegis system of the single cruiser, and F-14s were capable of defending the carrier from bomber and/or missile attacks with their powerful AWG-9 radars and weapons systems, and long-range AIM-54 Phoenix missiles. A CVBG was usually rounded off with a fleet stores and replenishment ship, and a tanker, both equipped for replenishing and refuelling combat vessels at sea. Thus, each CVBG comprised between six and 10 ships, which – together with interceptors embarked on the carrier – were capable of establishing deeply layered defences. On average, during this period the USN operated a total of 16 supercarriers, of which two were usually undergoing periodic maintenance. Therefore, for most of the 1980s, there were about 14 CVBGs around, roughly half of them either starting an overseas deployment, in the middle of it, or returning to the homeport at any point in time.

The cruiser USS *Columbus* (CG-12), seen after her refit as an Albany-class guided-missile cruiser. (USN)

Task Force One, including USS *Enterprise* (CVAN-65; foreground), USS *Long Beach* (CGN-9; centre), and USS *Bainbridge* (CGN-25; background), during Operation Sea Orbit in 1964. (USN Photo)

Project 683

In 1960, TsKB-18 and its Chief Designer, Zosima A. Deribin, presented the idea of a modified Project 651-class, with a redesigned submarine equipped with a nuclear plant based on two nuclear reactors. Design work was carried out, but Project 670 submarines with missiles capable of being launched underwater eventually proved more promising, so Project 683 was cancelled. Equipping Project 651s with nuclear reactors was intended to fix the primary problems associated with targeting Carrier Task Forces, allowing high speed for the final attack and a high cruising speed for intercepting moving formations.

Project 603

In September 1967, the Soviet Navy assigned to the Volna Central Design Bureau a study project to equip the Project 651 with the D-9 strategic weapons system. However, only a year later, in mid-1968, all work on this study was cancelled.

Julietts in Service

Project 651-class vessels provided excellent service to the Soviet Navy. Average serviceability was 76 percent, which was much higher than for contemporary nuclear-powered boats. Nevertheless, there were issues with a few of the boats. For example, the serviceability of K-63 was as low as 36.8 percent, spending no fewer than 3,302 days undergoing repairs and overhauls, as opposed to a mere 1,509 days in operational service. K-156 was slightly better, spending 2,490 days undergoing repairs and 3,315 days in service. However, other units were usually in excellent condition, the best of all being K-318: its serviceability was 92.44 percent, with only 595 days undergoing repairs and overhauls, against 7,277 days in service.[7]

Table 2: Project 651-Class Submarines	
Propulsion	2 diesel engines, D-43, 8,000hp 2 electric motor, PG-141, 6,000hp 1 diesel for charging batteries, 2D-42, 1,750hp 2 engines for creeping navigation, PG-140, 1,000hp
Length (m)	85.9
Beam (m)	9.7
Draught (m)	6.29
Displacement (surfaced/ submerged, tons)	3,174/3,750
Operational Depth (m)	240–300
Speed (knots)	18
Crew	78
Endurance	18,000nm at 7 knots 27.8nm at 18 knots submerged 810nm at 2.74 knots (creeping mode) 90 days
Weapons Systems	4 x 4K48 missiles (P-6) 6 x 533mm (forward), 6 torpedoes 4 x 406mm (aft), 12 torpedoes

A Project 651-class submarine seen in the process of loading P-6 missiles inside the port of Sevastopol, in the 1970s or 1980s. (Efim Sandler collection)

During 20 consecutive years, from 1966–86, at least one Project 651-class was always deployed to the Mediterranean.[8] In 1970, five patrols were carried out by the submarines in support of allies of the USSR while successive crises took place between Israel and Arab nations, and the US Navy also increased the number of its vessels in the area. This year marked the peak of the Project 651-class's deployment worldwide, with seven units on combat patrols during the whole year.

The organisation of the vessels, as has been stated, involved continuous movement between fleets. In the Northern Fleet, Julietts were assigned to the 35th Division, where at least 11 units served at one time or another, before the fleet received better and more modern submarines and the Project 651s were sent to other fleets, such as the Baltic Fleet. They served in two different units in the Pacific Fleet, the 29th Division, 4th Flotilla and 124th Brigade, 6th Squadron, while with the Baltic Fleet they served under the 16th Division.

The submarines deployed to the Mediterranean came from North, Baltic or Black Sea Fleets, while patrols in the Indian Ocean and around the Philippines were carried out by units from Pacific Fleet.

During its years of service with the Soviet fleet, the Project 651-class had no serious accidents, as happened with other units of the fleet. This does not mean, however, that accidents and failures did not happen in these units. For example, the lead unit of the class, K-156, during its first patrol in the Mediterranean, suffered a total failure in its diesel engines, which resulted in the submarine remaining in the Mediterranean awaiting spare parts and technicians for four months, supported by a repair vessel of the fleet. This vessel never again made an extended combat patrol.

The 16 units of the class made 61 combat patrols in all possible scenarios, with patrols in the Barents Sea, North and Central Atlantic, Indian Ocean, Philippine Sea and Mediterranean Sea. The principal area of deployment was the Mediterranean, due to its particular characteristics. With the carriers of the US Sixth Fleet in a closed sea, the Project 651-class had the option of trailing the task force and being readied at any moment to launch its missiles, with very little warning time. Thirty-three of the 61 patrols were carried out in the Mediterranean, including visits to the ports of allied countries that the USSR maintained in the region, such as Algeria, Syria or Egypt.

The second unit, K-85, started it first patrol to the Mediterranean in 1966 with a series of defects that could be traced back to the shipyard, including failures in the diesel engines and the lack of a second periscope. During its travels the problems with the diesel powerplant increased and the only periscope that was operational suffered from internal condensation due to a lack of correct watertight components and improper installation. Eventually, while the submarine was in the central Mediterranean, the Soviet Navy ordered it to return to a home port to fix the problems before restarting its combat service. A couple of years later, between August and November 1968, the same submarine was deployed for 93 days to the Mediterranean in a preventive and supportive movement to the situation in Czechoslovakia.

A P-6 missile shortly after exiting the forward launcher of a Project 651-class boat. The missile could be equipped with either an 800kg conventional warhead or a tactical nuclear warhead with a yield of 100–350kT. (Author's collection)

During its second patrol in the Mediterranean, between May and November 1974, K-77 trailed the Sixth Fleet's aircraft carriers USS *America* (CV-66), USS *Forrestal* (CV-59), and USS *Independence* (CV-62), creating a great deal of stress for the screening vessels. Two years later, this same submarine carried out a patrol near Puerto Rico.

Some of the patrols made by this class were of lengthy duration, such as the deployment carried out by K-68 in 1974 and 1975 in the Mediterranean, which lasted for more than nine months, or that conducted by K-120 in the Indian Ocean for seven months in 1978. This was a situation that would start to become common in the Soviet fleet.

In 1977, all the units of the class were redesignated. Initially designated as K, for their great range, this designation was later exclusively used in the Soviet Navy for nuclear submarine, the Project 651-class being switched to the conventional submarine designation that started with the letter B.

In the last decade of the USSR, the Project 651-class were surpassed by other more modern classes and became obsolete due to their ageing main armament. From 1981, the decision was taken to transfer the majority of the units operating with the Northern Fleet to a new assignment with the Baltic Fleet. Six submarines were

A row of Project 651-class boats of the 35th Division seen in a base on the Kola Peninsula during the summer. (Efim Sandler collection)

SOVIET STRATEGIC MISSILE FORCES (RVSN)

Khrushchev's ideas about the use of strategic weapons created an earthquake within the Soviet armed forces. The new holy grail of the armed forces was strategic nuclear weapons, and a new branch in the armed forces was created to bring together all of the systems' operatives within all the branches. The new branch, known as the Strategic Missile Forces, was an Army subdivision with a land operation mentality that left the Navy in a very bad situation.

All nuclear weapons in any branch of the armed forces with strategic capacity were put under the direct control of the Strategic Forces, and all programmes that did not fit in with this idea were cancelled. For the Soviet Navy, this new player in the Ministry of Defence proved a mortal enemy. Within a few months, the Soviet Navy had lost its reason to deploy far away from the Soviet coastline and its military role was auxiliary to the Soviet Army. Furthermore, the budget for new programmes, vessels and submarines was drastically cut.

The changes were carried out in December 1959, with the Navy forced to transfer all the bombers and reconnaissance aircraft in its inventory, due to their strategic capacities. The submarine programme also suffered greatly. The P-5 was seen as a strategic missile regardless of its range being below the 1,000km specified by the new branch as the range limit for strategic missiles. This forced the Navy to play only an auxiliary nuclear role, with its SSB/SSBNs in poor shape due to the inefficiency of their missiles.

Admiral Sergei Gorshkov, the Commander-in-Chief of the Soviet Navy, was now only able to continue developing new weapons and platforms under the umbrella of tactical and strategic naval missiles. The creation of the Strategic Forces branch had disturbed the research and development programmes in all the naval design bureaus, for missiles or submarines.

A Project 651/Juliett-class SSG, seen next to a Don-class submarine tender in the Mediterranean during the mid-1980s. Submarine tenders were of immense importance for the functionality of the Soviet Navy's Fifth Eskadra in this part of the world. (US Navy)

The front part of the launchers on a Project 651-class boat, seen after being loaded with P-6 missiles, and in the process of being retracted. (Efim Sandler collection)

transferred to the 16th Division of Submarines of the Baltic Fleet based in the Estonian port of Liepaja. This movement was not made to improve the capabilities of the Baltic Fleet, but only because the limited and ageing submarines could still serve a useful purpose in this enclosed sea. In 1991, with the fall of the Soviet Union, the units were transferred to the 58th Brigade of Submarines, with which they finished their operational life, thereafter being sold under another country's flag as scrap or as a floating museum for Western investors.

4
ECHO SERIES

Nominally at least, with the creation of the RVSN in 1959, the Soviet Navy ended its role in operations against land targets, completely reorienting towards anti-carrier operations. During the following years, it began applying the technology of nuclear propulsion to create not only a genuine Soviet concept of the SSGN, but also one of the most powerful naval weapons systems of its time.

Project 659

Project 651-class submarines proved highly popular in service. They were cheap to build and easy to maintain; indeed, a number of boats could be kept on station along the coasts of the USSR at all times. The Soviet Navy next focused on developing the capability to menace Western aircraft carrier groups far away from its bases. In Severodvinsk, in September 1955, the keel was laid for the first Soviet-made nuclear-powered submarine, the Project 627-class boat designated K-3 (ASCC/NATO codename 'November'). The USSR thus became the second global superpower to design such a vessel, the US having done so several years earlier, but the design and construction of the K-3 demonstrated the resolution of the Soviet government to bridge the gap, and quickly. The centrepiece of the new submarine was the 'I Generation' nuclear reactor known as the HEN.[1] This included two type VM-A pressurised-water nuclear reactors (PWRs), each producing 70MW and each powering one steam turbine that, via two-stage gearing, delivered 35,000hp to two propulsion shafts. Other machinery included two PG-116 creeping motors, two DG-4000 diesel generators and two banks of batteries with 112 cells each. The K-3 was capable of reaching an impressive top speed of 27 knots.

The nuclear power plant for the November-class submarines was an adaptation of the civilian system used on the world's first nuclear-powered surface ship, the icebreaker *Lenin*. The configuration of each reactor included four circuits in cascade, for removing heat and the transfer of this to the secondary loop to produce steam, while two other systems were dedicated to removing heat from the entire reactor. The water pressure inside the primary circuit of the reactor was 200kg/cm^2, while the steam was heated to 355°C and its pressure was 36kg/cm^2. The reactor core was heavily shielded: its radiological protection made up about 50 percent of its total weight. The fuel consisted of U-AI alloy, which was 20 percent enriched uranium: essentially, the best contemporary metallurgy could deliver. The Project 627-class submarines had a double-hull configuration, with nine internal compartments. To minimise costs and production

A nuclear-powered submarine of the Project 659-class ('Echo I'), seen following modification to the Project 659T standard. Note the sleek lines of this design, especially in comparison to its successor, Project 675 ('Echo II'). (US Navy)

The Project 627-class submarine K-3 *Leninsky Komsomol* was laid down on 24 September 1955 in Severodvinsk, marking the start of the Soviet nuclear submarine shipbuilding programme. (Soviet MOD)

times, their design was heavily standardised. They were expected to have an operational endurance of 50 days and to be capable of remaining submerged for 1,500 hours and had a 120-strong crew.

On 26 August 1956, the Council of Ministers approved the creation of nuclear submarines equipped with submarine-launched cruise missiles (SLCMs) for attacks on major land bases in the Pacific, using P-5 missiles. The result was the Project 659-class, designed by P.P. Putintsev of TsKB-18, with N.A. Klimov as Deputy Chief Designer. This was followed by the Project 675-class of nuclear-powered submarines, codenamed 'Echo' (later 'Echo I') by the ASCC/NATO.[2]

The Soviets invested heavily in homogenising as many elements of the Project 627 and Project 675 classes as possible. Both were powered by HEN power plants and – to minimise construction costs and time – had similar internal designs, including the double-hull configuration and nine internal compartments. Nevertheless, their design requirements were different, resulting in different hydrofoil designs. For example, the November class was optimised for better hydrodynamics and top speed when submerged, while the Echo I was required to have greater stability when surfaced, to better support missile launching procedures. The Echo I had to carry three pairs of launchers for P-6 missiles inside its hull, which resulted in a beam of 9.2 metres. The combination of such requirements produced a hull angled at the corners between the deck and its sides, in turn resulting in poor performance when submerged, but with a better buoyancy reserve than the Project 627-class vessels.

Echo Is were armed with a total of six launchers for P-5s, plus four 533mm torpedo tubes in the bow and four 406mm tubes aft. As in the case of earlier boats equipped with P-5s, the launch procedure required the submarine to surface and set up the firing and lasted the usual 20 minutes. Launch containers were integrated into the hull and took four minutes to be raised into the firing position, while the targeting procedure and other preparations took another 12 minutes. This configuration enabled the submarine to unleash a salvo of six missiles within a short period of time (the usual sequence was tubes 6, 3, 2, 5, 4 then 1, enabling every missile to launch without interference from the fumes of the previously launched weapon).[3]

Construction of the Project 659-class submarines began in early 1957, when the basic requirement was completed and forwarded to the Ministry of Shipbuilding and the Navy staff for approval. TsKB-18 decided to initiate work on its own even before official permission to proceed was granted. Consequently, the detailed engineering stage was completed by October 1957, enabling construction of the first boat to start in the Zvezda shipyard of Komsomoslk-na-Amur, in the Far East, only a few weeks later. In this fashion, the USSR obtained its second shipyard capable of manufacturing nuclear submarines, in turn enabling the one in Severodvinsk to remain focused on other projects. The construction of the first Project 659-class submarine took two years and 11 months; that of the fifth – and the last – just one year and four months: the average was 717 days.[4] Construction of a sixth vessel was cancelled when the costs began jeopardising the build-up of the RVSN.

The first Project 659-class submarine, K-45, was commissioned in 1960 and ran missile launch tests between January and May 1961. However, none of these tests met expectations. On the contrary, the test firing of 2 January in particular revealed many problems with the hydraulics and heating systems of the missile containers and other equipment. In March 1961, during a dive to great depth, the missile containers developed several leaks. Following repairs and the application of improvements, another test series was conducted in April the same year, but test-launches on the 16th and 26th of that month brought about similar results. It was only after additional repairs that four firings with satisfactory results were achieved on 24 May 1961.[5]

Echoes in the Pacific

All the Project 659-class submarines served in the Pacific, where their endurance enabled them to menace the west coast of the USA, forcing the USN to redeploy its anti-submarine warfare forces away from the Atlantic. Thanks to their new weapons, the modern SSGNs were capable of attacking targets anywhere from Japan to the Philippines, via Hawaii to the Panama Canal. For this reason alone, their appearance had a strategic impact.

However, the withdrawal from service of the P-5 missile in 1966 suddenly endangered the entire class, even though all the submarines were less than 10 years old; some had only been in operational service for three years. Consequently, the Naval Staff ran multiple studies trying to find a new role for the Project 659 class. The task of finding a solution was eventually assigned to a team from TsKB-18, led by O.Y. Margolin, and the result was an upgrade that became known as the Project 659T. Undertaken at the Zvezda shipyard in Bolshoy Kamen, this modification included the removal of the P-5 weapons system and related installations and launchers: in its place, torpedo storage was increased to 24 rounds. The Echo Is ceased serving as SSGNs and were converted into nuclear-powered attack submarines (SSNs).[6]

All the Project 659T boats were organised into the 45th Submarine Division, with their home base in Krashnikov Bay, Vilyuchinsk, from where they

Table 3: Project 659-Class

Propulsion	2 x PWR WM-A of 70MW 2 x Turbogenerators GTZA-601, 17,500hp 2 x Electric Motors PG-116, 450hp 2 x Generators GPM-21, 1,400kW 2 x Auxiliary Generators DG-460, 460kW
Length (m)	111.2
Beam (m)	9.2
Draught (m)	7.1
Displacement (surfaced/submerged, tons)	3,731/4,920
Operational Depth (m)	240–300
Speed (surfaced/submerged, knots)	15.1/26
Crew	104
Endurance (days)	50
Weapons	6 x P-5 missiles in 3 twin launchers 4 x 533mm torpedo tubes forward (models 53–61, SET-65) 4 x 406mm

ran regular patrols deep into the Pacific, and into the Indian Ocean and the Red Sea. In 1971, K-45 carried out a patrol in the Tonkin Gulf, off Vietnam, to shadow operations by USN carrier battle groups, while in 1979, K-66 monitored naval operations during a border war between the People's Republic of China and the Socialist Republic of Vietnam.[7]

Unlucky K-122

Equipped with the HEN powerplant, the Project 659-class vessels suffered a number of accidents – usually related to the performance of that system, but also that of various controls and their crews. Indeed, only months after the first boat of this kind reached the Pacific – K-122, in June 1963 – it suffered a loss of control while submerged and underway at 14 knots. Subsequent investigation concluded that there was an issue with the manufacturing quality of the horizontal rudder. In May 1966, fire erupted in the regenerative elements of the turbine system on K-66: this was quickly extinguished though and the submarine had its reactor cores replaced for the first time a year later.

In May 1970, during Exercise Okean 70, K-122 suffered a series of accidents. On 7 May, due to the confusion and resulting mismanagement of its skipper, Captain 1st Class V.F. Kopyev, K-122 hit an underwater mountain, damaging the sonar. The boat survived this experience without any leaks and continued its mission, only to slightly later, while underway at 30 knots and a depth of 170 metres, run out of control and rapidly descend to 270 metres. Kopyev managed to surface the boat and a subsequent inspection found a defect in the horizontal rudders. Five days later, a fire erupted in the turbine compartment and several crewmembers were badly affected by smoke, forcing Kopyev to order the boat to the surface again – this time for ventilation. A post-patrol investigation put all the blame on the skipper and he was dismissed from his position by Admiral N.N. Amelko.[8]

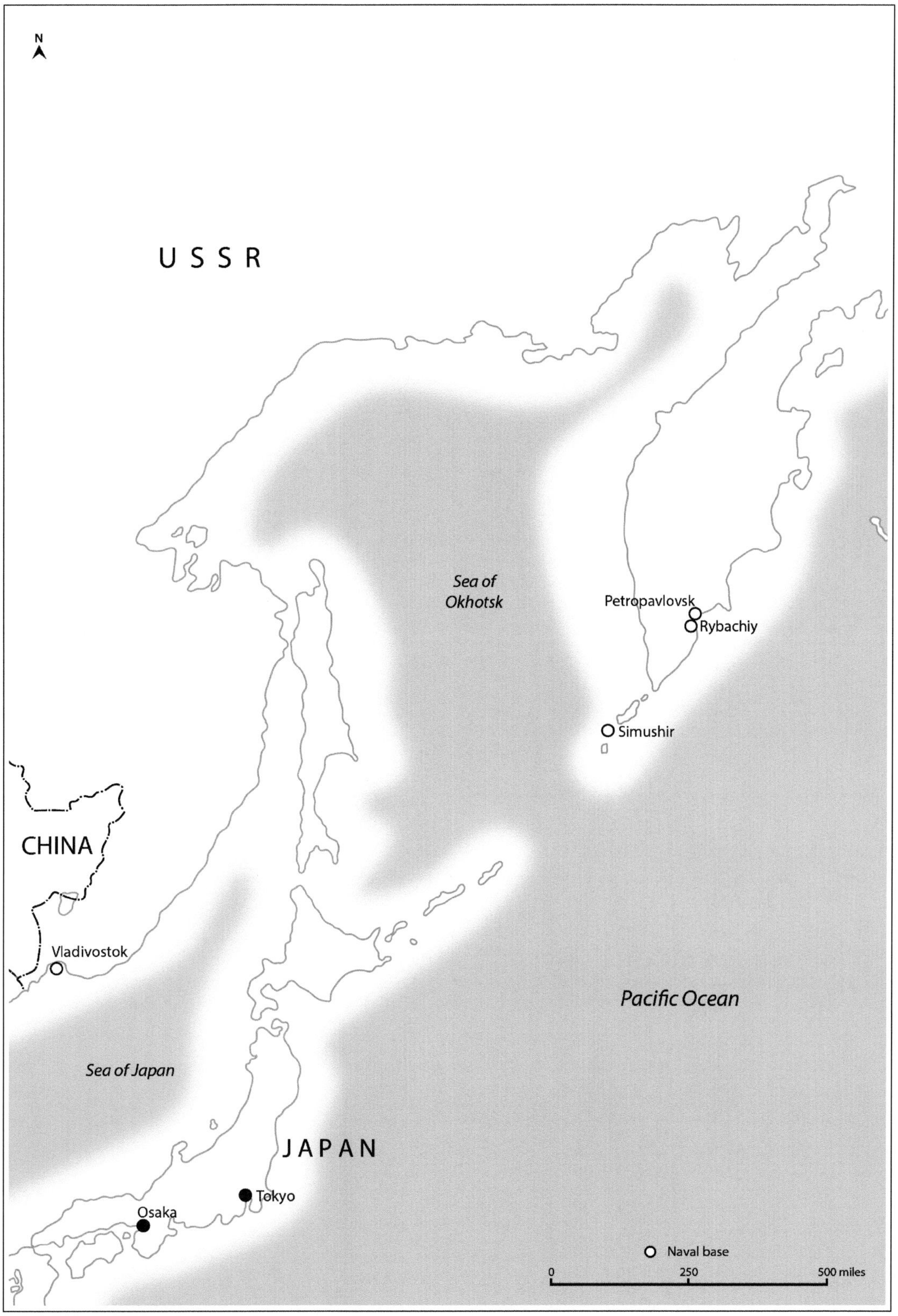

Major Soviet naval bases in the Pacific. (Map by George Anderson)

On 10 October 1974, the fifth unit of the class, K-151 – fresh from its upgrade to the Project 659T standard – was hit by its sister ship, K-66, which damaged the horizontal rudder. As a result, K-151 had to undergo emergency repairs in the Chazma Bay shipyard that lasted nearly a year: it returned to service just in time to take part in Exercise Okean 75 in April 1975. Then in August 1975, the same boat suffered a fire while on a patrol in the Philippine Sea. After several trouble-free years for the class, on 16 December 1979, the crew of K-45 detected increased levels of radioactivity. Nevertheless, the submarine continued its duties, and it was only in April 1980 that the reason for the increased levels was found – a leak in the primary cooling system.

An extremely rare photograph of a Project 659-class submarine in the process of launching one of its P-5 missiles, before the entire class was converted into SSNs. The number applied on the sail (551) was not related to the hull number or designation, but assigned depending on the task – and, often enough, to confuse possible observers. (Efim Sandler collection)

A Project 659/Echo I-class submarine underway at high speed on the surface of the Pacific Ocean. (US Navy)

Several months later, K-122 suffered another series of mishaps: this time its last, for as result of these the vessel was eventually decommissioned. While in its home port of Pavlovsky, with the crew enjoying well-deserved liberty, its skipper, Captain Sizov, received an order to sail out for a patrol station near the Japanese island of Okinawa. The boat reached the designated zone in late July, replacing its sister ship, K-151, and initially everything was routine. Then, on 19 August, fire erupted in the hydroacoustic station, and although this was quickly extinguished it resulted in the removal of all autonomous breathing equipment from the stern compartment forward, which Sizov failed to rectify. Two days later, on 21 August, while the crew was transferring equipment from one turbogenerator to another, an explosion occurred in compartment seven, which began to fill with smoke. By the time that part of the crew was evacuated to compartment eight, several were heavily affected by inhalation of toxic fumes. Amid growing confusion, the freon-supported firefighting system failed, allowing the fire to spread through compartments six, five, four and eight. Sizov then ordered a shut-down of the reactors, the submarine to surface and the crew trapped in compartment eight to be evacuated through the hatch in the exterior of the vessel. Unfortunately, due to the increased pressure caused by the fire inside, it proved impossible to open the hatch, and the situation repeated itself in compartment nine. Eventually, one of the sailors managed to open one of the rear torpedo tubes while working in total darkness, allowing 48 crewmembers – two of them unconscious – to be evacuated from the submarine. By that time, however, nine of the crew were dead and another five were missing.

Although on the surface, K-121 was unable to communicate due to the loss of electric power, even the emergency generator having been affected by the fire. As the conflagration continued, it turned some of plating on the external hull white-hot. Eventually, an LNG carrier flying a British flag passed by and saw Sizov signalling for help. The merchant vessel stopped and its crew provided food, water and blankets for the stricken submarine's crew, while transmitting messages to the Soviet Navy headquarters via the USSR's embassy in Tokyo. The following morning, a Soviet training ship from the Marine College in Vladivostok arrived on the scene and began evacuating non-essential crewmembers and the bodies of the deceased. Three days later, the submarine tender *Borodino* turned up with a reserve crew and a team of engineers, by which time K-122 was completely paralysed and had to be towed back to Pavlovsky.

A subsequent investigation concluded that all the officers lacked training in firefighting, and thus the crew was poorly trained too. Consequently, not only Sizov, but his deputy, Captain Savenkov, and the commander of the 45th Submarine Division, Captain 1st Class Zavavukhin, were all reprimanded.[9]

Despite the submarine having suffered massive damage, the HQ of the Soviet Navy initially wanted to have K-122 repaired and returned to service. Related works were undertaken between November 1980 and April 1981, but the results were considered unsatisfactory to the degree that the status of the vessel became 'uncertain'. After idling around its anchor for several years, K-122 was eventually officially decommissioned in October 1985.

In comparison, the remaining known accidents involving Project 659/Echo I-class submarines were minor. For example, on 10 September 1981, K-45 collided with the Soviet trawler *Nocokachalinsk*, resulting in a 6-metre-long breach of the external hull that necessitated emergency repairs in Bolshoy Kamen, during which a fire erupted that killed three dockyard workers.[10] At least as serious was K-66's problems with the primary cooling systems of both reactors, which prompted the Soviet Navy to prematurely decommission the vessel later the same year, while in 1989, a similar problem resulted in the retirement of K-59.

5
ECHO OF AN ECHO

As previously mentioned, in August 1956 the Council of Ministers of the USSR made a number of highly important decisions regarding the future of the Soviet Navy. One of these, issued on 17 August, was a decree authorising the design of a new nuclear-powered submarine armed with cruise missiles that could target both ships and land targets. Designed by TsKB-18 under the leadership of Pavel P. Pustyntsev, the new class received the designation Project 675, along with the ASCC/NATO codename 'Echo II'. Basic design and planning were completed and submitted for approval in October 1958, and construction began in 1959.

Nominally based on the design for the Project 659 vessels, the new class had a longer sail and – because it carried four twin launchers instead of three – a longer hull. The weapons system was designed to operate two different missiles: P-5 or P-5D as strategic weapons, and P-6 for anti-ship operations. Pustyntsev and his team applied a number of other improvements regarding electronics and combat management.[1]

Like their Project 659 predecessors, the Project 675 submarines had a double-hull configuration with 10 compartments. The outer hull was built of steel that was 4–16mm thick, while the pressure hull was made of AK-25 steel that was between 22mm and 35mm thick, which enabled the vessel to operate to depths of 240–300 metres. All the external surfaces were covered with anechoic rubber tiles to reduce sonar returns.[2]

The propulsion plant was based on the same VM-A reactors as in other vessels, with two units installed per submarine. With this plant being the first operational with the fleet, there were many incidents and accidents. The increased length in the Project 675-class submarines led to an increase of the submerged displacement to 5,760 tons, compared to 4,920 tons for Project 659 vessels, but the Project 675 class retained the same powerplant. The unavoidable result was a lower top speed of just 15 knots on the surface and 23 knots when submerged. This was to become one of the main problems of the new class.[3]

A front view at the bow of a Project 675-class submarine. (Efim Sandler collection)

The rare sight of a Project 675-class submarine with all four double launchers for P-5/P-6 missiles in the erected position. (Author's collection)

Two crewmembers in front of a Project 675-class submarine, the front launcher of which is seen loaded and in the raised position. (Efim Sandler collection)

The centrepiece of the Project 675-class was its P-6 weapons system, including four pairs of launchers for 4K48 missiles, all designed for anti-ship operations. This total of eight missiles provided a quantity gauged as having a good chance of penetrating the air defences of an average CVBG of the US Navy. That said, the launching procedure still had to be undertaken on the surface. Other weaponry on the class included four 533mm torpedo tubes forward and two 406mm tubes aft, with every boat able to take up to 20 torpedoes on board. The crew numbered 137, with 22 officers, 25 non-commissioned officers and 90 sailors.

Construction of the submarines was shared between two shipyards. Severodvinsk Shipyard, in the Northern Fleet area, was responsible of the first units being built. As the only nuclear-capable shipyard in the USSR at this time, it was decided to expand the nuclear projects to other shipyards to ease Severodvinsk's workload and expand geographically the nation's nuclear capacity. Increasing the number of nuclear-capable shipyards would also increase the total yearly output of nuclear submarines commissioned by the Soviet Navy.

The other shipyard chosen to be involved was the Amur Shipbuilding Plant (or Shipyard No. 199), in Komsomolsk-na-Amur, in the Far East, primarily to implement nuclear project technology in the Far East. The Project 675-class was the first nuclear submarine project of the Pacific Fleet and was to receive support from this shipyard. Severodvinsk, as the lead shipyard, provided much support to help launch this program through personnel, training, tools and procedures. A total of 29 units were constructed in both shipyards, with the first keel laid in 1961 and the last commissioned by the Soviet Navy in 1968. Sixteen vessels were constructed in Severodvinsk, with 13 built in the Komsomolsk shipyard, as shown in Table 4. The output rate of nuclear units for a new shipyard was impressive, reflecting the scale of the effort undertaken by Soviet industry.

Table 4: Project 675 Class: Construction Rate

	1963	1964	1965	1966	1967	1968
Severodvinsk	3	4	6	3	-	-
Komsomolsk	1	1	4	3	3	1
Total	4	5	10	6	3	1

These numbers provide evidence of the huge effort invested by the Soviet naval industry in the arms race with the United States and its allies. No fewer than 10 Project 675-class units were delivered by 1965 alone – at the same time other nuclear submarines were also being constructed in the country, in addition to numerous conventional submarines and surface ships.

The importance of the whole SSGN programme can also be seen from the fact that the first generation of nuclear submarines (HEN) comprised 55 units.[4] Of these, 34 were assigned to the SSGN role – more than 60 percent of the global production – with the rest shared between SSNs and SSBNs.

From the start of the development of the SSG/SSGN concept within the Soviet fleet in 1957 until 1969, the fleet had deployed 59 submarines in this role. During this time, the Soviet Navy was able to deploy at sea approximately 514 missile launchers based exclusively in submarines. This was an outstanding success for the naval arm and a real threat to the USSR's opponents. As will be seen later in this chapter, the US Navy had no option but to react to this new threat.

Construction time for the Soviets averaged 666 days per submarine, roughly one year and 10 months. In Severodvinsk, this time was reduced to 644 days, while in Komsomolsk it averaged 693 days. Taking into account that this was Komsomolsk's first nuclear project, the latter figure was impressive. The average time on the slipway and in dock was 411 days, with 254 days moored at a wharf for outfitting and for sea trials.

After the creation of the RVSN, the SSBN programme was halted. Some of the blocks, components and equipment bought and stored for the Project 658 Hotel I vessels were redirected for the Project 675-class programme, allowing some time benefits thanks to the common engineering design.

The spread of these submarines between the two main oceanic fleets of the USSR, and the large number constructed, meant that the Project 675s were the backbone of the SSGN forces of the Soviet fleet for several decades. The platform also provided numerous ship classes for the crews for training and developing tactics and operational use of this new type of naval weapon.

Conceptualisation

As on all early Soviet SSGs, the weapons system was centred on the P-6 missile. However, the Project 675-class was much more flexible

Table 5: Project 675-class	
Propulsion	2 x PWR WM-A of 70MW 2 x Steam Turbines 60-D1 2 x Generators GPM-21, 1,400kW 2 x Auxiliary Generators DG-400, 400kW
Length (m)	115.4
Beam (m)	9.3
Draught (m)	7.1
Displacement (surfaced/submerged, tons)	4,500/5,760
Operational Depth (m)	240–300
Speed (surfaced/submerged, knots)	15/23
Crew	137
Endurance (days)	60
Weapons	8 x launchers for 4K95 or 4K48 missiles (P-5 and P-6 weapons systems) 4 x 533mm torpedo tubes forward (models 53-61, SET-65) 2 x 406mm

A quartet of Project 675-class submarines seen in their base. (Efim Sandler collection)

in this regard: its weapons system was designed to deploy all the missiles of both the P-5 and P-6 systems, including the 4K95 (P-5, P-5D), 4K44, 4M44 and 3M44 (P-35), and 4K48 (P-6).

From the beginning of the SSG/SSGN projects, the main idea was to allow the submarine to be equipped with SSMs (surface-to-surface missiles) capable of threatening a carrier battlegroup or any other naval forces that the Soviet Navy may confront on the high seas anywhere around the world. The P-5 was a strategic missile, but regardless of its intended main role, it was the ideal platform for developing a long-range anti-ship missile. With this objective, its designer V.P. Chelomey continued developing the missile.

In 1956, the Council of Ministers of the USSR had assigned to Chelomey the design and development of two missiles with OTH (Over the Horizon) capabilities.[5] The experience gained through the P-5 and P-5D projects provided a basis for continued development of the missile. However, a problem arose with the category of targets between the various missiles. While the accuracy of the P-5 was initially low, when equipped with a nuclear warhead against a strategic land target, such as a city or naval base, the targeting process and overall accuracy were not a big problem. But with the P-6, both targeting and accuracy were big concerns for the designers due to the fact that the target would be a mobile naval platform in the middle of the ocean.

The first thing to do was to locate the target in the ocean. This problem, as it remains in the early twenty-first century, was a major one, because a naval formation of vessels sailing in radio silence and able to avoid other vessels is a hard target to find. The USSR had a strategic necessity to be capable of locating NATO naval formations and carrier battlegroups of the US, and to a lesser degree of the UK and France. The first step in doing so was based on Second World War technology, using HF/DF.[6] This technology is based on antennas installed in strategic locations that were able to locate emissions from vessels at sea and provide a relevant bearing from the antenna. To be useful information, there was a need for emissions to be located by more than one group of antennas in different locations, to triangulate the origin of the emissions and provide a fixed coordinate. However, this technology was very inaccurate, and in the beginning it was only possible to find an initial position of the target. After a vector or area had been produced with the HF/DF information, a reconnaissance aircraft had to be sent to the area to fix the position of the target and send this information to the submarines for them to launch an attack.

Yet even if all this process had been done properly and the enemy did not offer any opposition, there remained the problem of coordination between the aircraft, a command post ashore and the submarine. All this communication was done through datalinks of information to allow all the elements to be connected in the proper frequencies. However, the enemy could jam the signals and disrupt or prevent the procedure.[7]

Supposing again that all this had been accomplished, a missile still had to be launched, fly to the target and strike the enemy vessel. During the flying time of the missile, the target could change its position; the missile needed an actual target position for a chance to strike home. If a hit was not obtained, the process of transmitting

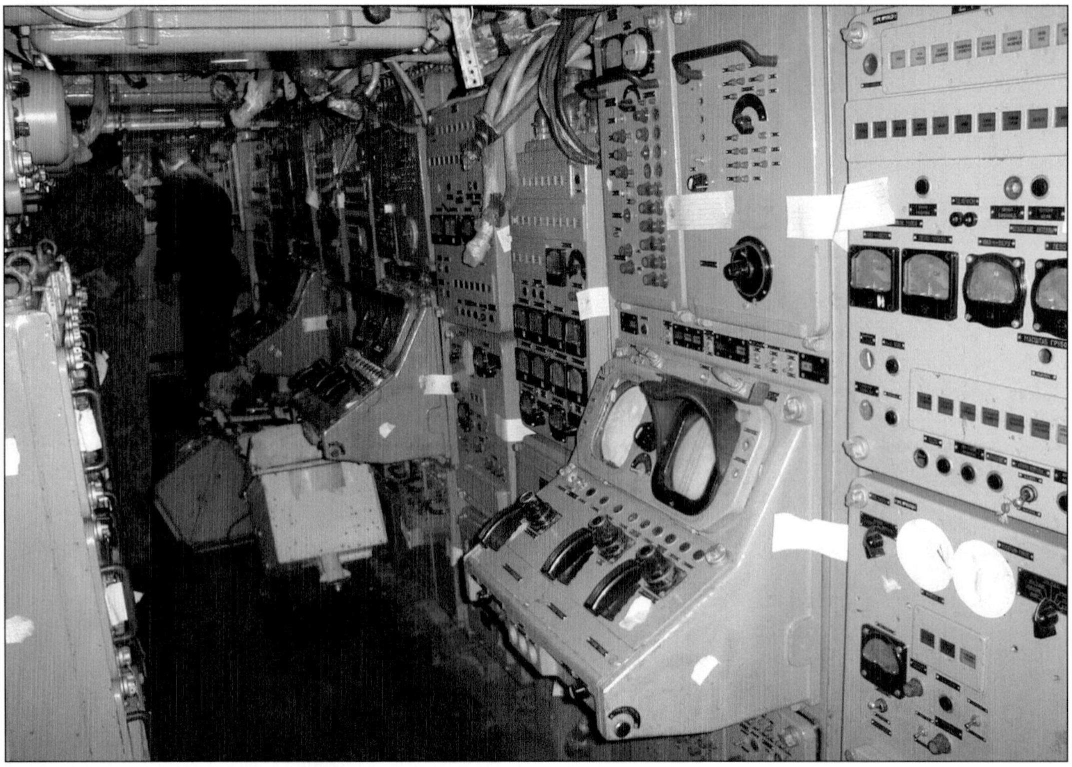

A view at the torpedo-control stations of the Project 675-class submarine. (Efim Sandler collection)

A P-6 missile being hoisted from its transport trolley into the launcher of a Project 675-class submarine. Notable are folding wings: these opened immediately after the missile exited the launcher. (Efim Sandler collection)

information from the aircraft to the submarine and from it to the missile had to start over again. The missiles now needed their own guidance system to complete their flight path against the enemy formation with precision, something more accurate than in its predecessor series due its current tactical use against vessels.

Targeting Problem

The targeting problem was a very difficult hurdle to overcome using the technology available in the 1960s. The Soviet solution to the problem put the emphasis on technologies and procedures that are still in use in this weapons system more than 50 years later. Multiple new technologies and systems were originated in the attempt to find the answer. The solution developed was vastly expensive, with a cost so high that it burdened the Soviet defence budget for decades, providing one of the first steps towards the later bankruptcy of the USSR and the fall of the Soviet Empire. What follows is an analysis of how the Soviets worked towards a solution with the Project 675 programme and the P-6 missile.

The first stage of detection could be carried out by an HF/DF land station or by a SIGINT aircraft that had located some emissions and started to work out a triangulation of the signals. Usually, this aircraft was the Tupolev Tu-16 reconnaissance bomber, that after having detected some emissions and obtained an approximate bearing and range called for the support of a reconnaissance aircraft, the Tu-95RT, that had a powerful surface-search radar (ASCC/NATO codename 'Big Bulge') and was able to manage transmissions with shore command posts or directly with submarines. The SIGINT aircraft was no longer necessary and could leave as it was only needed in first stages of detection until the reconnaissance aircraft arrived in the area. The type of communication used, based on datalinks, was the MRSC-1 Uspekh system. The Uspekh, based in the Tu-95RT, provided the information for the submarine, where the captain could evaluate the tactical situation and make a decision about the launching of missiles and his own position relative to the hostile forces.

After the decision to launch had been taken on board the submarine, the crew would start the prelaunch procedures while still submerged, feeding the missiles with the flight path and target information for the attack. Then the Project 675-class vessel needed to surface, raise the launchers and deploy its own fire-control radar (ASCC/NATO codename 'Front Door/Front Piece'), installed in the front part of the sail. All these actions required at least 20 minutes with the submarine surfaced before it could start the launch procedure.

One of the early Project 675-class submarines seen in the Zapadna Litsa base. (Efim Sandler collection)

Collective Targeting

There were several methods of launching missiles: either one, two or four could be launched in each salvo. Against an enemy formation, the latter option was preferred for this weapons system because the greater number of missiles in the air increased the probabilities of successfully penetrating the enemy's air defences.

According to various sources, two P-6 missiles could be launched in 90 seconds, while four missiles required four minutes to be launched. After launch, the missiles reached a cruising altitude of 3,000 metres at a speed of Mach 1.2 (around 800 knots). A range of 245nm implied a flight time to the target of 18 minutes. During this time, a vessel moving at 25–30 knots could change position by between 7½ and 9nm, so there was a great risk that the missiles may find nothing at the original target position. For this reason, the Soviet Navy developed the possibility for the submarine operator to update the course of the missiles in flight through information provided by the Tu-95RT in the area. The system was known as Video Data Link Drambuie, with the Tu-95 sending updated information to the submarine and the operator resending coordinates to the guidance system of the missiles. However, only one of the launched missiles would have its own radar operational: the others would be switched off to avoid detection by the enemy. The second and following missiles, undetected by the target, improved the probability of a successful impact.

Just before the terminal phase, where the missiles switched on their own active-radar seekers and homing systems, the operator checked the radar image from the missiles and selected the most valuable objective in the formation. From this point onwards, the missiles were autonomous and started to descend for the final attack. The final step involved the missiles attempting to dive 10–20 metres into the sea, with the intention of exploding just below the keel of the target to maximise the effect of the explosion.

To launch a second salvo of the remaining four missiles, the Project 675-class vessel needed an additional 15 minutes, which implied that for a full salvo against a formation, the submarine must remain surfaced for at least 40 minutes some 245nm from the target: this was a long time, during which it could be detected by enemy ASW aircraft.

The P-6 could be equipped with a conventional warhead of 800kg or a tactical nuclear warhead of 100–350kT. According to Soviet doctrine of the time, two to four nuclear warheads were estimated as sufficient to destroy a CVBG. There was little confidence in the effectiveness of conventional warheads, with captains and officers of the Soviet Navy not rating their chances of success in a conventional attack on a carrier battlegroup.

The MRSC-1 Uspekh communication system was modernised during the following decades. The Uspekh-U was basically the same system but allowed for Kamov Ka-25 and Ka-27 helicopters to serve as OTH target acquisition platforms, as the Tu-95RT had with the original system. With the large number of these helicopters deployed with the fleet, the OTH target acquisition platforms increased exponentially and provided a more numerous and flexible network for supporting the SSGN submarine fleet equipped with P-6 missiles.

In the 1970s, a similar idea was developed with target acquisition platforms based on satellites. A constellation of satellites was launched in orbit to support the system. US-P SIGINT satellites provided the first contacts in the oceans, followed by US-A radar ocean reconnaissance satellites (RORSAT) equipped with a nuclear electric power generation plant. Through the Kasatka communications system, installed in the submarines, the satellites were able to provide targeting data directly to submarines, with the possibility of receiving this information while still submerged. The system was operational from 1979 and was still partially in operation with the Russian Federation Fleet at the time of publication. Despite all the advanced technology involved, the system had some serious handicaps. Firstly, the submarine was forced to remain surfaced while transmitting information to the missiles, making it susceptible to being detected and attacked by enemy aircraft. Curiously, the ASW torpedoes of Western navies were not able to attack a surfaced submarine, and to fill this gap the US Navy started the development of a new weapon that resulted in the universal SSM missile, the Harpoon. ASW aircraft could also attack surfaced SSGN submarines, as of course could other vessels.

Furthermore, the whole P-6 attack procedure was based on datalinks, with communication between different platforms and the missiles. The availability of this communication channel was limited to 12 channels in a particular area due to the technology available at the time. All these datalinks were susceptible to jamming actions from hostile forces and to disruption by enemy attack. Finally, the

Table 6: 4K88/P-6 Missile	
Warhead	Conventional: 800kg Tactical Nuclear: 100–350 kT
Propulsion	4 RATO Booster 66,000lb Liquid-fuelled Turbojet TRD 4D48
Range (nm)	245
Speed (Mach)	1.2
Length (m)	10.8
Wingspan (m)	2.5
Weight at launch (tons)	5.6
Guidance Systems:	INS/Doppler radar navigation system with an active-radar terminal attack guidance system supported by active-seeker radar

P-6 was a big missile, being 10 metres length and having a wingspan of 2.5 metres, meaning that it created a good radar contact. The development of air defence systems in the US Fleet allowed the Soviet missiles to be detected and destroyed, using new SAMs and CIWS (close-in weapon system systems), before they reached the target or started their terminal phase of attack.

The most important reaction by the US Navy to this new Soviet threat came with the development of advanced AEW aircraft, CAP (combat air patrol) aircraft and long-range air-to-air missiles. The US Navy invested in the development of an advanced airborne platform for its carriers that resulted in the AEW E-2 Hawkeye. This aircraft had a powerful radar able to provide surveillance around the carrier formation some 250–300km from the vessels. CAP, initially based on the F-4 Phantom, was improved with the F-14 Tomcat, equipped with AIM-54 Phoenix missiles and the AN/AWG-9 radar with long-range detection and the capacity to follow six targets at the same time. The combination of these new assets with the US carrier air wing increased the probabilities of detecting, tracking and shooting-down any incoming threat, whether aircraft or missiles. The long-range CAP aircraft were also able to disrupt missions by Soviet SIGINT and reconnaissance aircraft, preventing them from obtaining the necessary information for submarines to attack.

The captains of the Project 675-class submarines now recognised that the probabilities of their missiles successfully crossing through the CAP, SAM and CIWS defences were minimal. On the other hand, the P-6 was still a very useful weapon against less well protected formations such as convoys or surface actions groups less powerful than a carrier battlegroup.

In any conflict between NATO and the Warsaw Pact, it was expected that hundreds of merchant ships would need to sail daily to Europe with vital supplies and heavy equipment for the military units deployed around the continent. As well as the high number of conventionally powered submarines and SSNs available to the Soviet Navy to attack these targets, the Project 675s were still a valuable asset against such vessels if they were able to voyage far into the Atlantic and reach the SLOC (sea lines of communications) where the merchantmen sailed.

The merchant ships' low speed and the vast area that had to be crossed, namely the GIUK (Greenland, Iceland, United Kingdom) gap, made it a potentially hazardous passage. But it was one of the sea regions most heavily defended by NATO forces, with the SOSUS (Sound Surveillance System) sonar system in operation and many long-range ASW squadrons being based in Iceland, the UK, Canada and the United States.

A weapon the Soviets could utilise against them was the P-6, a liquid-fuelled missile equipped with RATO solid fuel for its launch from the submarine. Like with the P-5, its wings were folded for storage inside their launch containers: the range of the 5,600kg weapon was estimated at 245nm, with a speed of Mach 1.2 (1,482km/h). The flight altitude varied from 7,000 metres in the cruise phase to 3,000 metres in the approach phase, and 100 metres in the terminal phase.

The guidance system was designed by the Granit Central Research Institute, with N.A. Charin as Director and M.V. Yatskovsky and I.Y. Krivtsov as Chief Designers. They developed all the operations for receiving and updating the target position and the missile flight path while in flight. Many experiments were carried out in the Central Aerodynamic Institute under the supervision of academic A.A. Dorodnitsyn, including model testing in aerodynamic tunnels and dummy models flying in helicopters and laboratory aircraft.

As already stated, the P-6 emanated from previous experience with the P-5/P-5D, but a lot of new design work had to be carried out on the new missiles to fulfil the requests of the Soviet Navy. These new tasks included OTH target selection, launching in different salvo configurations, in-flight management, manoeuvres to beat air defence systems, guidance systems, an RF-homing head system and new radome, made of dielectric materials. Guidance during the mid-course phase was based on an INS/Doppler, with a supporting active-radar seeker in the terminal phase.

A P-6 missile launching from one of two aft launchers of a Project 675-class submarine. (Voeno Tehnichky Zbornik)

An aerial view of a Project 675/Echo II-class submarines on patrol in the northern Pacific in the mid-1980s. (US Navy)

The first tests were carried out in October 1959, while the first OTH launches from a submarine, supported by a Tu-16RT Badger, were performed between July and September 1963, the first ever launch of this kind.

Development of the anti-ship P-6 missile was carried out in parallel to that of a sister missile, the P-35 (ASCC/NATO SS-N-3b Sepal for versions fired from surface vessels, and SSC-1b Sepal for those fired by coastal artillery units). These other missiles were developed at the same time and deployed on board surface vessels (Project 58 and Project 1134 cruisers) as well as with coastal artillery units. This 'family' of SSM missiles allowed the Soviet Union to achieve a milestone in the history of naval combat.

At the Military Defence Council of 1969, the Commander-in-Chief of the Soviet Navy, Admiral Sergei G. Gorshkov, characterised the invention of the P-6, and in general all the submarine-launched anti-ship cruise-missile systems as the greatest national achievement made by the Soviet Union in the history of naval warfare.

Modernisations, conversions and resulting sub-classes

The numerous platforms of the Project 675-class offered the Soviet Navy the opportunity to test a variety of different technologies. As the years passed and new submarines, more modern and more silent, entered service with the fleet, the Echo II vessels were modernised with new weapons and technologies. Some of them left the combat role and assumed special project positions. Some vessels of the class offered sufficient space for new weapons systems, which increased their number of years of service with the fleet, allowing Moscow to have more platforms at sea.

The majority of the units had two refuellings of their nuclear reactors during their operational service, which implied that the reactors still had the capacity to provide propulsion. One area that was seriously lacking in the Soviet naval industry was its modernisation and overhaul projects. Usually, funds were allocated to new-builds, while retrofits and modernisations remained a much lesser priority, not receiving the resources for shipyards to carry out such work. This was an endemic problem, both then and later in the Russian Federation.

There were questions around whether the modernisation of this class was worth the money that would need to be invested. From a military and technological point of view, the answer was probably 'no'. Another point of view that needed to be considered was the political one, both internal and external. Externally, if the large number of Echo II vessels started to be decommissioned early, it would create a substantial fall in the theoretical number of submarines available to the Soviets in the event of war. The US Navy would probably have noted this reduction and could thus start to apply more pressure on the remaining units. Internally, the reduction of a sizeable percentage of submarines would leave the Soviet Navy with fewer crews and bases and less money in the budget; and it was the budget that was the crucial factor. Regardless of whether a vessel was operational or not, useful or not, or capable of fighting in a war or not, the budget was made according to the number of vessels. That was something that Admiral Gorshkov knew perfectly well, and he thus managed to receive as much funding as possible for his fleet from Moscow.[8]

There were numerous different conversion projects for the Echo II class, some of which are summarised below. It should be borne in mind, however, that some units were never modernised or retrofitted with new weapons systems.

Project 675K

An upgrade of the systems of several vessels. Initially, this included the installation of new batteries, a new Nakat-M navigation radar, a new antenna for communication with the Kasatka-B system, a new MGK-100 Kerch sonar system and the integration of the updated Uspekh-U system. Only two units, K-47 and K-125, underwent this work in the Severodvinsk shipyard.

Project 675MU

A testbed platform for a new missiles system, with K-28 selected for its implementation. The vessel remained in the Severodvinsk shipyard between October 1968 and January 1975, being installed with new launchers and systems for testing the P-500 Bazalt missile (ASCC/NATO codename 'SS-N-12 Sandbox'), including new sonar and navigation radars, the Argon-K missile control system and Uspekh-U targeting system. Tests were carried out successfully and the missiles entered service with the Soviet Navy. The submarine could still load only eight missiles served the rest of its operational life with this configuration.

Project 675MK

The implementation of the above-mentioned systems in serial configuration for the rest of the units assigned this transformation.

Table 7: Submarines of the Project 675MK Class

Unit	Modernisation started	Modernisation completed	Commissioning year
K-94	December 1972	September 1976	1976
K-175	December 1973	November 1977	1977
K-184	October 1975	December 1978	1979
K-57	October 1976	December 1979	1980
K-104	October 1976	February 1981	1981
K-128	April 1977	December 1981	1982
K-189	December 1976	May 1982	1982
K-23	March 1977	October 1984	1984
K-56	June 1978	September 1986	1986

A Project 675MKU-class submarine as tracked down by the US Navy in the late 1980s. (US Navy)

Nine submarines were selected to be modernised with the new P-500 missiles, Kasatka-B and new Molniya communication systems and the Argon-K control system.

Four shipyards were involved in fulfilling the schedule of the transformations due to the large number of jobs that each vessel required.[9] The containers of the missiles needed to be enlarged to fit the new missiles, while the new control systems allowed the submarines to launch a salvo of eight missiles with the launching sequence of 4-7-3-8-1-6-2-5. These conversions were carried out between 1972 and 1986, with the vessels commissioned with the fleets between 1976 and 1986. It was a massively expensive overhaul for the Echo II fleet, regardless of the increased military efficiency provided by the new systems. This class was now old and more modern platforms in the construction halls offered better options. Nevertheless, that was the way the Soviet Navy operated its fleet.[10]

Project 675MKU

This was the last modernisation of the class, involving the use of new P-1000 Vulkan missiles that shared common architecture with the P-500 system. The modernisation was started during the death throes of the USSR, and the programme suffered from the collapse of the country, leading to it practically being cancelled. A total of five units were assigned to this modernisation in the Severodvinsk and Bolshoy Kamen shipyards.

K-1 performed the first launch of the P-1000 in December 1983, and in the summer of 1985 launched 18 test missiles, of which 10 were successful. During the following years, prior to its retirement from the fleet in 1992, K-1 completed three patrols with the new missiles on board. It is unclear if any of the other units fulfilled any patrols with the new systems.

Table 8: Upgrade of Submarines to the Project 675MKU Standard

Unit	Modernisation started	Modernisation completed	Commissioning year
K-1	February 1981	December 1985	1986
K-35	December 1984	December 1987	1988
K-34	1982	1988	1989
K-10	September 1984	1989	May 1989 (cancelled)
K-22	December 1985	December 1990	1990

Project 675N

One unit, K-170, was renamed KS-86 after the completion of work in the SPR-10 repairs shipyard at Polyarny in the Northern Fleet area. The work required a large amount of time and resources, the conversion lasting from January 1973 to December 1980. This submarine was covered in secrecy due to it serving with 29 Independent Brigade of Submarines of the Northern Fleet. This unit did not follow the regular Soviet Navy chains of command, its orders coming directly from the higher authority of the Kremlin or the state intelligence agencies (the KGB or GRU). The conversion was intended to create the capacity to operate with special extra-deep divers (known as hydronauts), the best-paid special forces of the former USSR and later Russian Federation. The vessel remained in service until 1991.[11]

Eleven units of the original class never received any major conversions. Although they underwent overhauls and modernisation of systems, they continued operating until the collapse of the USSR with the P-6 as their main weapon, having served during practically the whole of the Cold War.

Operational History

The service life of the Project 675-class submarines was marred by numerous accidents. The propulsion plant of the first generation of the type caused some of the worst accidents in the naval forces, and lead to the deaths of many officers and sailors. However, its deployment by the Soviet Navy was the first of its kind in the world, marking a milestone in the history of the Soviet fleet.

With 29 submarines commissioned by the Soviet Navy, the Project 675-class was one of the most common and widely used submarines during the Cold War. Fifteen units served with the Northern Fleet, while 14 were based with the Pacific Fleet.[13] The average serviceability of the class was 72 percent, with a figure of 74

P-500 ('SS-N-12 SANDBOX')

The same decree that initiated the research and development of the P-120 (ASCC/NATO codename 'SS-N-9 Siren') initiated the work on a new missile for SSG/SSGNs of the first generation, the P-500.[12] Initially, Chelomey used data from his earlier missiles and aimed for a surface-launched weapon (and one that would be compatible with surface vessels, too), resulting in the P-350 – the general size, weight and storage system of which were similar to the P-6, but which never entered service. The continuation of his work resulted in the P-500: the first Soviet submarine-launched anti-ship missile with a range over 500km (270nm), and the first to introduce the 'wolfpack' method of attack (later perfectioned in the P-700 Granit). As usual, the weapon could receive mid-course guidance updates, and had active terminal radar homing. The P-500 could be armed with the GSKB-47 warhead, weighing 1,000kg, or a nuclear warhead with a yield of 360Kt – either of which was armoured to increase their survivability against enemy CIWS. Furthermore, it had ECM equipment to interfere with enemy fire-control radars on the final approach. Powered by a new turbojet engine, the KP-17-300, the P-500 had a top speed of Mach 2, but was limited to about Mach 1.5 when programmed to fly at low altitude. This necessitated parts of its airframe be made of titanium.

The first series of flight tests was undertaken at the Nenoshka Test Range between October 1969 and October 1970, when it demonstrated a range of 550km (297nm). Between 1971 and 1974, the Project 675MU submarine K-28 embarked test rounds for several test cruises. Following successful certification, the P-500 entered operational service a year later. Series production was conducted at the Strela Works in Orenburg, and a total production run was estimated at more than 500, of which no fewer than 400 were still operational with the Soviet Navy as of 1990, and 150 as of 1995. Indeed, the P-500 was still used for training purposes in 2007, by when about 50 were still available.

While a weapon of clearly superior performance in comparison to the earlier P-6, P-500 still required launch from the surface, and preparation for launching lasted between 20 and 30 minutes – which was obviously a growing disadvantage. The Soviet Navy continued investing in such weapons, despite their obsolescence, because the contemporary Soviet Minister of Defence, Marshal Andrei Antonovich Grechko, insisted on developing a strong conventional force for a possible war in Europe, atop of already controlling a massive nuclear force. Under expected conditions, the GenStab assumed that older platforms could still operate effectively against NATO's sea lines of communication in the Atlantic – because a conventional war was expected to last longer and the USA would then have to introduce a convoy system to resupply its own troops, and those of NATO, in Europe – while modern submarines were to focus on combating CVBGs. Moreover, because P-500s were deployed on several classes of Soviet Navy surface warships, they offered the advantage of commonality.

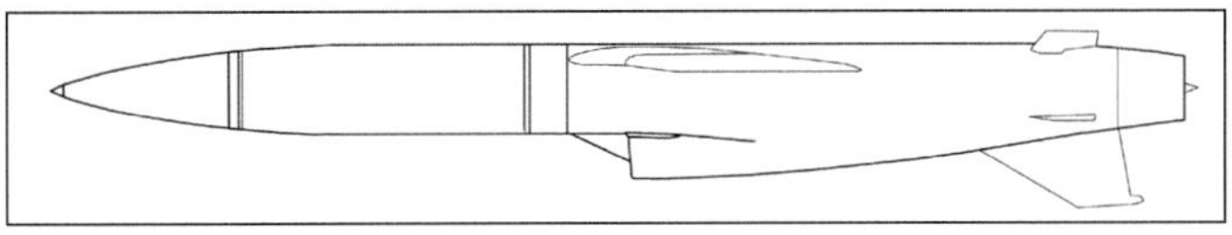

A diagram of the P-500 Bazalt missile. It had a 550km range at the speed of Mach 3, with a payload of 1,000kg: the latter included either a 350kt nuclear warhead, or a 950kg semi-armour-piercing high-explosive warhead. It could receive mid-course guidance corrections from the Tupolev Tu-95RT bomber, Kamov Ka-25K or Kamov Ka-31 helicopters, and had active-radar homing for terminal guidance. (Drawing by Tom Cooper)

percent for units of the Northern Fleet and 70 percent for those with the Pacific Fleet.

The level of effectiveness of the Soviet naval industry had a big impact on the availability of these units. Pacific shipyards were new to the nuclear business and had a worst efficiency than the better-invested and trained Northern Fleet shipyards.[14] The average days in overhaul for Pacific units was 2,634 days, while in the Northern Fleet shipyards the submarines required an average of just 2,407 days, a reduction of more than seven months per submarine, thereby increasing the availability of units for service with the fleet.

As operational units serving with the relevant fleets, the full class sailed 5,729,177 nautical miles: 3,497,420 with the Northern Fleet and 2,231,757 with the Pacific Fleet. The average nautical miles sailed per submarine was also better with Northern Fleet units, with 218,588nm against 185,979nm for those with the Pacific Fleet.

The full fleet of submarines executed 248 patrols, with 154 under the Northern Fleet and 94 with the Pacific Fleet. This further highlights the better maintenance and readiness in the Northern Fleet, whose units had an average of 9.62 patrols per submarine during their operational service, compared to 7.23 patrols for Pacific Fleet vessels. The number of patrols was a measure of the capability of the units to confront the enemy during any hostilities.

As a class, the Project 675 sailed in practically all possible scenarios against the Western nations and other countries hostile to the USSR. From 1964–89, at least one patrol maintained a continuous presence in the Atlantic Ocean. The same was the case in the Pacific region from 1965 until 1989. The class also carried out patrols in the Mediterranean Sea, involving Northern Fleet vessels from 1967–70 and 1974–89. The Indian Ocean received great attention from the class during the 1970s and 1980s, with deployments to ports in Yemen and Somalia. Pacific Fleet units were commonly deployed to the Philippine Sea, the Sea of Japan and in the 1980s to Vietnam, to the former US naval base at Cam Ranh Bay. Cuba and the Caribbean were also visited by formations from the Northern Fleet, especially in the 1970s.

The patrols reached their peak between 1966 and 1968 in the Atlantic Ocean, with eight submarines making patrols in each of those years. In the Mediterranean during the late 1970s and early 1980s – in particular 1978, 1981 and 1984 – four submarines were deployed each year. Deployments in the Pacific reached their maximum in 1968, with nine simultaneous patrols, while the following year there were eight patrols. The Indian Ocean received maximum attention in 1980 with a total of three patrols.

The class was thus a common platform in all of the principal maritime areas during the Cold War and was equipped with offensive systems that created a major threat to NATO and other Western fleets, especially for the US Navy, which had to take this menace very seriously.

The units serving with the Northern Fleet carried out several remarkable actions that deserve at least some comment to underscore the importance of these submarines, not only to the Soviet Navy, but also to all the other countries involved. The units in the Northern Fleet were assigned mainly to the 11th and 7th Division of Submarines, and later in the 1980s some with the 50th

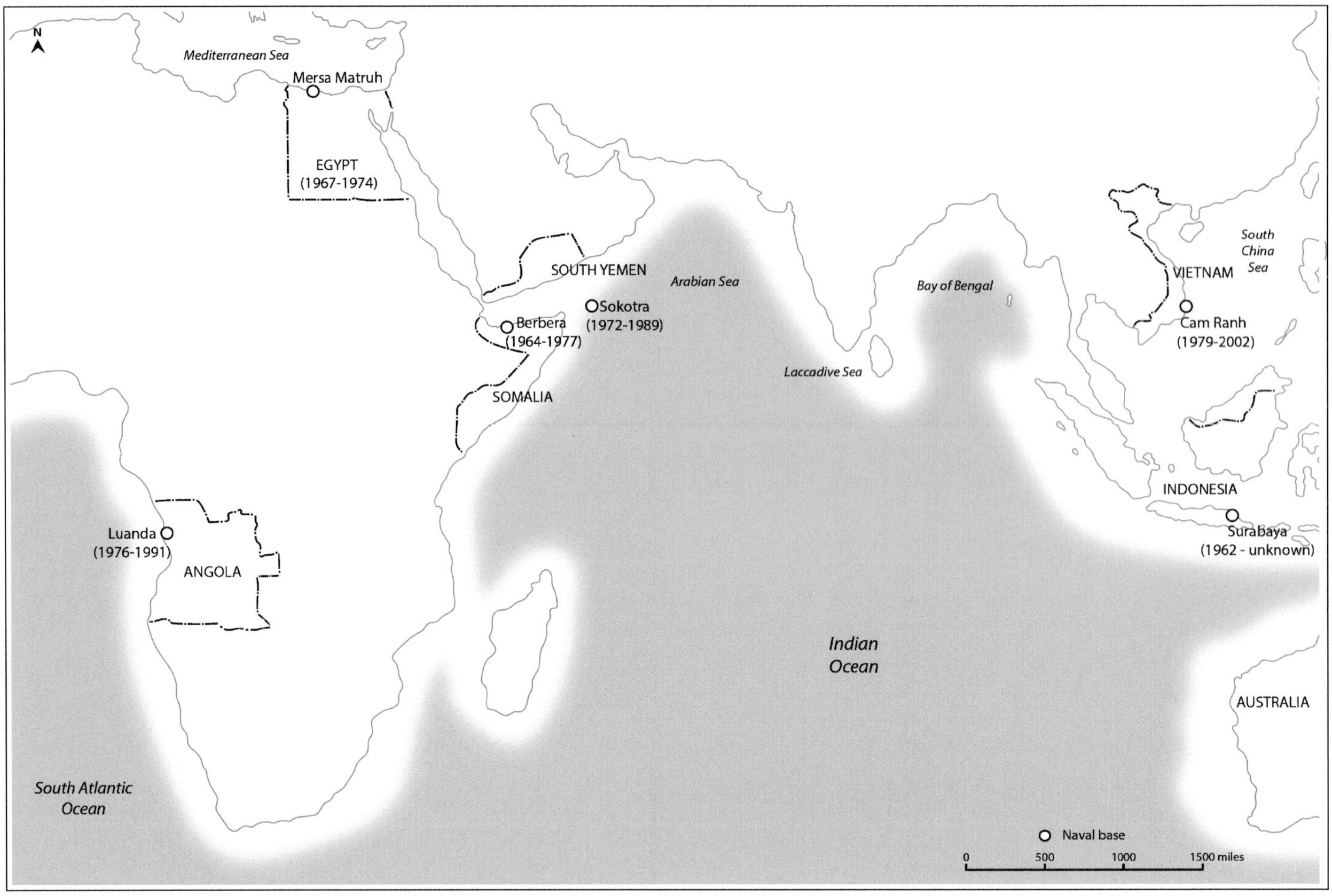

The USSR rarely managed to establish a permanent naval presence in the Atlantic Ocean, Mediterranean Sea and the Indian Ocean. Time and again, however, it did secure the right to use the port facilities shown on this map, including Mersa Matruh in Egypt, Luanda in Angola, Somalia, South Yemen, Vietnam and Indonesia. This represented a major problem for its SSGNs though, which had a long way to travel just to reach their stations at the crucial points of entry to the Indian Ocean. (Map by George Anderson)

A Project 675/Echo II-class submarine underway on the surface at high speed in the southern Pacific. (US Navy)

Division, while K.170 – after a full overhaul – was sent to serve with the 29th Independent Brigade of Submarines of the Northern Fleet, which was under the command of the GRU and the Higher Naval Intelligence Staff of the USSR. Some of the most important actions these submarines were involved in are listed below.

On 12 August 1965, the K-166 launched the first salvo of four P-6 missiles in the White Sea, earning the system a memorable success for the future of the fleet. In December of the same year, its sister ship, K-35, was visited by the Soviet cosmonaut Yuri Gagarin, who appeared to be impressed with the submarine technology that he saw and the submariners whom he met. The K-116, built and commissioned by the Northern Fleet, received an order to be transferred to the Pacific Fleet in 1966. The route selected for this mission was a southerly one, with a circumnavigation of the Drake Passage at the southernmost point of South America and then a voyage across the Pacific. Under the command of Rear Admiral Sorokin, K-116 was joined by K-133, a Project 627-class SSN, which was also transferred to the Pacific Fleet. The voyage was carried out without surfacing, sailing 21,000nm in 52 days, from 2 February to 26 March 1966. Rear Admiral Sorokin was decorated as a Hero of the Soviet Union for this achievement.

Some units made patrols armed with P-5D strategic missiles, making training launches with this missile type. It is known that at least K-74, in August–September 1966, and K-1, in 1972, each launched a full salvo of eight P-5Ds.

Another extreme cruise was planned to measure the crew and equipment's resistance during a lengthy submerged voyage in environmental conditions that differed from those that the Northern Fleet was used to. Between 24 March and 24 October 1967, a formation of Soviet vessels performed a voyage to equatorial latitudes to test the endurance and resilience of the crews and their equipment. The P-6 missiles stored inside their containers were tested for the effect of the voyage on its system and efficacy. The formation comprised conventional submarines K-128, B-21 and B-36 of the Project 641 Foxtrot-class SS, PMS-20 Ship Base of the Project 1886 class, PM-93 missile workshop ship of the Project 323A class, and an oceanographic vessel. The surface units provided supplies and support for the trip. K-128 suffered several incidents during the trip, as listed in Table 9.

A Project 675/Echo II-class submarine underway at minimal speed on the surface of the Pacific Ocean in the early 1980s. (US Navy)

Yuri Gagarin, the first Soviet Kosmonaut, is seen here during the visit of the K-35, accompanied by its contemporary skipper, Captain 2nd Class Ernst Bulyon. Gagarin requested that Bulyon perform a speed dive, but the latter ordered a dive to the periscope depth only: this proved enough, for Gagarin concluded he would prefer to fly to space than step into a submarine ever again. (Efim Sandler collection)

On the morning of 5 June 1967, at the start of another Arab–Israeli War, the K-131 – a submarine of the Northern Fleet – was on patrol in the Adriatic under the command of Captain 1st Rank Vadim Kulinchenko. Alarmed at the news of the Israeli onslaught, Moscow ordered him to immediately move to the coast of Israel and prepare for a missile attack by the end of the same day. Obviously, this was an impossible order, for the submarine not only had to pass the coasts of Italy, Greece and Turkey, but travel at a speed of 57 knots per hour in order to reach its position on time. Kulinchenko thus did his best and while moving into the eastern Mediterranean found the ships of the Fifth Eskadra and joined them. Unsurprisingly, the submarine failed to reach the coast of Israel even before the war was concluded through a UN-negotiated ceasefire, five days later.[15]

In 1969, after years of theoretical studies and tactical development, K-131 and K-135, both boats of the Project 675-class class, launched a successful attack of two salvos against a target from two different directions. This was the first time that such an attack confirmed the feasibility of the P-6 missile and the Project 675-class class.

The following year, K-135 took part in the fleet exercise Okean 70, after which it visited Cuba accompanied by four surface units, one tanker and the conventional submarine B-109 of the Project 641-class. Visits to Cuban ports by formations of Soviet vessels or submarines alone continued in 1972 with K-1 and in 1973 with K-172. K-1 repeated the visit in the summer of 1973, also inserted in a formation. Such deployments of nuclear submarines to the Caribbean obviously worried the chiefs of the US Navy and the US Department of Defense but provided valuable information while they tracked the Soviet submarines.

Pacific Fleet units also made important deployments and created moments in Soviet naval history. The structure of services in this fleet was more complex, with more organic structures involved. Units usually started to serve with the Pacific Fleet under the 26th Division of Submarines, but later there were also the 10th, 45th and

A Project 675-class submarine seen navigating in heavy seas next to a supply ship in the Mediterranean. (Efim Sandler collection)

29th Divisions. In the 1980s, some units were sent to the 8th, 42nd and 38th Divisions; during deployments in Vietnam, they were integrated with the 38th Division of Submarines based in Cam Rahn Bay Naval Base.

During a patrol in December 1966 and January 1967, K-48 located, trailed and made simulated torpedo and missile attacks against the US Navy's nuclear-powered cruiser USS *Brainbridge* (CGN-25) in the Philippine Sea. In 1969, border clashes between the USSR and China seemed to be leading to a war situation. For this reason, the Soviets, not knowing if or when war would come, deployed the Project 675-class vessels K-56 and K-34, among other types of submarine and kinds of ship, to patrol in the Sea of Japan, prepositioning for any future action, but ultimately their use was not necessary as tensions eased.

Another encounter with the US Navy took place in 1968 in the South China Sea. On this occasion it was K-10 that found the carrier battlegroup centred on the USS *Enterprise* (CVAN-65, later CVN-65), with the nuclear-powered escorts cruisers USS *Bainbridge*, USS *Long Beach* (CG-9) and USS *Truxtun* (CGN-35). K-10 trailed the formation for 13 hours while conducting simulated torpedo and missile attacks on the carrier, obtaining valuable acoustic intelligence from the encounter.

After the mining of North Vietnamese ports by US forces in 1972, the USSR deployed submarines to the area as tensions heightened. Between May and June, four Project 675-class vessels – K-184, K-189, K-57 and K-7 – took station in the South China Sea and Philippine Sea.[16] The K-184 encountered and trailed USS *Guardfish*, an American SSN, at the beginning of this patrol. In turn, the K-57 had the dubious honour of carrying out a failed torpedoes exercise in September 1980 with a supervisor from the Soviet Navy on board. The supervisor was the future Commander-in-Chief of the Soviet Navy, Admiral Chervanin. It was unusual for a Project 675-class submarine to perform badly during such exercises. Three years later, in February 1983, K-57 hosted the then Commander-in-Chief of the

A Project 675-class submarine seen while approaching a supply ship on the high sea. By taking fuel for auxiliary machinery, and food, the boat could remain on station for several additional weeks – a particularly pressing issue during the late 1960s and through the 1970s, while the Soviet Navy still had too few SSGNs to permanently occupy all the stations in the Pacific that it wanted to control. (Efim Sandler collection)

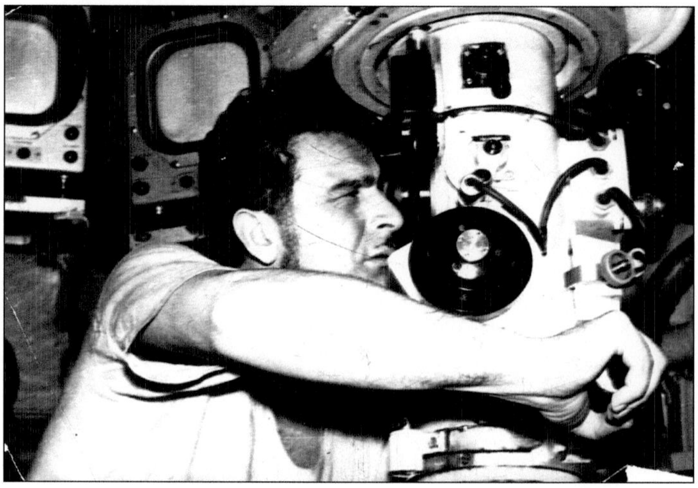

The deputy commander of a Project 675-class submarine monitoring the surrounding waters through the observation periscope of the boat. (Efim Sandler collection)

Another Project 675-class boat tied to a supply ship in the Mediterranean. Notable are the details of the rear deck and the third pair of missile launchers. (Efim Sandler collection)

Soviet Navy, Sergei G. Gorshkov, during a visit to Aden in Yemen. Also in 1983, K-7 was able to trail the nuclear-powered supercarrier USS *Nimitz* (CVN-68) during exercises in the Pacific, being praised for its actions by the Soviet Pacific Fleet.

Accidents involving SSGNs of the Project 675-class

The high speed at which the Project 675-class submarines were rushed into service and the high tempo of their operational deployments resulted in a wide range of accidents, from fires to literal meltdowns of their nuclear reactors. Some incidents were the responsibility of their designers and builders: others were caused by their crews. The most dramatic of these incidents are described below, while a number of other minor accidents are provided in Table 9 at the end of this chapter.

A memorial for the victims of the accident involving K-131. (Efim Sandler collection)

Early on 24 June 1970, K-108 – commanded by Captain 1st Class Boris Bagdasaryan – was taking part in an exercise off Petropavlovks when it collided with another submarine. The starboard propulsion shaft and propeller were bent and control over them was lost, causing the vessel to start descending out of control. After unsuccessfully trying to get the submarine to rise to the surface by blowing tanks and other methods, Bagdasaryan ordered his crew to reverse the port shaft. Luckily, the clutch survived the strain and K-108 eventually managed to surface. Meanwhile, the sonar picked up sounds from what appeared to be another submarine, leaving the collision zone at a speed of 15 knots. Heavily damaged, K-108 called for help from the Pacific Fleet while taking a course for its home base.

It was eventually discovered that the other submarine was USS *Tautog* (SSN-639), commanded by Captain Buele G. Balderston – a recipient of the Presidential Mention in Dispatches for monitoring a Soviet cruise-missile exercise in the same area sometime earlier. On this occasion, however, Balderston came too close and hit the starboard propeller of K-108 with his sail as the Soviet submarine began to submerge. The Soviet vessel suffered not only critical damage to its propeller shaft, but also to its external hull in the stern area, all of which necessitated extensive repairs. As far as is known, *Tautog* suffered heavy damage to its sail and lost all its antennas and periscope. Fortunately, nobody was killed or seriously damaged in the accident.[17]

A Project 675/Echo II-class submarine underway in the Pacific in the early 1980s. (US Navy)

The sail of K-22, seen from USS *Vogue* (FF-1047), while breaching the surface and wobbling immediately after the collision on 28 August 1976. The submarine was shadowing USS *Moinester* (FF-1097) but was unaware of USS *Vogue*'s presence. (Efim Sandler collection)

K-22 at the anchorage off Kythera following its collision with USS *Vogue*, 150nm south-west of Souda Bay, Crete, with obvious traces of damage to its sail and bow. (Photo by Eugene Ivkin)

Collisions involving Project 675/Echo II-class submarines occurred several further times thereafter. On 19 September 1973, K-131 hit K-320 of the Project 670/Charlie-class during an exercise in the White Sea. Once again, both crews were lucky as damage was only limited – though this accident did result in the reprimand and dismissal of several officers. Less than a year later, on 14 June 1973, K-56 was returning from a missile-firing exercise in the Sea of Japan, escorted by Project 1134/Kresta I-class cruiser *Vladivostok* (which carried the commander of the Submarine Division and numerous officers from other submarines). While checking the seas around the vessel, the crew switched on the surface radar and made a few quick sweeps, finding no other contacts. Two hours later, the radar was flicked on again – initially with the same result. Then four new contacts appeared, all in the proximity of the submarine. The commander ordered evasive manoeuvres, but it was too late: the fishery research vessel *Akademik Berg* hit the starboard side of the SSGN while underway at a speed of nine knots, breaching both the external and inner hull and causing a 4-metre-wide hole, through which both compartments one and two were flooded. The water that entered compartment two reached a battery tank, causing a fire that killed all 27 crewmembers there: 22 crew in compartment one were able to deal with the flooding and prevented any further damage. Eventually, K-56 had to be towed back to its home port, where the submarine spent the next eight months undergoing repairs. A commission that investigated the accident concluded that the skippers of both vessels had violated normal procedures.

On 20 August 1973, K-1 hit the bottom of the Hagua Banks in the Caribbean Sea at a speed of 16 knots and depth of 120 metres. Although the crew managed to return the boat to the surface, it then struck a reef. The two collisions caused structural damage to all torpedo tubes and the sonar equipment, and it was only in June 1974 that K-1 completed a new set of state trials prior to returning to operational service.

On the morning of 18 April 1976, K-116, assigned to the Pacific Fleet after being transferred from the Northern Fleet, left Avacha Bay escorted by the minesweeper MT-80. The escort was unable to reach a position to properly cover K-116, the submarine proceeding at 10–12 knots. At the same time, the motor vessel *Volsk* entered Avacha Bay without receiving any advice from the port authority to alter its course.

MT-80 was not in position to protect K-116 from the *Volsk*, while K-116's radar operator only located the other vessel very late. The captain then ordered the submarine to reduce speed to 5–6 knots and start evasive manoeuvres, but the *Volsk* hit K-116 at nine knots. The submarine was forced to return to base for repairs. In the dry dock, damage was ascertained to be a penetration of the external hull with a hole of five square metres and a dent in the pressure hull. The degaussing coils were also destroyed in the impacted area. Repairs after this accident – which would have been easily avoidable if normal protection measures had been taken by all parties involved – took from May 1976 until April 1977, immobilising a nuclear-powered submarine for practically a whole year.

A view of the wrecked front of the sail of K-22. Clearly, the radar antenna was a total loss. (Efim Sandler collection)

under its own propulsion to Severodvinsk shipyard. Repairs were carried out to the structure of the forward hull, sonar system, sail structure, augment system in the forward side of the hull and the forward pair of missiles containers. The captain of K-22 was dismissed from his position for the role he played in this accident.

K-56 embarked on one patrol in the Pacific in 1977, during which a major leak was found in the port side nuclear reactor, forcing it to return to base with only one reactor operating. The submarine entered the SRH-30 shipyard in January 1978 for repairs to various pieces of equipment, including the leaking reactor. While undergoing a pressure test to locate the leak, a non-return valve failed to work properly and caused an emission of radioactive water inside compartments five and six, creating a major contamination problem.

Another collision involving an Echo II-class vessel – which became a very famous naval incident – took place in the Mediterranean in August 1976. K-22, an Echo II, was finishing its assigned patrol in the Ionian Sea, 150nm to the south-west of Crete, when on 28 August, around 1628 hours, it detected a US frigate through its periscope. The captain decided to continue trailing the warship as an exercise for his crew. All approximations and estimations of distance, bearing and course of the frigate were done based on the captain's observation, the speed of the vessel and sea conditions preventing the sonar from being useful during this time. K-22 started to approximate the frigate at different positions and speeds, the captain realising that the frigate had located his submarine. The observed frigate was the Knox-class USS *Moinester* (FF-1097), but unobserved by the captain of K-22 was another US frigate nearby, the USS *Vogue* (FF-1047) of the Garcia class. While K-22 continued its movement, it was closing in dangerously on the second frigate. At 1825 hours, in his fourth periscope observation, the captain finally detected the *Vogue* at very close range and ordered an emergency dive and the periscope down. Despite this manoeuvre, K-22 struck the *Vogue* below the hangar area on the starboard side, the submarine being damaged in the bow area of the hull and the forward part of the sail.

Neither of the vessels were at risk of sinking, but the Commander of the US Sixth Fleet and other USN skippers offered assistance to the surfaced submarine and the Commander of the Soviet Fifth Eskadra. In a very polite manner, all such offers were refused by the Soviets. USS *Vogue* had to be towed to Crete, and later to Toulon, where it was repaired in the French Navy shipyards for two months before returning to the United States.

K-22 limped to the Soviet anchorage off the Greek island of Kythera, where it received emergency repairs allowing it to sail

A full decontamination of the submarine was carried out, after which the cause of the leak in the nuclear reactor was found to be a crack in the envelope of the reactor and some thread-bars used for tightening and sealing. The State Commission that was overseeing the work ruled that it was impossible to repair the crack and the leaks in situ in compartment six, so it was decided to replace the nuclear reactor with a new one. Meanwhile, the Soviet Navy decided that the time required in the shipyard for the repairs would be utilised to modernise the submarine to the Project 675MK standard.

The full conversion plus the changing of the port side nuclear reactor was carried out between January 1978 and 28 September 1986, a repair of eight years in a vessel with 12 years of service when it suffered the reactor malfunction. After this lengthy repair, the submarine was commissioned by the Pacific Fleet and made one more patrol in 1988 in the Vietnam area before being dismissed from the Navy in July 1992.

Returning to K-116, which had suffered the collision with the *Volsk* in Avacha Bay in 1976, it underwent repairs until April 1977, after which, from July 1978 to July 1979, it received a second replacement of the fuel elements in both nuclear reactors. On 2 July 1979, K-116 left the shipyard and sailed on the surface to Vladimir Bay, despite the worries of many of the crew that the repairs had not been completed satisfactorily. During its journey, a major leak of cooling water from the primary loop took place, flooding the reactor compartment, depressurising the core of the reactor and boiling a large amount of the primary water. This led to a leak of radioactive gases and aerosols throughout the submarine's compartments, affecting all crewmembers on board.[18] K-116 was unable to sail under its own power and had to be towed back to the shipyard. The State Commission that checked the status of submarines made an official request to the Pacific Fleet Commander-in-Chief to retire

P-1000 VULKAN

Developed as an improved version of the P-500, the P-1000 became a matter of quite some controversy in the West – though only once it was discovered by Western intelligence services, towards the end of the Cold War. Unsurprisingly, this weapon never received an ASCC/NATO reporting name.

Following the line of the P-6 and P-500 – and meant to replace all the older missiles of these types in service on submarines and surface vessels – the P-1000 incorporated extensive use of titanium alloys to reduce the weight and improve survivability. The 11.7m long and 4,800kg weapon could accelerate to the speed of Mach 3, but still reach a range of 750km (405 miles). Its flight testing began in 1983, and by the end of the year the first rounds were loaded on the Project 675MKV class submarine K-1. Further development was protracted though and it was officially certified for operational service only in 1987.

The deployment of the P-1000 required the installation of the Kasatka-B weapons systems, and the Legenda satellite communication system. Early on, the Soviet Navy wanted to rearm all of its Project 675-class submarines upgraded to the Project 675MKV standard with it, and five are known to have been subjected to related upgrades between 1977 and 1990.[22] However, the work was completed on only four of them, and one was cancelled with the boat still in the shipyard. Worse yet: despite all the expense, all the Project 675MKV submarines were withdrawn from service between 1992 and 1994 – with which the operational service of the P-1000 also ended.

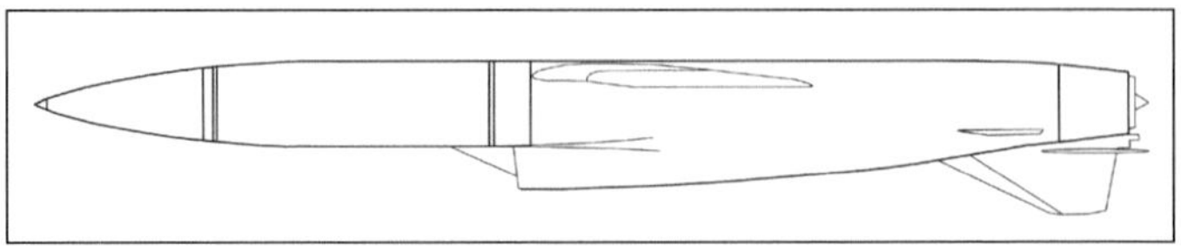

A diagram of the short-serving P-1000 *Vulkan* anti-ship missile. It had the same maximum range and speed as the P-500, but the weight was increased by 1,200kg. Eventually, it was installed on only three Project 675-class vessels: the K-1, the K-35 and the K-22. (Drawing by Tom Cooper)

K-116 from service due to the amount of contaminated water that had affected all the equipment in the reactor compartment and the contamination throughout the vessel. Furthermore, due to the lack of cooling in the reactor, some of the fuel elements had suffered a meltdown, creating a serious problem for the refuelling process and other maintenance.[19] The vessel was eventually placed in reserve in 1982 and left the fleet. This was the first accident in the Echo II class that led to the loss of a unit.

On 20 March 1981, K-184 went to sea to take part in a combined exercise with the Project 670 Charlie I-class SSGN K-43. The exercise was based on a deep dive test coordinated between both submarines. The procedures and steps for the coordinated dive were worked out on board K-184 instead of at the headquarters of the division. At 1835 hours, both submarines rendezvoused on the surface and the procedures for the exercise were transmitted via VHF with some errors, which were unnoticed by K-43. At 1918 hours, the dive test started, but neither of the submarines followed the correct procedures, resulting in mutual contact between them being lost at 2036 hours.

At 2119 hours, K-184 resurfaced and spotted a green light that it identified as a merchant vessel, when in reality was the already surfaced K-43. Meanwhile, K-43, thinking that its partner was still to emerge on the surface, started to manoeuvre outside what it believed to be the danger area. However, the new course it took put it on a collision course with the surfaced K-184. At 2154 hours, the officers of the watch in K-43 detected some flashing lights at a bearing of 70–80 degrees on its starboard side, which was the dangerously close K-184, and two minutes later ordered an emergency reverse turbine. Nevertheless, at 2200 hours, K-184 struck its exercise partner on the starboard side.

Fortunately, no injuries were caused during this collision and the submarines suffered only material damage to their external hulls. Both skippers were, however, reprimanded, and the captain of K-184, Captain 2nd Rank Moskalenko, was dismissed from his position.[20] Both submarines required time in drydock to fix their structural damage.

K-10 suffered one of the least known submarine collisions of the Cold War. On 21 January 1983, it struck another submerged submarine in the bow. The damage was considerable, though no casualties were reported. The submarine returned to base and entered drydock and was subsequently assigned for repairs and transformation to the Project 675MKV standard, but this was cancelled due to lack of funds and problems with the naval budget in the last years of the Soviet Navy. During an inspection in the drydock of the forward damage, steel elements of the other submarine were found in its structure. Mystery surrounds the identity of the other vessel, as no other nation has admitted suffering an accident involving one of its submarines at this time.[21]

On 18 June 1984, a tragic incident happened for the Northern Fleet while K-131 was in the Barents Sea returning from a patrol. An electrician was working on equipment in compartment eight when his clothing and equipment set on fire. The team in the compartment tried to save the life of the electrician while others started to fight the fire. The flames spread to compartment seven and a large volume of toxic fumes was produced. By the time the fire was brought under control and extinguished, 13 members of the crew had been killed due to inhalation of the fumes.

The K-431 Catastrophe

The most serious incident involving the Echo II class, indeed probably one of the biggest nuclear accidents in the whole Soviet leet, happened in the summer of 1985 in Chazma Bay near Vladivostok. The vessel involved was the former K-31, which at the time had been renamed to the new designation K-431, which became the name associated with the incident.

The submarine was undergoing the second refuelling of its reactors,[23] but during tests, after the fuel rods had been inserted and the reactor closed again, it was found that the starboard side reactor was not watertight and something appeared to be in the seal of the reactor, making it impossible to tighten it properly.

The Executive Officer of the vessel decided to try to fix the problem in his own way, not following normal Soviet Navy procedures that required all work to start again in the starboard side reactor to look for the cause of the problem. The delays that this work would have caused to the vessel's delivery influenced all the officers of the submarine, as well as the work supervisors of the shipyard.

Early on the morning of Saturday 10 August, the Executive Officer organised the work with crewmembers, with assistance

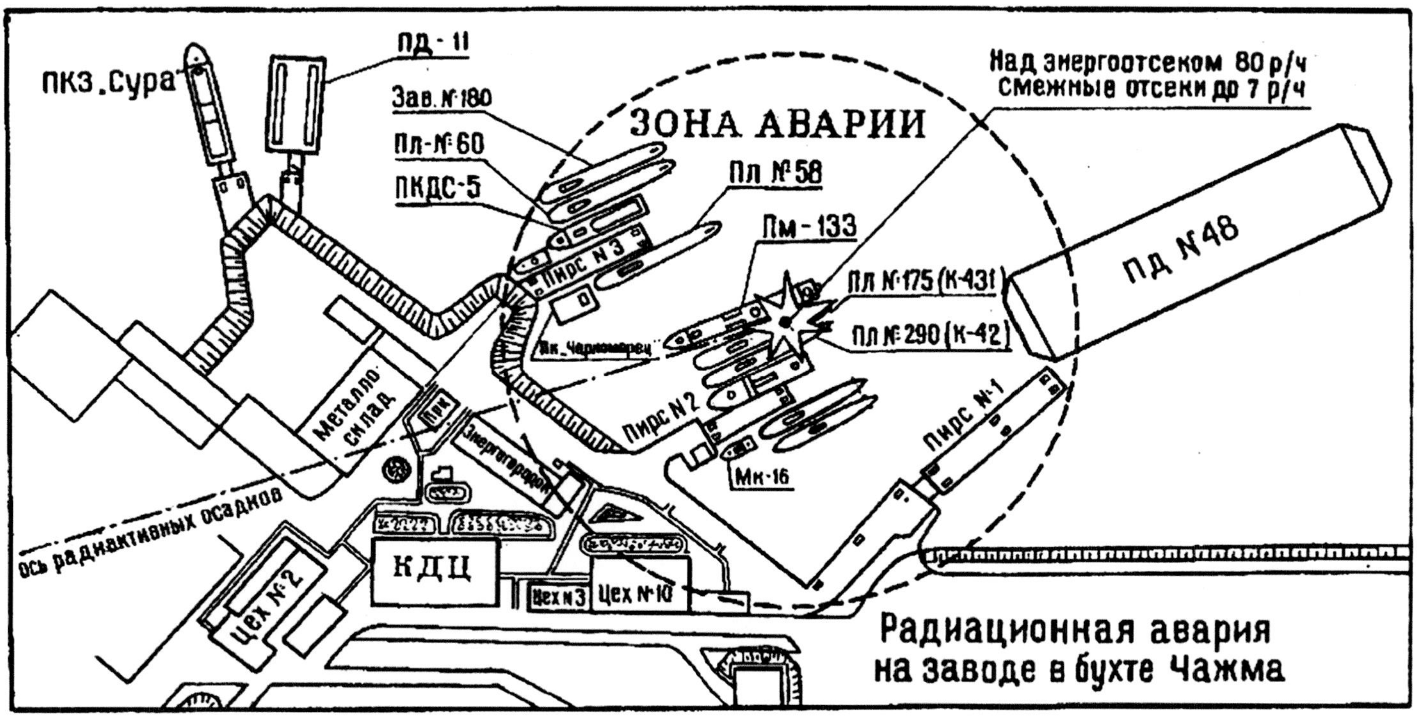

The position of K-431 at the time of the terrible accident in Chazma Bay on 10 August 1985. (Voeno Tehnichky Zbornik)

from a few shipyard workers. The procedure involved the raising of the cover of the reactor, opening it and allowing an inspection of the seal of the cover. The design of the reactor allowed the raising of the cover, together with the control rods of the reactor, to a maximum height to avoid a self-sustained chain reaction in the reactor. This safety height was set by a welded-on component to limit the raising movement. However, unknown to the Executive Officer and other crewmembers was that this piece had been cut by the crew to allow better access for the inspection of the seal, within which was an electrode rod that had been forgotten during previous work and was now disrupting the proper sealing of the cover of the reactor, preventing it from becoming watertight. While this was happening inside the submarine, the movement of another vessel inside the port caused a wave and consequent movement inside the submarine. The lifted control rod, together with the reactor cover, starting to move out of the safety position and allowed the reactor to suffer a catastrophic accident. An uncontrolled self-sustained chain reaction created heat and steam sufficient to cause an explosion inside the reactor while it was completely open.

The cover of the reactor was a piece of steel weighing some 12 tons, but the explosion lifted it into the air in the engine room: the explosion and the impact of the falling cover instantly wrecked the engine room. The external and inner hull were punctured by fuel elements from the reactor – a few of which were thrown 80 metres away, together with much radioactive debris – and damaged to a degree where the submarine was flooded, starting with the engine room and stern compartment. A radioactive cloud approximately 6,000 metres long and hundreds of metres wide was released over the Dunai peninsula in the direction of Vladivostok: radioactive particles were later found 30 kilometres away from the shipyard. All vessels, installations and equipment which were in Chazma Bay at the time received heavy doses of radiation, as did all the personnel that promptly launched intensive efforts to contain the catastrophe – to little avail. Contaminated seawater soon began exiting the engine room and circulating back into the bay. Fires on board K-431 continued in multiple areas for several hours.

Alerted about the explosion, the Division Commander Rear Admiral Viktor Khramtsov, rushed to Chazma Bay. During his journey he still had hopes that the explosion involved other equipment aboard the submarine and not the nuclear reactors. When he reached the shipyard, fumes and gases covered the whole area, making breathing difficult. When Khramtsov and his staff located K-431, it was sinking slowly at the pier. Helped by everyone who was at hand, they cut the mooring ropes with fire axes and ordered the tugs to pull K-431 to a sand bank to avoid a full uncontrolled sinking. Thereafter, the teams on board were able to circulate seawater in an open loop to the reactors, cooling the core but spreading tons of contaminated water into the bay. No attempt was made to repair the submarine due the scale of the damage caused by the explosion and fires. The contamination was so high that such work was unthinkable. K-431 was thus completely lost to the Soviet Navy, remaining in Chazma Bay until it was possible to tow it to the naval base in Pavlovsk to await dismantling.

The dismantling process for the submarine was beyond the normal procedures due to the accident it had suffered. Nevertheless, in January 2010 a contract was assigned to the Zvezda shipyard by the Russian state atomic energy corporation Rosatom, and during April, May and June that year a Joint Commission from Rosatom and Zvezda visited the vessel to evaluate the work and measure radiation levels. Protests were lodged by workers and citizens of the nearby Pavlovsk city due to the risks caused by the dismantling of the submarine. The work was eventually carried out, the submarine being scrapped on an ad-hoc basis. However, the effects of this terrible nuclear accident will reverberate well into the twenty-first century.

Eight officers and two sailors lost their lives during the accident, while more than 300 people suffered from radiation poisoning, with 39 of them having serious radiation sickness.[24] Despite this, the accident could have been far worse than it was; thanks to the heroic actions of officers and sailors present during that awful Saturday morning, the world was saved from another Chernobyl. However, the Soviet Navy lost the services of another nuclear submarine due to this incident.

K-431, once the fires caused by its catastrophic explosion were extinguished. Note at least two flotation devices keeping the hulk upright and on the surface. (Voeno Tehnichky Zbornik)

The following month another Echo II-class submarine was at the centre of a further nuclear accident, but this one with less tragic consequences. On 29 September 1985, K-175 was in Yemen carrying out a patrol when, after an incorrect procedure by the crew, the primary loop was depressurised, and a radiation leak occurred. The vessel's officers decided to fix the problem locally and they were able to continue with their assignment.

A year later, in November 1986, with the same submarine deployed in Cam Ranh Bay naval base in Vietnam, it suffered a meltdown in one of its reactors and the release of radioactive gases and aerosols into the environment. The contamination was so heavy that it was deemed the vessel could not be repaired and it was placed in reserve. K-175 was eventually transported to the Soviet Union in a floating dock vessel to be dismantled, which meant yet another submarine out of service for the Soviet fleet.

The last accident that involved the loss of a submarine of this class took place on 26 June 1989, when, after 23 years of service with the Northern Fleet, the former K-172 – now redesignated as K-192 – developed a leak in its primary cooling loop while on the way back to its home base in Gadzievo, near Murmansk in the far north of the USSR. The boat was immediately taken to the surface, about 350km from Bear Island in the Barents Sea. The leak caused a loss of cooling water and an increase in temperature in the core. To ease the situation, it was decided to divert all the available fresh water on board to the reactors in an open loop, discharging the contaminated water into the sea. This provisional solution managed to maintain the reactors at a high, but not dangerous, temperature. Soviet merchant vessel *Konstantin Yuon* arrived to help and provided fresh water to the submarine so that the cooling system of the reactors could continue to function. Finally, the order was given to shut down both reactors to reduce the still increasing temperatures in them.

The support vessel *Amur* also came to offer help for the stricken submarine, starting to provide a continuous flow of fresh water. This vessel also had a treatment plant for nuclear-contaminated water, many Scandinavians having been concerned about contamination levels. At this stage, human error caused more damage to the submarine's reactors.

While the *Amur* was connected, on board K-192 it was decided to try to repair the leak in the primary circuit, which was defined as micro-crack in a joint weld of pipes in the primary loop. Consequently, the flow of fresh water from the auxiliary vessel was shut down. However, when it became necessary to restart this flow, the operator was not at his position. The reactors' temperatures thus started rising again, and with the scale of the emergency growing, seawater was pumped directly to the reactors once more. With the high variation of temperatures, the fuel bars started to crack and a fracture began to appear in the cladding of the fuel elements. The *Amur* thus received water with such high radiation levels that it was unable to deal with it.

The submarine then started to flow seawater, in an open loop, directly to the reactors in a final attempt to cool them down. The situation was brought back to some level of control, and K-192

An unknown Project 675/Echo II submarine, nicely showing the recesses in the outer hull, necessary to deflect the blast from missile's boosters at their launch. This was to become the final class of Soviet SSGNs which had to surface in order to deploy its primary weapons, and one that served the training of an entirely new generation of Soviet Navy's submariners. (Efim Gordon collection)

Table 9: Further Accidents of the Project 675 Class

Date	Unit	Place	Type of Accident	Description
10/03/1963	K-47	Motovka Bay	Near miss	While surfacing, the vessel was very close to and collided with submarine K-113.
November 1965	K-74		Engineering	The blades of the turbine and condenser were destroyed during operation.
1966–1967	K-34	Komsomolsk-na-Amur	Reactor engineering	During the installation of the reactor in the shipyard, equipment was damaged, and the boat's delivery was delayed by 6 months.
04/06/1967	K-128	Northern Fleet	Nuclear plant	Due to an electrician's error, a blackout was caused, forcing the submarine to surface. Problems developed in cooling the reactor and with the main cooling pumps. External help was necessary, with extra fresh water to cool down the reactors.
09/09/1967	K-116	Northern Fleet	HVAC system	A full failure of the HVAC left the vessel with rising temperatures in the compartments, forcing it to surface and request external assistance before returning to base.
April 1968	K-172	Mediterranean	Contamination	126 crew members suffered mercury contamination, from an unknown source, while on patrol. The vessel was later decontaminated.
1969	K-166	Northern Fleet	Radioactive leak	While at sea, a leakage of radioactive gases and aerosols was detected, forcing the submarine to return to base.
12/10/1970	K-166	Northern Fleet	Explosion	Blowing high-pressure air into a ballast tank, inadvertently mixed with hydraulic oil, caused an explosion that destroyed weapon equipment.
29/09/1971	K-184	Sea of Okhotsk	Radioactive leak	A radioactive leak in compartment 6 spread to 2, 3, 7 and 8. Venting was carried out and the submarine returned to base. A US P-3 surveillance aircraft overflew the vessel while it was surfaced.
1975	K-172	Northern Fleet	Nuclear plant	Loss of flow in the primary circuit.
25/01/1975	K-57	Pacific Fleet	Accident	During painting work, fumes were released, and the firefighting system activated. Two crewmembers were killed due to asphyxia.
07/12/1975	K-35	Northern Fleet	Explosion	While charging battery bank 2, hydrogen mixed with air and caused an explosion, resulting in two crew being injured.
24/09/1976	K-47	Northern Fleet North Atlantic	Fire	An electric short circuit caused a fire in compartment 8. Three crewmembers died due to carbon monoxide poisoning while firefighting.
1977	K-48	Pacific Fleet	Engineering	During a deep dive test the stern tube seal of the shaft came loose, with more than 500 litres per hour of water entering the vessel.
1977	K-56	Pacific Fleet	Nuclear plant	A leak in the port side reactor forced the submarine to return to base.
June 1979	K-10	Pacific Fleet	Explosion	While charging its batteries, an explosion took place with several of the crew injured.
1981	K-131	Northern Fleet Mediterranean	Collision	The vessel collided with the sea bottom while patrolling in the Mediterranean.
28/09/1982	K-131	Northern Fleet	Explosion	While painting water ballast tank number 2, an explosion occurred due to build-up of fumes. Two crew were killed and four injured.
11/08/1983	K-94	Pacific Fleet	Nuclear plant	Leakage in the primary circuit.
21/03/1984	K-94	Pacific Fleet	Nuclear plant	Leakage in the primary circulation pump.
24/09/1984	K-47	Northern Fleet	Nuclear plant	Leakage in the primary circuit.
1985	K-90	Northern Fleet Barents Sea	Nuclear plant	Heavy leak in the steam generator.

(Continued overleaf)

Table 9: Further Accidents of the Project 675 Class (*continued*)				
March 1986	K-184	Pacific Fleet	Nuclear plant	High levels of salt were detected in the secondary system, forcing the submarine to return to base for two weeks of repairs.
22/12/1987	K-48	Pacific Fleet	Explosion	An explosion in the battery banks while charging damaged various equipment.
13/05/1991	K-74	Northern Fleet	Weapons	A missile was launched by error, with one crewman killed.
29/06/2002	K-104	Northern Fleet	Accident	During the dismantling process in floating dock PD-63, the submarine fell from the keel block. There were no injuries.

was finally able to reach its base on 28 June. The contamination and damage to the fuel elements were so severe that the vessel was taken out of commission by the Soviet Navy. It had been a very close near-miss accident that could have produced another major nuclear accident in the North Atlantic. During the decommissioning process of the submarine, its reactors continued to provide many problems due to the damage suffered during the incident.

This accident had been so serious, demonstrating the poor condition of the first-generation HEN nuclear power plants, that the whole Soviet Navy started to check the status of the HEN submarines, which ultimately led to the decision to retire several more such units.

As has been highlighted above, management of the first-generation nuclear plants and the submarines they were in was seriously lacking. One of the main reasons for this poor performance was said to be the pressure mounted by the Soviet High Naval Staff to put into service as many nuclear submarines as possible. This led to a large number of nuclear submarines that were full of flaws, from their design to their manufacture in the shipyards. The collisions that occurred, however, can only be explained by the poor training of officers and lack of control by the submarine divisions.

Table 9 details other accidents that involved this class of submarines; as can clearly be seen, the number of such incidents was very high.

Between 1989 and 1994, all the remaining units of the class with the fleet were decommissioned. The Project 675-class was an unreliable platform but offered an opportunity for the Soviet Navy to train its crews and develop tactics and doctrines. They were built in sufficient number to be deployed across the world's oceans and create a permanent presence in opposition to the US Navy. They were the first submarines that epitomised Admiral Gorshkov's concept of the 'battle of the first salvo', with the only option being to launch an attack against the US carriers and little probability of surviving that initial attack.

Unfortunately, the cost in lives and accidents in these submarines was very high, with Soviet officers and sailors forced to go to sea knowing that they were serving on troublesome vessels that had often caused the death of their crewmembers.

6
THE UNBEATABLE PAPA

As previously described, through the late 1950s and during the 1960s, the Soviet Navy's submarine fleet went from the idea of fitting anti-ship missiles in its submarines to an entirely new weapons concept: the SSGN. By the mid-1960s, its submarines were equipped with nuclear propulsion; they were provided with the capacity to search for and track their primary objectives – CVBGs of the US Navy – and to strike these from when surfaced. During this period, the missiles evolved as much as the submarines did – from ad-hoc designs to weapons systems with internal guidance systems, new propulsion systems and other equipment. This development increased the capability of the Soviet Navy by a magnitude: for the first time ever, it was able to link-up its SSGNs with other units and to deploy them anywhere around the globe, always ready to launch the opening salvo of missiles in the event of war, and – through gaining operational surprise – with a high probability of penetrating defences of enemy aircraft carriers, to the strategic advantage of the USSR.

The deployment of so many nuclear-powered, missile-armed submarines contributed significantly to the impression of the Soviet Union's military research and development enjoying 'unlimited' funding and resources, and for the capacity of its engineers and scientists to not only develop revolutionary concepts, but actually field some of the best technology available at the time. Precisely at that point, they went a step further and developed the Project 661-class (ASCC/NATO codename 'Papa'): the epitome of the contemporary Soviet SSGN design optimised regardless of the cost. Together with the Project 705 Lira nuclear-powered attack submarines (ASCC/NATO codename 'Alfa'), they earned a special place in history as not only some of the fastest submarines ever built, but through forcing Western navies to react with the development of new weapons and tactics of their own.

Project 661

The roots of the Project 661-class can be traced back to 28 August 1958, when a joint decree of the Central Committee of the Communist Party of the Soviet Union and the Council of Ministers of the USSR ordered the design of a new, nuclear-powered submarine class, with innovative technologies that granted it an exceptionally high speed, and the innovative capability to launch its anti-ship missiles while still submerged. The design bureau selected for this task was TsKB-16 Malakhit, which had previously been working on cruiser designs. The studies, research and development for this program, given project number 661 and the nickname 'Anchar', pushed the limits of what was technologically possible so far, and did not just result

The Project 651 class (ASCC/NATO codename 'Juliett') was a diesel-electric-powered SSG, of which 16 were constructed between 1960 and 1968. They displaced 3,225 tons surfaced and 4,203 tons submerged, were powered by two 4,000hp diesel engines and could reach a maximum speed of 16.8 knots surfaced or 18 knots submerged. Their original armament included four P-6 missiles (these were replaced by P-500s and P-750s), six 533mm torpedo tubes forward and four 406mm tubes aft. The Julietts were assigned as follows: K-124, K-77 and K-81 to the Baltic Fleet; K-58, K-67 and K-318 to the Black Sea Fleet; K-63, K-73, K-120 and K-270 to the Pacific Fleet; and the rest to the Northern Fleet. Submarines of the Project 651-class undertook a total of 61 patrols, of which 35 were in the Mediterranean: the class proved more effective when deployed in shallow and enclosed waters than did nuclear-powered SSGNs. (Artwork by Ivan Zajac)

The Project 675 class (ASCC/NATO codename 'Echo II') was a nuclear-powered SSGN, of which 29 were constructed between 1960 and 1967. They displaced 4,415 tons when surfaced and 5,760 tons when submerged: built around two VM-A reactors (70MW each), their powerplant could accelerate them to a speed of 14 knots on the surface, and 22 knots submerged. Original armament included the P-6 weapons system with eight launchers and the capability to deploy both 4K48 (P-6) and 4K95 (P-5) missiles. Radar for fire control was provided by Argument and Uspekh systems. P-6s were eventually replaced by P-500s. Other armament included four 533mm torpedo tubes forward and two 406mm tubes aft. The class received numerous modifications: Project 675K (applied on K-48) was a mid-life upgrade in which batteries were replaced and compartments rearranged; Project 675MK (K-1, K-22, and K-35) added the Kasatka-B satellite targeting system; boats upgraded to the Project 675MKV standard received the Argon-675 fire-control system and P-1000 missiles; while the K-86 was converted to a frogman carrier. Project 675-class boats made 248 combat patrols (about 55 percent of all the patrols undertaken by SSGNs). (Artwork by Ivan Zajac)

The Project 670A class (also known as Skat; ASCC/NATO codename Charlie I) was an SSGN of which 11 were completed between 1967 and 1972, all of which served in the Pacific Fleet. They were powered by one MV-4 reactor with an output of 89.2MW, displaced 4,300 tons surfaced and 5,100 tons submerged, and had a maximum speed of 20 knots on the surface and 24 knots submerged. Their Amethyst weapons system included eight launchers for P-70 anti-ship missiles – which could be fired while the vessel was submerged – and a floating radio buoy to receive commands, target designation data and satellite navigation data without coming to periscope depth. Other armament included four 533mm torpedo tubes forward and two 406mm tubes aft: the usual complement included two nuclear anti-ship torpedoes and two Tsakra (SS-N-15 Starfish) anti-submarine torpedoes. Boats of this class made 80 combat patrols in the 1970s and 1980s. K-43 was leased to India from January 1988 until January 1991, known there as Project 06709/INS *Chakra*. (Artwork by Ivan Zajac)

A further development of the Project 670 class (ASCC/NATO codename Charlie I), of which 11 were constructed, the Project 670M class (also known as 'SKAT-M'; ASCC/NATO codename Charlie II) was an SSGN of which only six were constructed, all in Gorkiy, between 1973 and 1980. The powerplant consisted of one VM-4 water-cooled reactor (89.2MW) and its length was 103 metres. Displacing 4,372 tons when surfaced and 5,500 tons submerged, they were capable of reaching maximum speeds of 20 knots on the surface and 24 knots submerged. While the weapons systems of the Project 670 class included eight P-70 Amethyst anti-ship missiles, the improved Project 670M-class vessels included an 8-metre insert in the hull forward of the sail, incorporating electronics and launch systems for targeting and firing eight P-120 Malakhit anti-ship missiles. Secondary armament included six 533mm torpedo tubes with 12 reloads (of which two were usually Tsakra nuclear anti-submarine torpedoes). Boats of this class are known to have undertaken only 38 patrols in the Atlantic and the Mediterranean, indicating low serviceability rates. All were scrapped between 1990 and 1994. (Artwork by Ivan Zajac)

The Project 661 class (also known as 'Anchar'; ASCC/NATO codename Papa) was an SSGN of which only one was constructed: originally named K-162, it was laid down on 28 December 1963, completed on 31 December 1969 and renamed K-222 in 1978. Powered by two compact light-water reactors (177.4MW each), with a 106.9-metre-long hull entirely made of titanium, and displacing 5,280 tons on the surface and 7,100 tons submerged, this submarine broke the underwater speed record on trials by reaching 44.7 knots (a record which stands to this day). The weapons system was centred on 10 P-70 Amethyst anti-ship missiles, all of which could be launched in two salvos, with a three-minute interval between salvos. Secondary armament included four 533mm torpedo tubes for SET-53 anti-submarine torpedoes. The sole vessel of this class was an experimental yet fully combat-capable submarine, but it undertook only two combat patrols, both with the Northern Fleet, before suffering damage to one of its reactors while they were undergoing maintenance in the shipyard in September 1980. The K-222 Anchar was placed in reserve in 1988 and dismantled at Sevmash, starting in 2010. (Artwork by Ivan Zajac)

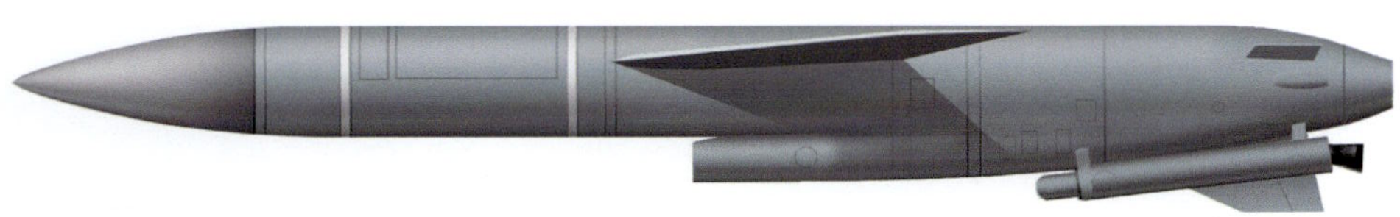

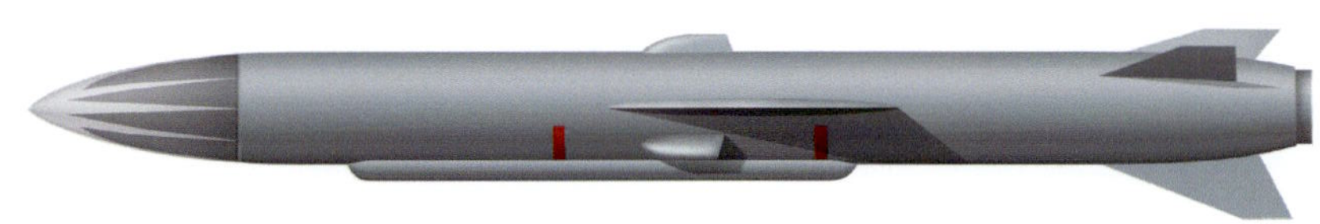

The two primary anti-ship missiles deployed by the Soviet SSGs and SSGNs of the first and second generation were the P-6 (left) and P-70 Ametist (right). Both were massive weapons, capable of delivering a tremendous punch. However, while the former emphasised range, the second depended on speed and the moment of surprise for its effectiveness. The P-6 could be launched from the surface only; the P-70 enabled the boats of the Project 670 and 670M classes to engage enemy warships from under the surface. (Artworks by Tom Cooper)

The Project 949A class (also known as 'Granit'; ASCC/NATO codename Oscar II) was an SSGN of which eight were constructed in Severodvinsk between 1978 and 1996, in addition to two Project 949/Granit-class boats. Powered by two OK-650B reactors (190MW each), they were capable of reaching a maximum speed of 30 knots submerged. Primary armament consisted of the Granit weapons system with 24 P-700 Granit missiles: secondary armament included two 650mm and four 533mm torpedo tubes (for which 28 reloads were carried, usually including several RPK-2 Vyuga anti-submarine missiles with nuclear warheads). Project 949 and 949A-class submarines were extremely powerful vessels, yet they undertook a total of only 12 patrols before 1991. While thus failing to demonstrate the full capacity of this type during the Soviet era, they remained in service after 1991, providing the Russian Navy with an opportunity to retain related skills. By 2015, the class had conducted another 40 patrols, of which about 60 percent were with the Pacific Fleet and 32 percent with the Northern Fleet, with two in the Mediterranean and one in the Caribbean. (Artwork by Ivan Zajac)

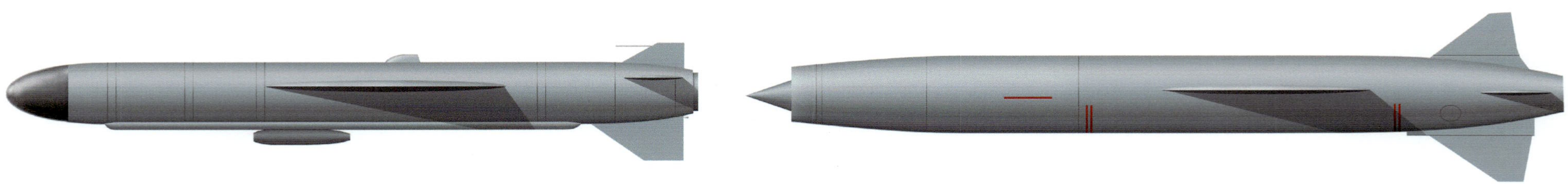

Entering service in 1972, the P-120 Malakhit weapons system (ASCC/NATO codename 'SS-N-9 Siren') became the core of the Project 670M-class (Charlie II). Each vessel carried eight such missiles, two of which were usually equipped with nuclear warheads, with the remainder being conventionally armed. All eight could be launched from a submerged submarine in a quick salvo. At 70km, the P-120's range was still relatively short, but the weapon travelled at Mach 0.9, and was equipped with a passive infrared seeker in the housing under the fuselage, in addition to its terminal active radar homing system. The P-700 Granit (ASCC/NATO codename 'SS-N-19 Shipwreck'; shown on the right) was the main weapon of the Project 949- and 949A-classes (Oscar II). The weapon was developed to be used in attacks conducted in coordination with Tupolev Tu-22M bombers. One missile in each salvo would use its radar in active and passive modes to 'scout' for targets and relay this information to the remainder. The P-700 could reach a maximum speed of Mach 2.5 if fired over the maximum range and travelling at high altitude, or Mach 1.5 in sea-skimming mode. This missile was armoured to provide a degree of protection against the Mk.15 Phalanx CIWS system carried by US and allied warships. (Artworks by Tom Cooper)

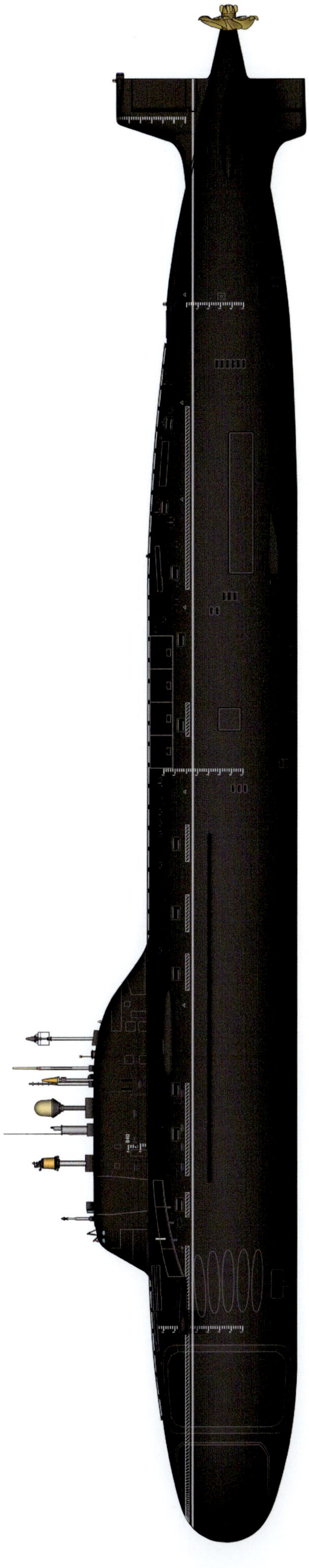

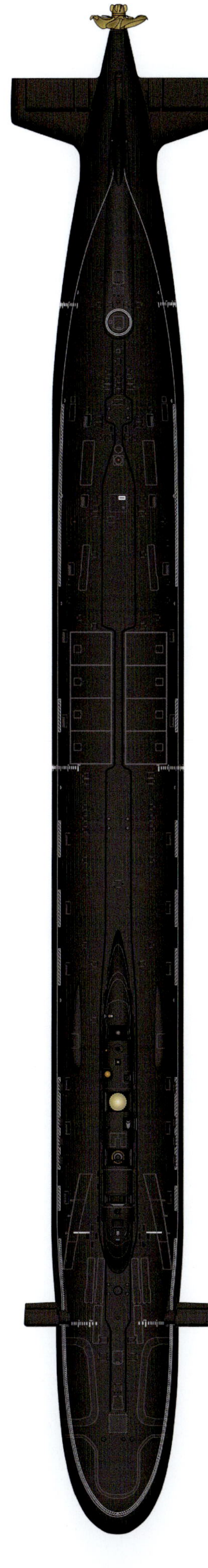

The Project 885 class (also known as 'Yasen' or 'Graney'; ASCC/NATO codename Severodvinsk) was the last SSGN designed during the Soviet era. Construction of the first vessel began on 21 December 1993, but experienced massive delays due to financial problems and constantly increasing costs of construction. It was thus only in 2013 that the K-560, named *Severodvinsk*, was finally commissioned into service. Three additional vessels of this class – K-561 *Kazan*, K-573 *Novosibirsk* and K-571 *Krasnoyarsk* – were undergoing sea trials from 2020–22. Powered by a single OK-650KPM pressurised-water reactor (200MW), and displacing 8,600 tons on the surface and 13,800 tons submerged, they are capable of reaching speeds of 20 knots on the surface and 35 knots submerged. The claimed top silent speed was 28 knots. The weapons system includes eight quadruple silos for a total of 32 Oniks anti-ship or Kaliber cruise missiles, and 10 533mm torpedo tubes. K-560 reportedly conducted one combat patrol in summer 2018 and another in spring 2020, while in October 2021 it performed two test-firings of Zircon cruise missiles from the White Sea to the Barents Sea, both from the surface and while submerged. (Artwork by Ivan Zajac)

The Soviet naval officer's uniform for summer use in the 1970s and 1980s was made of dark blue cotton. The jacket was usually decorated with a submariner badge, sometimes with the insignia of the fleet (if worn, then on the left shoulder), and the uniform was topped with an officer's cap, decorated with the Soviet Navy officer's badge. The illustrated shoulder- and sleeve stripes identify his rank as that of a Captain 3rd Rank. (Artwork by Anderson Subtil)

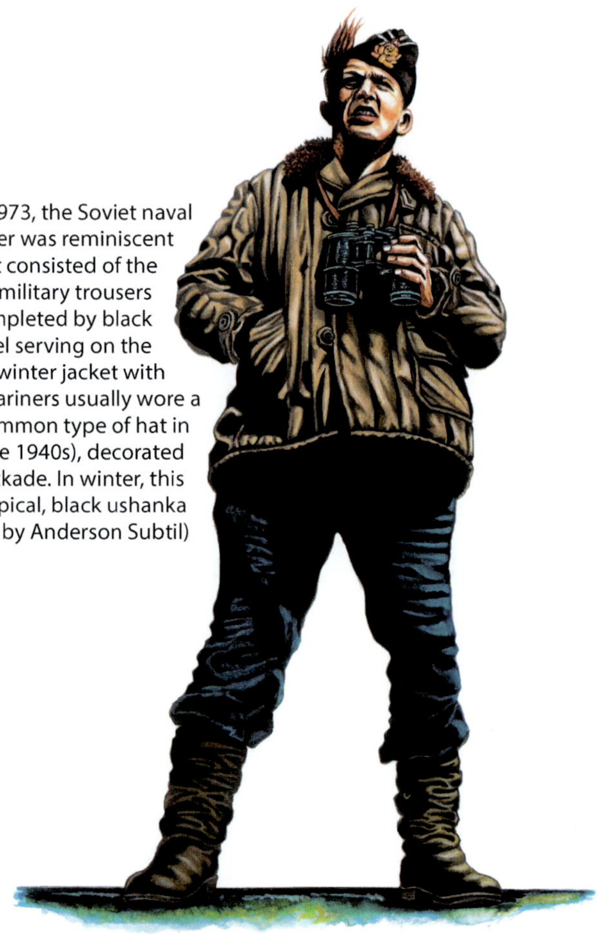

As of the 1960s and until 1973, the Soviet naval officer working uniform for winter was reminiscent of that from earlier times: it consisted of the winter working short jacket and military trousers made of cotton, both in blue, completed by black leather boots. Atop this, personnel serving on the sail would frequently don the winter jacket with fur. When on duty, Soviet submariners usually wore a black Pilotka cap (the most common type of hat in the Soviet armed forces since the 1940s), decorated with a hat badge with naval cockade. In winter, this was frequently replaced by the typical, black ushanka fur cap. (Artwork by Anderson Subtil)

In addition to light blue overalls, the Soviet Navy's uniform for sailors serving on submarines in the 1970s and 1980s – and that of the Russian Navy in the 1990s – consisted of an oiled jacket and trousers – which served as overalls – in black material. A black mask with warm liner, flash mask and warm gloves were usually carried in the bag on the side. A black Pilotka cap is also worn here. (Artwork by Anderson Subtil)

While their vessels wore no insignia (even the application of designations was rare: at most temporary 'hull numbers' were assigned for the duration of various exercises), the tight-knit community of Soviet submariners proudly wore memorabilia, mostly in the form of small metal badges, usually applied on jackets, sometimes on caps. In addition to the Soviet Navy flag, those of the submariners were frequently dominated by dolphins. This collage shows patches worn by the crews of K-168 (later K-222), the sole boat of the Project 661-class (known to the NATO as 'Papa', as also indicated in this collage). The second row shows badges issued for the submarine's 10th anniversary of operations, and the third row those for the 30th, 35th and 40th anniversaries. (Efim Sandler collection)

The Project 651-class ('Juliett') submarine K-77, seen underway on the surface of the Mediterranean Sea. This conventionally powered class was a fall-back in the event of a major failure of the much bigger, and heavier armed Project 675-class nuclear-powered submarines. Its primary armament consisted of only four P-6 missiles. Nevertheless, Julietts served with distinction, providing sterling service not only with patrols in the Mediterranean Sea, but through helping train an entirely new generation of Soviet Navy submariners. (US Navy)

A close-up and rear-view of the front section of two Project 651/Juliett-class submarines, detected and tracked by the US Navy in the Mediterranean Sea during the 1980s. Notable are the large cut-outs in the hull (which served as blast-deflectors at the missile launch) and sonar arrays atop and around the bow. (US Navy)

The Project 675/Echo II class was the first custom designed SSGN of the Soviet Navy. No fewer than 29 were constructed and, despite extensive problems with their propulsion system, it provided sterling service to the Soviet Navy well into the 1980s. This example was photographed while underway on the surface of the north-western Pacific, at relatively high speed. Notable are the cut-outs for jet-blast deflectors behind each pair of launchers for P-6 missiles. These were clearly anything but favourable for the quiet operation of this class, but in the 1960s the Soviet Navy paid little attention to this aspect of submarine operations. (US Navy)

The front section of a Project 659/Echo II class submarine. Notable are scorch marks in the jet blast deflector, indicating that the vessel has recently fired one of its powerful weapons. Conducting intensive patrols throughout the 1970s and 1980s – including several deep into the Atlantic, and off the coast of Hawaii – Project 675 submarines were mainly involved in tracking surface ships. That said, in 1967, the K-135 detected and tracked the George Washington-class nuclear-powered ballistic-missile submarine USS *Patrick Henry* (SSBN-599) for nearly six hours. From the mid-1970s, 14 boats of this class were overhauled and upgraded to carry P-500 Bazalt missiles (ASCC/NATO codename 'SS-N-12 Sandbox'), which had a range of 550km (297nm). Despite this upgrade, and that of Project 675MKV, the class was obsolete by the mid-1980s, and rapidly withdrawn from service towards the end of the decade. (US Navy).

Two close-up photographs of the unlucky submarine K-175 of the Project 675M/Echo II class (recognisable by bulges on the launchers), taken by the US Navy after its accident off the coast of Vietnam in November 1986. Notable is the smoke emitted from the hull behind the sail, the wider centre section of the hull, details of her missile launchers, and the gear along the deck. (US Navy Photo)

A rare colour photograph of the K-168/K-222, the sole boat of the Project 661/Papa class – and (still) the fastest submarine in the world. Notable is the sleek design of its hull, and the sail that caused such massive volumes of noise when it operated at high speed. (Efim Sandler collection)

An elevated view of K-43, a Project 670M-class submarine, while the vessel was leased to the Indian Navy under the designation INS *Chakra*, from January 1988 until January 1991. (US DoD)

The Project 949/Oscar-class submarine K-186 Omsk, seen in Vladivostok in 2008. (Efim Sandler collection)

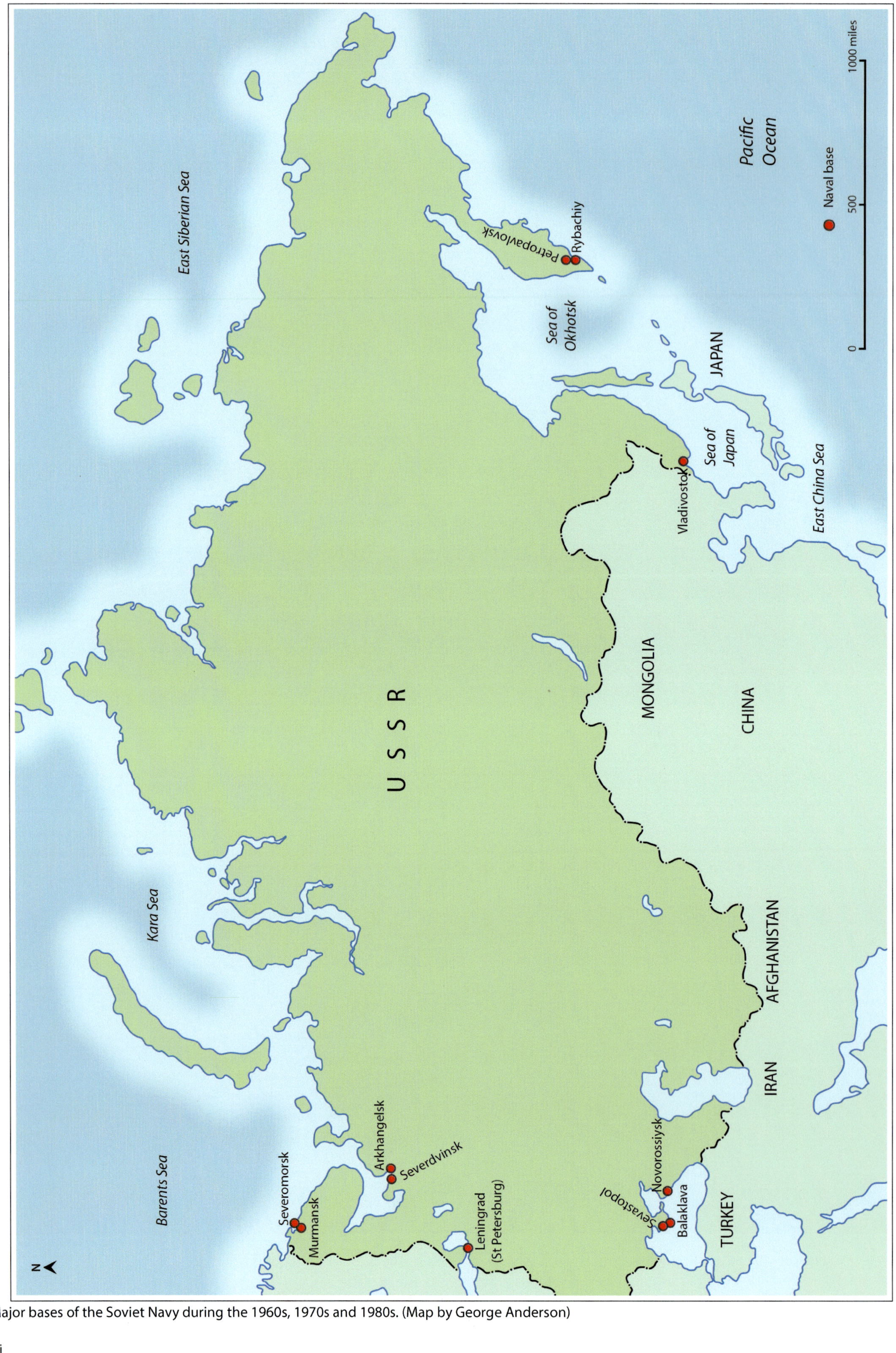

Major bases of the Soviet Navy during the 1960s, 1970s and 1980s. (Map by George Anderson)

in a new class of SSGNs, but actually resulted in the emergence of entirely new technologies for several future classes of warships. They produced a school of thought about the optimal use of SSGs and SSGNs, too: henceforth, these were defined as platforms capable of tracking their primary prey – the quick-moving CVBGs of the US Navy – over unlimited ranges with maximum discretion, and then striking them at the selected point in time. From the point of view of Soviet designers, there were multiple ways of achieving this capability:

- Unlimited range and autonomy were achieved using nuclear propulsion. In the early days of nuclear propulsion, the plants were inefficient, so the designers decided to request a new model of nuclear plant to be used on board the Project 661.
- The issue of high underwater speed was related to the previous item and implied the full redesign of the hydrodynamic hull shape of the new submarine. Weight also needed to be reduced to improve the power-to-mass ratio. This required research of new materials for the hull, with the added objectives of increasing the maximum diving depth, helping to improve the chances of survival under enemy attack and avoiding the risk of easy detection at high speed by sonar.
- The subject of discretion was the most important when attacking the anticipated targets. The submarines needed missiles with underwater launch capacity to avoid swift detection by search aircraft and helicopters and aircraft of combat air patrols of the enemy task group, far away from the outer screen of ASW frigates. MAD equipment installed in enemy airborne platforms also needed to be avoided by the submarines, which could only be done by changing the material of the hull to a non-ferrous one. The maximum potential depth of the platform was also a very important factor.

The improved output of the nuclear powerplant installed in a relatively small hull required an improved level of automation for safe operation – especially at high speed: this resulted in minimising the number of crew. Curiously, the level of noise emission was not a priority, continuing the tradition of the first generation of Soviet nuclear reactors of speed over silence.[1]

The Chief Designer for Project 661 was N. N. Isanin, supervised by the Chief Observer provided by the Soviet Navy and the Ministry of Defence, Captain 2nd Rank Y. G. Ilynsky, and, later on, Captain 2nd Rank V. N. Markov.

No fewer than 14 different configurations were studied before an entirely new hull shape was selected: Project 661 received a rounded outer hull, reminiscent of Western designs. The stern area alone was redesigned several times until it gave the desired increase in speed: the eventual solution was to change the flow in the suction area of the propellers, thereby increasing their efficiency. Together with lower displacement, low external surface, and the low mass of the high-power nuclear reactors, this reached the required speed of 38 knots. Still, such parameters created a huge challenge for the designers used to working with big submarines with much larger powerplants and double hulls. At the time, Soviet industry had next to nothing ready and available for use on Project 661. Nevertheless, solutions were in sight, starting with two new types of nuclear reactors: PWRs, using highly enriched uranium as fuel for higher efficiency; and liquid-metal cooled reactors (LMCs), which offered incredible benefits for their naval application.

Unfortunately for the Papa class, based on the concept of using an alloy of lead and bismuth to transfer the heat from the reactor while keeping its dimensions minimal, and preventing the necessity of high-pressure equipment, the LMC was only available in the form of an experimental design, and could not be readied in time.[2] Therefore, the submarine received a newly-designed VM-5M PWR, delivering 80,000hps: at the time, this was the most powerful reactor in the Soviet Navy, yielding twice the power of any other nuclear plant in the world. Other improvements were added to the machinery spaces, greatly increasing their efficiency. For example, the pumps of the primary reactor circuit were optimised to work with high thermic loads, while the main electricity consumers were designed to work with a voltage of 380v/50Hz. Finally, the emergency generator – a diesel plant in earlier times – was replaced by two heavy banks of silver-zinc batteries.

Nevertheless, once the submarine was constructed, its displacement was higher than expected: the reason was the requirement to accommodate 10–12 anti-ship missile launchers in a double-hull configuration. This caused a great controversy over the number of shaft lines and reactors installed. One faction of designers demanded the application of the Western practice of using one reactor and a single shaft (which was certain to make the submarine smaller, crewed by a lesser complement, and cheaper, while improving its operational safety). The faction that won could be described as 'traditionalists', who insisted on two reactors and two shafts in the name of improving survivability and technical availability throughout the operational life. This solution added much to the weight, for the two propellers (with five blades each), required the 'toberas' – a shroud around them – necessary for Arctic operations where they had to be protected from damage by ice.

Golden Fish

The other main point of interest was the selection of the material for the hull. From the innovative ideas that emanated from the original decree, three types were considered: aluminium, steel and titanium. Aluminium was quickly discarded due its poor resistance to corrosion and poor performance under high pressure during deep diving at high speed. New steel alloys promised better performance than earlier ones but were still undergoing research. There only remained the titanium option. As of the 1960s, the USSR was pioneering research and development of the industrial application of titanium for military projects and was the only country capable of manufacturing large plates and of the necessary welding procedures. However, even the Soviets had never before faced such a challenge as constructing an entire submarine hull from titanium.

Unsurprisingly, several problems emerged in the process, even if, overall, this material was to provide numerous benefits, including higher resistance to pressure and corrosion, despite lower density compared to steel. In other words: a vessel with a titanium hull was able to dive deeper and do so at higher speed, while offering higher resistance to underwater weapons, a lower overall weight, and less adverse corrosion effects.

The primary problem with titanium was its cost: not only the cost of producing large plates made of it, but of arranging an entirely new industry necessary to handle these plates, and new technologies of welding and constructing submarines – because something of this kind had never been attempted before (the only components made of titanium by this time were those for aircraft and spacecraft: nobody had ever attempted building something as big as a submarine before). Nevertheless, in 1959 the State Commission for Shipbuilding approved the use of titanium for Project 661.

Like everything else about Project 661, the decision to use titanium for construction of the hull was taken without understanding the resulting costs. Quite literally: the vessel had to be built without a budget limit in order to make all the necessary processes possible.[3]

A double-hull configuration was also approved, which was one of the classic Soviet design rules for submarines – even if this resulted in another increase in the cost – as did the fact that everything including titanium (from machinery for handling the materials, via welding procedures to consumables, new unfolding machines capable of working with 60mm thick plates, new workshops, and new factories) had to be newly-designed and newly-built. As if this was not enough, the welding required perfect cleanliness of the material and surrounding area, and an atmosphere rich in argon gas to avoid any contamination of seams. Moreover, vital for the resistance of the seam was the heating process during the welding. To reach the required level of quality, the Severodvinsk shipyard invested massively in new installations, equipment, tools and training of the workforce, so much so, that, because the submarine was thought to be cheaper if build from gold, Project 661 was nicknamed the *Zolotaya Rybka* – or 'golden fish'.

Final Design

Once the basic outline was defined, in February 1960, authorisation was granted to proceed with the detailed engineering phase. Amongst others, this required the precise definition of the weapons system, which created additional problems. Project 661 was originally required to accommodate 12 brand-new P-70 anti-ship missiles (ASCC/NATO codename 'SS-N-7 Starbright'). This required a redesign of the forward hull, which was constructed in a 'figure of eight' shape, with two different pressure hulls, each 5.5 metres in diameter (the inner hull in the remaining submarine had a maximum diameter of 9 metres), one above the other, providing the necessary space in the outer hull. However, even this allowed only the installation of 10 launchers (five on each side of the vessel), because these had to be positioned at an angle of 32.5 degrees. The latter was necessary due to the inability of the P-70's designer, the TsKB-34, to create a vertical launch system.[4] All 10 missiles could be launched in two salvos of five missiles each, with a gap of three minutes in between: this was expected to offer a high probability of overpowering the defences of the CVBG and disabling the carrier.

The configuration of the forward hull affected the size of the torpedo room, which was much narrower than in earlier Soviet designs. Because of this, although capable of releasing such weapons from a maximum depth of 200 metres, the vessel was armed with only four 533mm torpedo tubes and carried just eight reloads.[5]

Construction

A decree from the Council of Ministers of the USSR approved the preliminary design and main elements of the project, and in May 1960, the final draft of the design was approved. As expected, the decree confirmed the extensive use of new technologies and a new technical approach to any problems detected, forcing all the designers and engineers involved to develop new procedures. This was probably the most revolutionary concept of the Soviet submarines project, developing new systems never previously thought of, requiring immense investments, and the involvement of more than 400 research institutes for the development of new materials, structural elements, weapons and other systems. Eventually, even the Central Institute for Research No. 45 – the main research bureau of the USSR, better known as the Krylov Institute – became involved in determining the theoretical effectiveness of the new submarine.[6]

The testing of new P-70 missiles required extra spending: the S-158 – a Whiskey Twin Cylinder-class vessel, was modified at the Nikolayiv shipyard to the Project 644-7 standard to serve as a testbed and received two silos for new missiles. Another two submarines, both of the Project 611-class, were used to test the MGK-300 Rubin sonar system, and the Radian-1 mine-searching sonar system.[7] This was still not enough, and thus two SSNs of the Project 627-class – K-3 and K-181 – were selected for the testing of automatisation, and the use of new control and navigation systems (Turmalin, Shpat and Sigma, respectively).

Once the construction was approved, the work in the Severodvinks shipyard began, with the first step being two half-size sections to perform various tests on – to make sure the selection of materials and designs was correct and fulfilled the designers' expectations. One section was tested in the pressure chamber, while the other was sent to Lake Ladoga near Leningrad, for shock testing. Both tests ended with unexpected results, revealing a problem in the welding seams. Apparently, during the cooling period of the welding, the shipyard did not follow the established time guidelines, and this led to impurities and defects that weakened the structure.

Around the same time, the management of the project began having growing concerns about the decision to use titanium – which put the project well behind schedule. The State Committee for

One of the earliest photographs of K-168, the one and only submarine of the Project 661-class. Notable are her sleek lines, and also the covers for the anti-ship missile launchers, ahead of the sail. (Efim Sandler collection)

Shipbuilding assembled a team of leading metallurgy experts to fix the problem: they quickly concluded that the design tools used for the structure were based on steel, and not suitable for the titanium structure. Moreover, they requested a new alloy because the factory manufacturing these, Komunar, was providing plates containing a very high degree of hydrogen (one of the main pollutants of titanium), which resulted in fractures. It has been estimated that nearly 20 percent of the hull had to be built anew. The first plates of the new material were delivered in November 1961, enabling the laying of the keel of the first unit, designated K-168, on 28 December 1963.

K-168 underway at high speed on the surface. Notable are the large surface of the fin and the rudder. (Efim Sandler collection)

The delay in the construction of the hull caused a delay in the construction of reactors, in turn resulting in the vessel remaining on the slipway until its launch day, on 21 December 1968.[8] Such a long construction time put immense pressure upon the entire project, causing even the leaders of the Soviet Navy, the Ministry of Defence and the entire shipbuilding industry to start questioning it. Indeed, by 1968, even the government in Moscow as concerned about its viability, and thus no second vessel of the Project 661-class was ever constructed.

Testing

Once the submarine was afloat and outfitted, the Navy carried out a series of inspections – which revealed yet additional problems. The most massive amongst these was the integrity of the hull: no fewer than 10 of the main ballast tanks were found not to be watertight. Combined with numerous defects in equipment, this resulted in the submarine being delivered to the Navy only in December 1969. The first series of sea trials began on 13 December and lasted for 13 days: the service then accepted the new boat, despite discovering additional cracks in the titanium, a leak in the tertiary loop of the reactor, and a failure of the hydraulic system – all of which had to be fixed in the shipyard. Moreover, there was growing pressure to complete two additional crucial tests by 31 December 1969: the launch of a P-70 missile and assessing the vessel's top speed.

To the good fortune of the crew, the weather spoiled the test firing, and thus – quite ironically – the Naval Staff did not insist on trials of the centrepiece of the brand-new SSGN: its missile system. Instead, it demanded only the speed trials. On 31 December 1969, members of the State Commission led by Admiral Ernst Buliyon embarked the K-168, commanded by Captain 1st Rank Y. F. Golubkov, with Captain 2nd Rank V. Samokhin as the deputy, and the flag of the fleet had been raised over the sail.[9] The test area was carefully combed for any US or British submarines known to have frequently monitored such tests, and then the green light was given. The area in question had an average depth of 200 metres, which meant that at high speed, in the event of any kind of problems, the vessel was certain to hit the bottom within less than 30 seconds. For the next 12 hours, the K-168 was underway at 90 percent of the power output of her reactors: nevertheless, it reached an astonishing speed of 42 knots (77.8km/h), thus clearly surpassing the specification for 38 knots – and establishing a new world record that remains valid today. As soon as the submarine returned to port, Admiral Maslov promptly signed its acceptance into the Soviet Navy and sent a famous telegram to the Soviet Prime Minister Leonid Brezhnev, informing him that the 'Blue Ribbon' – a symbol of high quality – was now in the hands of a Soviet submarine.[10]

Admiral Ernst Buliyon: skipper of K-35 (Project 675/Echo II-class) in 1963–1968. On 31 December 1969 he served as the chairman of the acceptance commission for the K-168 and was on board when the submarine reached the speed of 42 knots. (Efim Sandler collection)

The speed achieved by the Papa was so high that it caused several unforeseen problems. Various external elements of the submarine – such as grids and handrails – were literally ripped off due to the force exerted over them. The external paint was badly damaged in the bow area, exposing the titanium directly to the seawater. Some external plates also suffered dents from the dynamic pressure applied. Obviously, much of this was understandable, for nobody expected the vessel to reach such a high speed.[11] However, a much more massive issue was the level of K-168's noise: while underway at 35 knots, this reached 100dB inside the control room, surpassing the maximum permissible level: the levels of noise in the machinery spaces were much worse.[12] The reason was the turbulent flow around the submarine hull. A related issue was that as soon as the submarine accelerated to high speed, its sonar systems were entirely

Table 10: Project 661-Class (Anchar)	
Propulsion	2 x PWR WM-5M of 177.4MW Steam production of 2 x 250 tons per hour 2 x Steam Turbines GTZA-618, 80,000hp 2 x Turbogenerators OK-3 of 3,000kW 2 bank of silver-zinc batteries of 152 cells
Length (m)	106.92
Beam (m)	11.5
Draught (m)	8.2
Displacement (surfaced/submerged, tons)	5,179/7,000
Operational Depth (m)	400/500
Speed (knots)	25/45
Crew	82
Endurance (days)	70
Weapons	10 x P-70 missiles in individual SM-97 launchers 4 x 533mm torpedo tubes forward (models SET-65, SAET-60M, 53-65K)

'deaf': they became unable to monitor the surrounding area, and the submarine was thus constantly at risk of collision, and unable to make use of its weapons. As such, it was essentially a useless toy and not a combat vessel.

New Speed Record

During 1970, the Soviet Navy continued with the Papa's testing, fixing the minor issues that continued to appear in the vessel. Another speed trial was held on 18 December 1970. Aboard on this occasion were Chief Designer Shulzenko and Rear Admiral Maslov as Chairman of the State Acceptance Commission, who agreed to an uncommon procedure for the test, which necessitated making some special arrangements in the machinery. Firstly, it was decided to use the maximum power available from the reactors, close to 100 percent. It was also necessary to block the emergency protection of the turbines and switch to manual control; a risky operation. In charge of the control post of the turbine was an engineer from the turbine manufacturer, the Kirov Factory, Alexander Skvortsov. As the test got underway, with a delivered power of 97 percent from the reactors and at a depth of 100 metres, the submarine achieved a new world record of an impressive 44.7 knots. Several days later, a satisfied Soviet Navy finally declared the K-168 to be operational: from inception of the project until that point in time had taken 12 years – for a single submarine. This was to prove something impossible to afford, even for the USSR.[13]

Weapons System

As with almost everything in Project 661, the missile system installed was new and offered new capabilities to the Soviet submarine fleet. Development of this missile, designated P-70, had been approved through a decree from the Council of Ministers of the USSR, No.363-100, on 1 April 1959. Although assigned to Design Bureau OKB-52 under the command of its Chief Designer, Chelomey, other design bureaus were also involved in the P-70 programme:

- KB-52: For the cruise jet engine and start system of the engine after breaking the surface
- NII-6: Solid fuel for the engines and the conventional warhead design
- TsKB-34: Chief Designer B.G. Bochkov, who designed the launchers
- NII-49: Chief Designer A.B. Mitrofanov, who designed the control system for the launch and the missile
- NII-3: Chief Designer N. Sviridov, who designed the MGK-300 Rubin sonar system and the interface for updating the missile guidance system

The main purpose of the P-70 was to allow the SSGN to execute an underwater launch of the missiles carried on board. This meant that the tactical surprise achieved would be greater, reducing the capacity of enemy forces to counterattack the submarine and reducing vital reaction time for enemy detection of the in-flight missiles.

As has been outlined in previous chapters, the missiles carried by Soviet SSG/SSGN forces were unable to be launched underwater because their main fuel was based on liquid propellants that could not burn in the sea. For this reason, Chelomey and his team developed a new idea to allow the missile to be launched from a flooded launch tube with an initial stage using solid propellants, which could operate under the sea's surface. A strap was installed around the missile, holding four rockets equipped with the solid propellant NMF-2, also used in strategic ballistic missiles (ICBMs); after the missile had broken the surface of the sea, the strap would disengage from the missile and drop into the sea.

At this moment, the main rocket of the missile would start and the four fins, folded during the underwater launching and transition, would be deployed and the missile start its normal flight. The folded wings provided the benefit of reduced volume for the stowage of the missile in the submarine, one of the technological leaps of the programme. The second stage pushed the missile to a speed where the turbine would have an incoming flow sufficient to start itself. This second stage also used a solid propellant, in this case 239L.

The missile had a very high level of performance. It had a cruising speed of Mach 0.9 and was able to fly between 40 and 60 metres above the surface of the sea thanks to an altimetric radar installed inside it. While its range was only 80km, much less than its predecessor the P-6/SS-N-3 – which could reach 460km – this handicap did not mean the new missile was a failure, with the doctrinal uses of the SSGNs developing over the years.

Comparing the technical characteristics of the P-70 and P-6, it was obvious that the P-70 was a small missile with a lot of improvements, which implied a refined design. Its launch weight was 3,375kg (including a 530kg warhead), against the 4,500kg of the P-6. The size had also been reduced, from a length of 10 metres in the P-6 to 6.7 metres in the P-70, while the diameter shrank from 0.9 metres to 0.55 metres. All this enabled the P-70 to have a reduced radar signature and put pressure on the enemy radar systems to detect it flying at low altitude.

With its new missile system, Soviet industry had again proved able to beat the West, namely the United States and it naval forces and industrial might. The P-70 was the world's first missile with

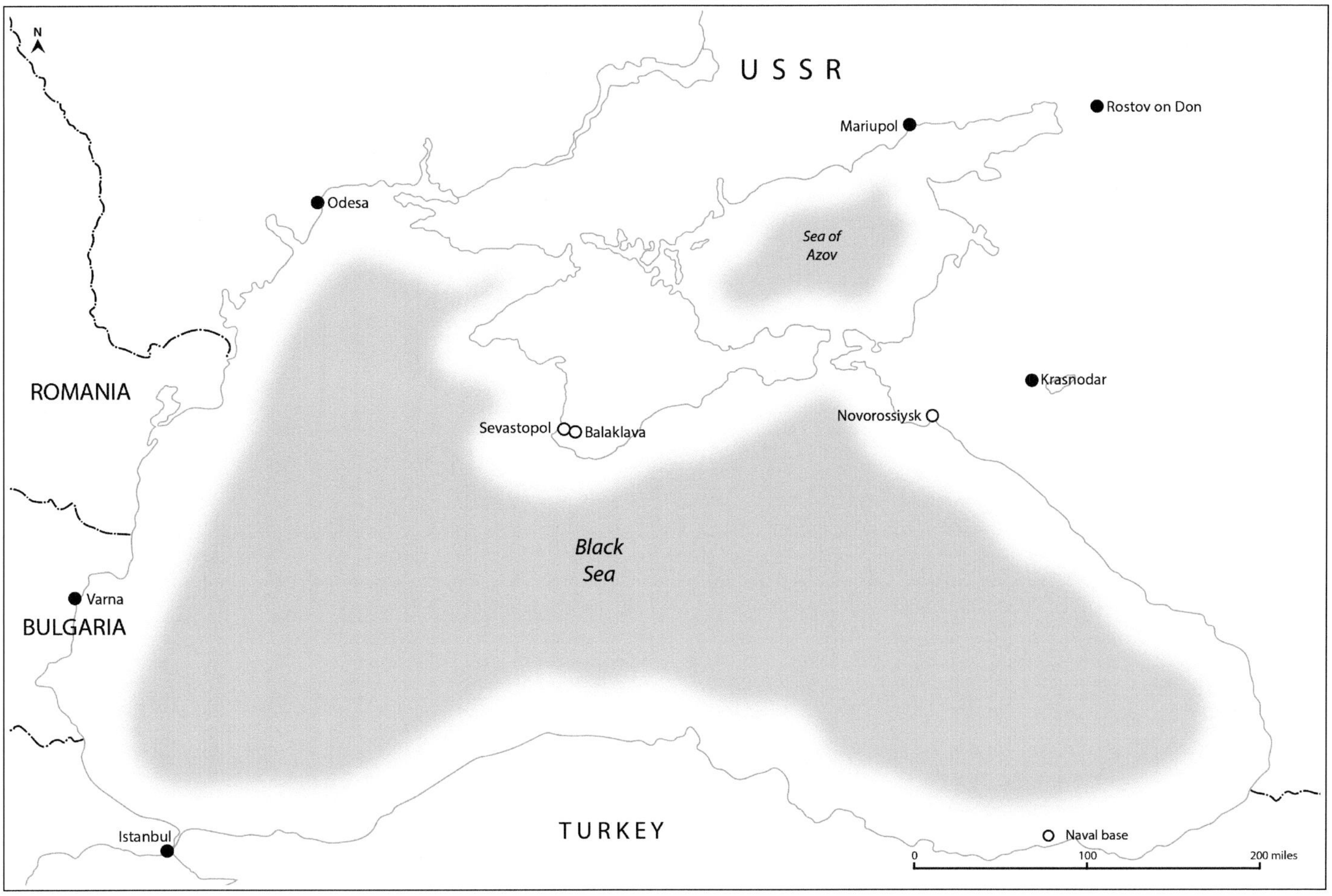

Major Soviet naval bases in the Black Sea. (Map by George Anderson)

an underwater launching capability, and the US spent more than a decade in pursuit of a system to match this Soviet success.[14] However, this success came at great cost for the Soviet Union.

The initial disappointment about the short range of the missile actually presented some tactical advantages. The Papa was expected to be in close contact with an enemy formation, so a greater range for its missiles would be of no use for it mission. Moreover, a short range meant a short flying time, and thus less opportunity for reaction by the enemy defences and surprise would be maximised in such conditions. What was also true, though, was that the submarine would be close to the outer screen of enemy ASW units, and there was consequently a high probability that the salvo breaking the sea's surface could be visually detected by any airborne ASW platform patrolling above the enemy formation, which could then launch a counterattack before the second salvo was fired.

Nevertheless, the short flying time, plus the low altitude of the missile path and its reduced radar signature, increased the theoretical probability of success for the attack. The Soviet Naval Staff thus developed a doctrine for using SSGNs equipped with the P-70.[15]

Between August and September 1960, flight tests were carried out for the P-70, measuring the aerodynamic behaviour of the platform and the range and efficiency of different compositions of propellants in the jet engine. After the completion of this stage, launches began from a static underwater silo on a test range near Balaclava in the Black Sea. The first underwater launching was carried out on 24 June 1961, followed by nine more launches, with the last two of this series completed in December of the same year. Thereafter, the whole programme was ready to transition to launches from a submarine.

The S-158, a submarine of the Whiskey Twin Cylinder-class assigned to the Black Sea Fleet was given the task of carrying out the flight testing. For this purpose, it was outfitted with two silos for new missiles. Work to transform the submarine into a testbed was carried out in shipyard No. 444 at Nikolayev between 1963 and 1964. Finally, between July and December 1964, underwater launching from the submarine took place. Six missiles were launched, three of them resulting in a direct impact, one impacting underwater in the area of the target, and two being failed attempts. The operational depth for launching the missiles was set at a maximum of 30 metres. The S-158 programme continued from March 1965 until September 1966, with 13 missiles launched from the platform, the last tests carried out under the command of the design bureau. During these test phases, a maximum range was established of 70km.

P-70 Missile

There were two different versions of the P-70's warhead: a conventional one, with the Soviet designation 4G66, consisting of a 530kg HE warhead, and the tactical nuclear version with a 200kT device. Usually, each submarine was equipped with a mix of 80 percent conventional warheads and 20 percent nuclear-tipped missiles.[16]

For guidance purposes, the P-70 was equipped with an automatic pilot that used the relative positions of the launching platform and the targets, with the information provided by the sonar system of the submarine. For mid-course guidance, the missile was equipped with a programmable INS. In the final phase of the flight path, the missile was equipped with a radar, working in the J-band, to try to lock onto the target vessel and explode underwater, under the keel, at a depth of 10–50 metres, with the intention of maximising the effects of the blast.

The missile had a database of energetic and geometric signatures of targets, to help to lock on onto the defined target. The warhead was fitted with limited anti-jamming devices to work in the electronic warfare environment, at least with the first production series, as the possibility of jamming equipment effectively disorienting the attacking missiles was high.

The K-168 underway on the surface: the submarine was made to not only test the idea of constructing a vessel of such size and entirely made from titanium, but also to bring its short-ranged P-70 missiles to bear with help of its high speed. The records it set in 1969 remain valid today. (Efim Sandler collection)

The effective range of the missile varied, depending on the information provided about the target. If the missile used information from the sonar system, the range could be limited to 50km, and it required target information from a third platform to determine its path and increase the range to 70–80km. Over the years, with improvements in sonar technology, the third platform requirement was no longer necessary. The operational characteristics of the missile mean that the P-70 could be considered the first operational SSM of the 'fire and forget' category, the lack of necessity for the launching platform to update the missile with target information making it much appreciated among submarine commanders. Despite this, the short distance of launching from the enemy made the survivability of the submarine a concern. Furthermore, the missiles could only be effectively stowed in the launchers for three months, after which they needed to be disembarked and updated in specialised workshops.

Unlike some earlier missile designs, which had been designed to be launched from various platforms – submarines, ships and aircraft – the P-70, with its underwater launch procedure, was only designed to provide service with the Soviet submarine forces. Total production of the missiles has been estimated at 200 units, with more than the half of that number available in the magazines of the Soviet Navy as of 1991.

All the target information for the combat management system, including missiles and torpedoes, was provided by the MGK-300 Rubin sonar system of the submarine. This was the first powerful Soviet sonar and was specifically designed for the detection of carrier battlegroups at ranges up to 1,000km, using convergence zones. The cylindrical array was 6 metres in diameter and 3 metres high, with more than 400 piezoelectric ceramic reversible active/passive transducer modules. It worked, for passive searching, in in the 4.0–6.5kHz bands.

Table 11: P-70 Missile (4K-66)	
Warhead	Conventional: 530kg HE Tactical Nuclear: 200kT
Propulsion	4 strapped boosters with solid fuel for underwater launch, with second stage in solid fuel and a jet engine for cruise speed
Range (nm)	80
Speed (Mach)	0.9
Length (m)	6.7
Wingspan (m)	0.55
Weight at launch (tons)	3.375
Guidance Systems	Through information provided by the sonar system, altimetric radar and J-band radar for terminal guidance

Question of Series Production

1970 was a fateful year for Project 661 in regards of its future, as the Naval Staff studied the possibility of launching series construction for the Northern and the Pacific Fleets. The main issue whether to go ahead with this decision involved in depth study of all the handicaps that the project had, as well as its benefits and the missiles provided to the fleet.

The short range of the P-70, together with the high level of noise radiated into the sea and the limited magazines for spare torpedoes, led Soviet strategists to request a full revision of the project before any increase in production. The noise emissions also blocked the normal operation of the submarine's sonar systems, which meant that in a wartime scenario the sole Project 661-class submarine would have lived a very risky life. The shipbuilding and industrial side of the project also needed to be considered: the high price of materials and procedures, the lack of a sufficient mass of skilled workers and the long delays suffered due to the application of new technologies created a generally poor opinion of the capacity of the shipbuilding industry to deal with this programme. It must be borne in mind that at this time, all the shipyards in the Soviet Union were in the middle of huge efforts to build a new fleet, including all kind of submarines and surface vessels. Resources deployed to this project would of course affect the overall capacity of the Soviet fleet.

In addition, the titanium problem had not been fully corrected. Quality control needed to be stronger in the Project 661-class: nevertheless, cracks and material failures continued to arise throughout its service life. For example, between October 1972 and January 1975, K-168 was in the Severodvinsk shipyard for a deep inspection of the hull's condition, which led to orders for a huge amount of welding when numerous cracks were found in the titanium. The titanium problem also had a cost issue. The budget for military programmes in the Soviet Union was high, but there was a limit as to what could be spent. The Project 661-class has been reported to have consumed an estimated 1 percent of Soviet GDP in the 1960s. No country in the world could (nor can, in our days) afford such an expensive series of submarines. Only a single unit, despite all its benefits, was also a luxury for the Soviet Navy. It is thus nothing short of a miracle that the Soviet government allowed the Navy and industry to proceed with this astonishing project.[17]

Despite support for the Papa from such prominent figures in the Soviet military hierarchy as the naval Commander-in-Chief, Admiral Gorshkov,[18] the decision was then taken to discard series production and to maintain the solitary unit as an experimental submarine in service with the Northern Fleet. The industry created around the Papa project, especially for titanium, was diverted to other industries, with titanium included as a common material for other submarine programmes thanks to the investment already carried out in Project 661. A new program was launched to design a series production version, designated Project 661M, with all the improvements and modifications previously carried out or suggested, to try to reduce the costs of the platform. Yet another version, known as Project 661A, aimed to modernise the vessel, with new and better-performing P-120 missiles, but this was never approved by the Soviet Navy.

A third project emerged in form of the design for Project 661B. This envisioned a change in the role from that of SSGN to SSBN, equipped with R-29 submarine-launched ballistic missiles (ASCC/ NATO codename 'SS-N-8 Sawfly'). With there being no way to reduce the level of noise for the design of this kind, this never advanced past the study stage.

Conclusions about Project 661

We have outlined the operational life and design struggles of a war machine, a submarine equipped with anti-ship missiles. This was only one example of the Soviet capacity for designing submarines and evolving a design to new levels never imagined previously by any other country.

The Papa was a unique object in a unique world. It represented the maximum that the Soviet shipbuilding industry could create with unlimited resources at its disposal. The research carried out under the umbrella of this project was immense. Future generations of submarines of all kinds, even today, benefit from this programme. Some of the technologies developed still cannot be employed by shipbuilding industry today due to the high costs associated with them.

The command from the original decree, expressly forbidding the following of previous design lines or ideas, created a huge step up in quality in the following generations of Soviet submarine designers, allowing them to gain high-level technical expertise with Project 661. This benefited the whole Soviet naval industry in the following decades, leading to more innovative designs.

An example that is easy to see is the development of a new industry involving titanium being applied to submarine and other vessel structures. New mathematical tools were developed to calculate titanium structures. In addition, factories and workshops were built to work with plates of titanium. All this work was applied in the later Alfa and Sierra SSN submarines. While it is true that the high cost meant the Soviet Union could not afford to build large quantities of this submarine, the Russian Federation is nowadays still the only country with the know-how to deal with this kind of project.

Titanium is only one of the fields where what the NATO called the Papa class revolutionised the Soviet Navy. High-speed submarines required new operational doctrines and tactics to be efficiently used by their commanders, and again the Soviet Union was the only country that took the necessary time and arranged a large enough budget to develop this. Western countries reacted to this menace by creating new weapons able to attack this platform, with huge programmes in new torpedo technology and ASW airborne platforms, but never developed their own high-speed submarines.

Underwater-launched anti-ship missiles were also a new feature in naval warfare, allowing SSGN submarines to effectively attack enemy warships or – what could be even worse for an opponent – the sea lines of communication used by merchant ships. From the middle of the last century, submarines equipped with this kind of missile could have attacked merchant vessels in the Atlantic with impunity, unless NATO established a well-equipped convoy system, which would have detracted vital resources from other areas. And no convoy system could have been 100 percent effective against a group of submarines fitted with this kind of missiles.

Unfortunately for the Soviet Navy, the Papa project also had some serious drawbacks. The cost of the project was unaffordable for a large series of submarines. Papa finally remained in the fleet only as an experimental platform for testing new technologies, doctrines, capabilities, and equipment.

As a lead ship of a class and the only one of its kind, several features suffered greatly from being newly born. Titanium building and maintenance programmes were only developed while the submarine was being constructed or operated, leading to long repair periods, many of them unexpected and creating pressure on the shipyard managers due to the Soviet Navy not understanding the reasons for all the problems that arose. In general, the performance of the submarine was loved by the Commander-in-Chief of the Soviet Navy, Admiral Gorshkov, but not by the commanders of the fleets and brigades, who never had Project 661 available on time due to an endless series of problems.

Overall, the sole Project 661 submarine was not really a combat platform, but a vessel made to an unbeatable design that broke all the limits as regards speed and equipped with some of the best anti-ship missiles of its time.

Project 661 in Operation

During its operational life, K-168 received three tactical denominations: K-18 from the beginning of the project until 27 January 1965, then K-168 until 15 January 1978, and finally, until the decommissioning of the vessel, K-222. In December 1970, it arrived at its home port in the naval base at Zapadnaya Litsa. Between January 1970 and December 1971, K-168 underwent extensive sea trials, pushing the machinery to its limits and trying to extract as much information as possible from the performance of the design. It sailed nearly 40,000nm, with 75 percent of them submerged.

The submarine remained the focus of experiments and tests throughout its entire operational life, and its only two operational patrols. One of these patrols was between September and December 1971 in the North Atlantic, where it employed its maximum range and speed in the open ocean. In the course of that patrol, it located the CVBG centred on the USS *Saratoga* (CV-60), returning to the United States from a deployment with the Sixth Fleet. During this encounter, K-168 shadowed the carrier at high speeds, showing its flag for the US Navy to see. The action created great concern in the Pentagon, although the high noise emissions of the Soviet submarine made it easy for all the US escorts and patrols to make ready a fire solution against the submarine in case it was needed. In a wartime operation, the Papa would have been discovered the moment it went into high-speed mode. Another patrol was made by the submarine in the Atlantic Ocean in 1981.

US NAVY AND NATO ANTI-SUBMARINE CVBGs

In addition to attack carrier battle groups, during the 1960s, in reaction to the growth of the Soviet nuclear-powered submarines, the US Navy developed the concept of anti-submarine carrier battle groups. These were centred on modified Essex-class aircraft carriers that embarked an air wing – the Carrier Anti-submarine Air Group – specialised in ASW, and usually including one or two squadrons of Grumman S-2 Trackers, a squadron or a flight of Grumman E-1B Tracers, and one unit of Sikorsky SH-3 Sea King helicopters. Depending on the carrier in question, such wing was sometimes complemented with a single squadron of Douglas A-4 Skyhawks that served for air defence purposes. About 20 carriers received hull designations in the CVS-sequence.

USS *Wasp* (CVS-18), with Anti-submarine Task Group Bravo, in the Mediterranean Sea on 19 August 1961. All the destroyers in this group belonged to the Gearing-class. The S-2 Trackers, A-1 Skyraiders, and Sikorsky HSS-1 Seabat helicopters were assigned to Carrier Anti-submarine Air Group 52 (CVSG-52). (US Navy)

HMCS *Bonaventure* (R22) underway in 1961 with S-2 Tracker anti-submarine aircraft on deck. (US Navy)

This pattern was followed by most of the NATO and allied navies that operated British-made Colossus- and Majestic-class ships. By 1965, the air wings of the Australian carrier HMAS *Melbourne* (R21), Brazilian carrier *Minas Gerais* (A11), Canadian carrier HMCS *Bonaventure* (R22), and the Netherland's HNLMS *Karel Doorman* (R81), were either reequipped with a combination of S-2 Trackers and SH-3 Sea Kings, or just the latter. Like CVSs of the US Navy, all the ships in question were operated as the centrepieces of CVBGs specialised in anti-submarine warfare. The Royal Navy and the French *Marine nationale*, went a slightly different way: the British refitted several of their Centaur-class vessels as helicopter assault carriers, while the French constructed two new attack aircraft carriers (R98 *Clemanceau* and R99 *Foch*) but, equipped these with a squadron of Breguet 1050 Alizé ASW aircraft and a flight of Aerospatiale SA.321 Super Frelon ASW helicopters.

Like practically all the classes of submarines of the Soviet Navy, the boat suffered one major accident related to its nuclear plant. In November 1980, as K-222 was in the Severodvinsk shipyard undergoing refuelling of her reactors and other routine maintenance, the tools for handling nuclear rods – unique within the entire Soviet Navy – were lost by the crew. Eventually, the Navy found itself with no option but to order the shipyard to refuel the submarine using the original drawings and supervised by naval personnel. On 30 November, in the middle of the procedure, all the crew members left the boat for their lunch break: only the shipyard technicians and workers remaining on board, which was strictly against Soviet Navy regulations. This decision was taken because the Navy did not want any more delays in the docking due to the embarrassing situation created previously when the loss of the tools was revealed. There was strong pressure to keep to the time schedule. While in the dockyard, electric power was provided to the control rods. At one point, all the control rods of the reactor began to lift: the problem was that the automatic safety system had been shut down, and no officers from the vessel were in charge or supervising the operation. The reactor thus started generating heat, without any cooling water to dissipate that heat due to the automatic system also not being connected. No alarms or acoustic signals were activated, according to witnesses. Pressure and temperature in the reactor started to rise, without being noticed by anyone on board. When the pressure caused a break in one of the pipes in the condenser of the primary loop, and radioactive steam and water started to pass through the machinery

K-222 tied to a pier at a base in the Murmansk area in the mid-1980s. (Efim Sandler collection)

spaces, the alarms sounded on board and the shipyard staff realised there was a major problem in the reactor.

Viktor Sitkov, the manager of the shipyard and in charge of the operations that were taking place at that moment, understood that something was very wrong and started to issue orders to avoid further damage or risk. The first step he took was to isolate the broken condenser and prevent more radioactive steam from spreading inside the submarine, after which he started the main pumps to fill the system with water and start cooling the core of the reactor. These actions led the reactor parameters to return to normal working pressures and temperatures.

The following day, Admiral Nikolay Mormul – a senior technical advisor to the Soviet Navy – was flown to Severodvinsk to inspect the damage. Although he found this was not as serious as in other accidents that had happened in the Northern Fleet, and could be repaired, the commission investigating this accident recommended that the Navy change the reactors for more moderns ones and to install an emergency generator in the submarine. Eventually, due to K-222's uniqueness, the decision was taken to only repair the damage and to carry out a series of reactor tests to determine whether any parameters had been exceeded. All the tests indicated that the powerplant was in good order and the Commander-in-Chief of the Northern Fleet, Admiral Vladimir N. Chervanin, agreed with the conclusions of the commission: he accepted the K-222 as operational and decontaminated.[19]

In 1988, the vessel was assigned to reserve status and moved to the naval base at Belomorsk, close to Severodvinsk, prior to its definitive retirement from the Soviet Navy and scrapping. That said, even the latter proved a problematic issue: due to the loss of tools, and with fuel inside the reactors for more than 20 years, the service had to find a specialised company capable of processing the rods. This took until 2008, by when the buoyancy of the boat was in jeopardy: without proper maintenance, cracks appeared in the external hull and seawater started to flow inside the ballast tanks. In the absence of money or personnel to fix this problem, emergency solutions were provided.

The scrapping of the vessel was carried out by the Severodvinsk shipyard, the original builder and the only one able to manage the titanium structure, from March 2010. The scrapping was also unique because it was done with the reactors still inside the submarine. Right to the end, Project 661 remained full of 'special' features. That was a sad, but not unexpected finale for an amazing vessel that established two world records in submerged speed, which remain unsurpassed, and put in place a firm technological base for future high-speed submarines. The benefits of this project for the Soviet/Russian shipbuilding industry still have no comparison.

7
CHARLIES

In parallel to the incredible, one-off Project 661 submarine, the Soviet Union was working on a new class of SSGNs designed to create the first serious menace for the CVBGs of the US Navy in the so-called 'battle of the first salvo'. While the Papa class was a single-vessel-class that was impossible to classify in the generation of submarines, the new class was to belong to the second generation of Soviet nuclear-powered boats. It came into being at the time submarines of the first generation were starting to provide operational feedback, revealing that the main concern was the lack of reliability of the nuclear plants, which in turn had affected their operational availability.[1] These vessels also served as learning tools for the fleet, enabling it to develop and refine its doctrine and tactics.

The two main points to be changed in the second-generation submarine-launched missiles were to improve the safety of the nuclear plants and avoid the necessity of surface-launched missiles. As has been seen in the previous chapter, underwater launching of missiles was now possible; the question now was how to deploy them wisely to the whole SSGN fleet. Meanwhile, the safety of nuclear plants was, under normal technical development, improving.

The decade had been marked by Soviet investment, practically without limits, in new submarine technologies such as titanium alloys for hulls and liquid-metal cooled reactors. This tendency in submarine warfare research also had an impact on the Charlie class.

Project 672

The one-off Project 661 was, for all its fantastic achievements, an extremely expensive project, but it must be understood that in these times there were numerous costly projects running in the Soviet shipbuilding industry. The missile installed into the Project 661 – the P-70 – was the most interesting anti-ship missile of its time due to its capacity to be launched underwater. The Soviet High Naval Staff thus requested a project for adapting this missile to a cheaper platform, one that could be built at less technologically advanced shipyards than Severodvinsk, which was involved in various other priority projects.[2] In essence, they wanted to create a project for a mass-production SSGN.

Since 1958, TsKB-143 had conducted a project for an SSGN design with minimal displacement that matched the new requirements of the Naval Staff. The result was Project 672, a submarine of nearly 2,500 tons but powered by a new nuclear powerplant that weighed only half that of the previous generation, while still yielding 40,000hps.

Its hull was expected to be built in titanium, for depths greater than 500 metres and a speed between 30 and 35 knots. However, when the designers tried to integrate the P-70 missiles into the structure of this new vessel, it was clear that it would not work due to the lack of space for the number of missiles envisaged to be embarked. The project was finally cancelled in 1960.

Under the Ministerial Decree of 1958 that allowed the creation of Project 661 and the new submarine technologies that we have seen above, other design bureaus were also involved in different projects for the Soviet Navy. One of them was TsKB-112, located in Gorkiy, that was working on a small mass-production SSN, Project 670 Skat, with nuclear propulsion and a limited crew embarked. In May 1960, it was decided to equip it with P-70 missiles and develop a new SSGN for the fleet.

TsKB-112 (later called Lazhurit), was a relatively young submarine design bureau, founded only in 1953, that had previously worked on the Project 613 conventional submarine. Between 1958 and 1960, its Chief Designer was V. K. Shaposhnikok, while V. P. Vorobyev took over afterwards. The Project 670 became its priority, not only because Vorobyev was highly enthusiastic about developing a submarine capable of striking an aircraft carrier with missiles, but because it was also of immense importance for the Soviet shipbuilding industry.

Single Shaft Design

A fundamental requirement for Project 672 was to carry eight missiles: this was the minimal number providing the theoretical capacity to damage the primary target, allowing for some missiles being shot down by air defences. This objective in such a small design had a major impact on the final platform, with the surfaced displacement increasing from the initial 2,500 tons to 3,574 tons. To avoid any further increase in size, weight and displacement, a revolutionary concept – from the Soviet point of view – was applied to the vessel's propulsion. Only one reactor was to be installed, with one shaft for propulsion. In a further attempt to save weight, the hull would not be double for the entire length of the vessel – again against normal Soviet philosophy – and mixture of materials would be used in the hull.[3]

The proposed propulsion was the most problematic decision. A new 89.2MW reactor, designated VM-4, was designed for the class, with an OK-350 steam turbine providing 18,800hp. This single-reactor configuration provided an output of 60 percent of the power provided by the standard double-reactor plant. The speed of the submarine was estimated with this power to be 26 knots.

The compartment of the nuclear reactor was also redesigned to improve its safety. The main circulation pumps of the third and fourth loops were installed outside the reactor compartment to allow the crew, unlike in previous classes of the fleet, to operate it in the event of an accident with the reactor or a blackout in this section.

The original propeller was of fixed pitch with five blades. In future modernisations of the class, to improve the noise emissions in the water, the system was changed to two propellers of four blades, 3.9 and 3.8 metres in diameter. One propeller line, under normal conditions, is less detectable than a twin configuration, due to less distortion in the water flow around the vessel. Two auxiliary waterjets allowed the vessel to continuing sailing at five knots in case of a nuclear plant failure. The submarine had a 500kW diesel generator installed, along with two banks of batteries with 112 cells in each.

A Project 670-class submarine next to its predecessor, a Project 675/Echo II-class boat. The sleek lines of the newer design are clear, possible thanks to the installation of all of its smaller but more advanced primary weapons within launchers in front of the sail. (Efim Sandler collection)

The hull and the materials used were some of the most controversial decisions of the project. The final submerged displacement was 4,980 tons, a small figure for a boat with nuclear propulsion. This decision had important consequences in the final performance of the Charlie-class submarines. The reserve of buoyancy, always higher in Soviet than in Western submarines, related to the chances of survival of the

A Project 670-class submarine in the process of being manoeuvred to the dock with help of two tugboats. (Efim Sandler collection)

A control station aboard a Project 670-class submarine: while smaller than the Project 675, the class offered better crew comfort. (Efim Sandler collection)

Noise emissions were one of the most important factors during the design of the submarine. The Charlie-class vessels were the first Soviet submarines that used an automatic system for closing the scuppers and ventilation during submerged navigation. The number, status and condition of the scuppers was a crucial factor in the noise emitted by a submerged submarine. The designers were unable to reduce the number of scuppers to a Western-design standard, but the Charlies had fewer hull penetrations than their partners in the Soviet fleet. Anechoic protection was installed, which appeared to provide the most successful protection of all the second-generation Soviet submarines.

platform after an attack, was reduced compared to the usual Soviet designs. Structural resistance to the effect of blasts from enemy weapons was also reduced, especially in the area where the double-hull configuration was not followed. This decision also affected the maximum depth that the vessel could reached on operation, estimated at 300 metres.

The mid-section of the vessel was the area without the double-hull configuration. The steel used in the pressure hull was AK-29 quality, with other materials used in different areas to improve the final performance of the structure. Titanium alloys were used in the forward section of the submarine, strengthening specific areas including the dome of the sonar array, and in the stern tube and seal of the shafts, while low-magnetic steel was used in the outer hull and water ballast tank. The sail and the retractable wings were built of aluminium alloys to save weight.[4]

Another decision which affected noise reduction was the installation of the main machinery over sine-blocks, which are flexible structures that avoid transmission of the machinery's vibrations to the hull and their reverberation to the ocean: the same installation protected the main machinery from the blast effect of enemy weapons.[5]

Weapons System

The submarine was equipped with eight launchers for P-70 missiles, installed forward of the sail between the pressure hull and outer hull.[6] The model SM-97A launchers were installed with an angle of 32.5 degrees to the horizontal of the vessel, and all were built in the 232 Bolshevik factory. A separate hydraulic system was installed solely for the operation of missile covers.[7] These eight covers were flush with the outer hull and hinged inboard when opened. This arrangement of the hatches and launchers avoided all the problems

An elevated view of the sail of the Project 670-class. Notable is its vertical front, necessary because of the installation of hydrophones, and the 'collar': attachments installed around its base, which helped decrease the noise emitted by the waterflow around the sail. (Efim Sandler collection)

A view of part of the control station of a Project 670-class boat – still dominated by so-called 'steam gauges'. (Efim Sandler collection)

that the Soviet Navy had suffered before with the Echo-class vessels and P-5 missiles while launching, as well as with the blast effects in the structure and crew safety. The missiles were now inside a safe area and could be launched with only minor concern for the safety of the vessel. Unfortunately, this arrangement affected the number of torpedoes that the vessel could load in its magazines due to the space taken up by the missiles. These were the first Soviet submarines equipped with such missile hatch covers, and subsequent classes have continued to use this system.

The lower end of one of two periscopes used aboard the Project 670-class, seen here in the fully raised position. (Efim Sandler collection)

The sail was small and streamlined, but there were some problems in the original design with the flow of water around this part of the vessel, which was later fixed with supplementary collars. The verticality in the forward side of the sail was very characteristic of this class, due to the hydrophones of the sonar system being installed there.

Apart from its missile armament, which will be detailed later, this class had only four 533mm torpedo tubes and two 406mm tubes, with 12 torpedoes for the former and four for the latter. This allowed it to retain its attack role even when all its missiles had been fired. The vessel's main weapons system was designed around the Rubin sonar, the most advanced in the Soviet fleet at the time. However, a lack of space once the missiles had been installed led to the decision to have the MGK-100 Kerch instead, of lesser performance but, smaller than the Rubin. The other electronic suites installed in the vessel were the MG-14 Arfa-G sonar system for mine detection and obstacle avoidance, MRP-21 Zaliv-P ESM (electronic support measures) system, Topol rader, Nikhrom-M identification friend or foe system and Sigma-670M navigation system. An automated Brest combat management system was also installed, allowing a reduction of the crew in this area.[8]

A satellite targeting system was approved, with a buoy to receive data while the submarine was submerged, but unfortunately for the Soviet fleet, the system was never deployed and the system was discarded.

Construction

The construction of the Charlie I was affected by the Soviet fluvial system. To increase the number of nuclear submarines that the state's shipbuilding industry was able to provide annually, some freshwater shipyards were modernised and prepared to start managing nuclear-powered submarine projects. One of them was the Gorkiy plant, where the shipyard was to launch the submarine and send it through the river system to the Northern Fleet for final outfitting and sea trials.

While this idea increased the number of nuclear submarines built per year, it also created a bottleneck in new projects. The limitations of the river systems, plus the size of vessel able to be built in the fluvial shipyards, meant they were generally of smaller displacement than those from the coastal shipyards. With this in mind, the Charlie I SSGN was designed as a small submarine. This also affected the final performance of the submarines, the lack of available space limiting the equipment able to be installed on board, as highlighted above with the sonar system.

The Gorkiy shipyard had just finished building Juliett SSGs and needed new projects to avoid under-capacity in its installations. The Project 670 Charlie I SSGN was assigned to this shipyard to help with the labour situation.[9] Some sources mention the length of the vessels as a limiting factor for those built in Gorkiy, but such an assertion appears to be incorrect as the shipyard was able to manage bigger submarines. More limiting was the navigational factor of the inland waterways.

The fluvial waterways used were the Volga, the Marinsky system and the White Sea–Baltic Channel completing the journey to Severodvinsk shipyard, where the submarines were outfitted and delivered to the fleet.[10]

The Gorkiy shipyard eventually built 11 submarines, with the first keel laid in 1964 and the last unit commissioned by the Soviet Navy in 1972. This meant a construction rate of 1.37 submarines per year. The build statistics of this class were impressive. The average build of the class lasted 986 days (two years and eight months), which was not bad for the first nuclear series submarine built in the yard, with an average time in dock of 721 days and 265 days for outfitting and sea trials until commissioning.

The main idea behind all the design effort and logistics chains involved in creating the Charlies was a mass-production submarine class, which in the shipbuilding industry meant the least time possible in construction of each unit, allowing the start of another vessel. The Gorkiy shipyard and the managers of the project fully fulfilled this objective. Analysing the last three units of the class, when all the improvements had been applied to the project, the total time required for finishing a vessel from keel to commission was 790, 598 and 406 days respectively.

A pair of Project 672 boats at the pier in their home base. Notable on the bow of the vessels are two vertical rows of torpedo tube covers: the uppermost pair covered the smaller 406mm tubes. (Efim Sandler collection)

Table 12: Project 670 (Skat)	
Propulsion	1 x PWR WM-4 of 89.2MW 1 x Steam Turbine OK-350 1 x Shaft, 18,800hp 2 x Turbogenerators TM-88, 2,000kW each 1 x Auxiliary Generator DG-500, 500kW 2 banks of batteries cells, 112 cells per bank
Length (m)	94.3
Beam (m)	9.9
Draught (m)	7.5
Displacement (surfaced/submerged, tons)	3,574/4,980
Operational Depth (m)	240/300
Speed (knots)	12/26
Crew	86 (23 officers)
Endurance (days)	50
Weapons	8 x P-70 missiles in 8 SM-97A launchers 4 x 533mm torpedo tubes forward (12 reloads, models SET-65, SAET-60M & 53-65K) 2 x 406mm tubes (4 reloads, models SET-450 & MGT-2)

These times compared favourably with the average of the class of 986 days, meaning these final units required 20 percent, 40 percent and 59 percent less time to be produced than the average. Comparing these figures with the initial units of the class, the percentage improvement is even better. All this merely confirms that the project was well-designed and organised for a mass-production submarine to be built in smaller shipyards. Furthermore, the submarine created was good enough for the needs of the Soviet Navy.

New Operational Concept

The equipment of the Project 670-class, with the underwater-launched P-70 missile, meant a change in the Soviet naval doctrine and in the US Navy's defensive countermeasures. Comparing the previous P-6 family of missiles with the performance of the new P-70, it can be seen that the threat had evolved to a new dimension. The P-6 was a long-range SSM with a datalink to its launcher platform, which could be guided during its flight. The idea was to hit the enemy fleet from as far away as possible. The new P-70 missile had other features that made it ideal for use with a mass-production platform. Foremost, it could be launched while the submarine was submerged. Because of this, its guidance system required the location of the launching point and target position prior to launch, to enable the missile to know where it was, and where it should fly to. In turn, once it fired missiles, the submarine was free to manoeuvre. The range of the P-70 was much shorter than that of its predecessor: only 40nm (74km). However, what was initially considered a big handicap was quickly converted into a new doctrine of attacking CVBGs.

The US Navy had reacted to the P-5 and P-6 menace by developing an air defence system around the carriers at the maximum effective range: the CVs were surrounded by destroyers equipped for anti-submarine tasks, and cruisers equipped with powerful radars and long-range surface-to-air missiles. Like the P-5 and P-6 before, the P-70 had the size and thus the radar cross-section comparable to that of a tactical fighter and this meant that it could be countered with similar weapons. Later on, the Americans discovered that

VIKINGS TO THE RESCUE

In reaction to the appearance of the Project 670-class, the US Navy – and allied services – was forced to develop new countermeasures. One was to add a second engine to the Kaman helicopters, resulting in the SH-2F version, which gave it a range of over 400 nautical miles (about 750km). Moreover, the US Navy intensified the development of a new anti-submarine aircraft. Originally designed to replace old and slow Grumman S-2 Tracker, the new platform was required to be jet powered, and thus faster, carry a bigger warload, and search for enemy submarines out to a range of 400nm in front of the carrier. The winner of the resulting contest was Lockheed, which – in cooperation with Ling-Temco-Vought – developed the S-3 Viking anti-submarine jet: probably the most dangerous opponent of the Project 670-class. The type entered service in the early 1970s, prompting a major reorganisation of US Navy's CVBGs: instead of classifying its aircraft carriers into 'attack' and 'anti-submarine' vessels, it retired the latter, and thus all remaining S-2 Trackers, without replacement. In turn, it equipped each of the former attack carriers with a squadron of S-3 Vikings, converting them into 'multi-purpose ships'. This change was most obvious in the resulting redesignation of hull numbers: prefixes of attack carriers lost the 'A' (i.e. were changed from CVA and CVAN to CV and CVN, respectively).

Finally, the US Navy not only reinforced the electronic warfare capabilities of all of its warships, but commenced research and development into an entirely new anti-air weapons system, which, eventually, was to result in the emergence of the – extremely expensive, yet ultra-fast reaction – Aegis, a decade later. That said, there was no doubt that, as of the late 1960s and early 1970s, once the Soviet doctrine of anti-carrier warfare was almost complete, the defences of CVBGs were still in the process of being bolstered to the necessary level: for the first time ever, the USA was reacting to a new threat from the USSR.

An S-3A Viking of anti-submarine squadron VS-21, on the deck of the aircraft carrier USS *John F. Kennedy* in the 1970s. Vikings formed the first line of anti-submarine defence of USN CVBGs during that decade and into the 1980s. (Photo by A. Molton, via Tom Cooper)

because the P-70 was not supported by the launching submarine's radar, they could easily jam its guidance system with electronic countermeasures, although this worked on 12 channels. As a consequence, by the late 1960s, the mass of weapons systems deployed by Soviet SSGNs was, effectively, obsolete.

This forced the Soviet Navy into developing a new concept of deploying its Project 670 submarines. Ironically, the solution was found not from operating this class, but from operations of the SSN units of the Soviet Navy. These were equipped with torpedoes only, and thus had to penetrate the ASW screen of the CVBG in order to approach to within the range of their weapons. Henceforth, the decision was taken for the Project 670-class to operate in similar fashion: they were to penetrate the ASW screen – consisting of old and relatively slow Grumman S-2 Tracker aircraft in the case of anti-submarine carriers, and of frigates equipped with Kaman SH-2 Seasprite helicopters in the case of CVBGs – and attack the carrier from a range of less than 40 nautical miles. The missile was equipped with an INS for the initial stages of flight and an active homing radar for terminal guidance. This meant that it was autonomous once launched. It was also very fast: its cruise speed was 600 knots (1,111km/h), and flight time 4–4.5 minutes. This meant that attack from such a short range left the defences with very little time to react: 3.5–4 minutes. However, as of the 1960s, all the types of SAMs operated by the US Navy were designed to combat incoming aircraft and anti-ship missiles from long range, and their weapons systems were not made for quick reaction. If the CVBG wanted to protect itself from such an attack, it had to spread its ASW screen further away from the carrier, in turn creating more space for possible attacks by SSNs. Thus, although an attempt to penetrate the outer ASW screen of the CVBG was of high risk for the Project 670-class, it also had a good chance of success.

Soviet Doctrine of Anti-Carrier Warfare

As of the late 1960s, the Soviet Navy already boasted a fleet of 52 SSGs and SSGNs, and had a large number of additional units under construction. Meanwhile, it had been in possession of heavy anti-ship missiles for over a decade, and thus in a position to expect that in the near future it might reach 'critical mass' in the number of units needed to keep them on station in all the oceans, and thus be able to cause critical damage quite early during any war. That said, the Soviet anti-carrier warfare doctrine did not depend on SSGs and SSGNs alone, nor was it purely offensive by nature. On the contrary, it remained defensive by nature, and its centrepiece was a large fleet of medium bombers equipped with powerful anti-ship missiles. Submarines were 'only' the second line of defence in that strategy, followed by the third consisting of surface vessels; submarines only equipped with torpedoes were expected to act as the ultimate weapon, one deployed against whatever was left of the CVBG after attacks by the other three means.

The ultimate result of this succession of ideas was the emergence of Admiral Gorshkov's doctrine of the 'battle of the first salvo', alluded to earlier. The essence of this doctrine was to keep the Soviet Navy's vessels – including surface ships, but especially SSGs and SSGNs – in close proximity to the carrier during peace, so that these could deliver a devastating attack at the start of any conflict, preferably, in coordination with bombers, and from multiple directions at the same time. Of course, the Soviets had no doubts that such an action would draw a strong response from the USA and NATO: indeed, they were aware of the fact that any of their surface vessels and any submarines tracking enemy CVBGs were certain to be at least damaged beyond repair, or sunk, at the start of any war. However, they were expected to cause sufficiently heavy damage to the CVBG before being taken out, to disrupt their further operations – at least in the Mediterranean, and possibly even in the North Atlantic.

From an operational point of view, the most difficult task of this doctrine was the coordination of attacks by the Soviet Naval Aviation and missiles from SSG/SSGNs. Because aircraft carriers were very loud vessels, which could be easily tracked by contemporary sonars from a range of 50 or more nautical miles, the Project 670-class was usually capable of tracking a CVBG during peacetime operations. In the event of war, the SSGN would slow down to a speed of five knots and unleash all of its eight missiles in two salvos, all flying at low altitude. However, aircraft needed precise information about the position of the target and had a tight schedule for launching missiles against it. Such information was difficult to obtain with the technology available at the time. Nevertheless, the Soviet reconnaissance systems' ability to obtain this level information was improving by the year.

Weak Spot

While the Project 670-class was relatively good in peacetime, it had one major drawback in its design that would become relevant at war. Its submerged speed was limited to 26 knots. As such, it was insufficient to chase a CVBG moving at high speed: even less so would it enable the submarine to outrun the enemy carrier in order to reach a suitable attack position. Furthermore, this lack of speed affected the ability to move out of the launching area and thus avoid a counterattack from the anti-submarine defences,

A rear view of a Project 672-class boat, underway at steering speed (3–5 knots). The submarines of this program were kept as small as possible: nevertheless, they could reach a maximum speed of only 26 knots and were considered much too slow for their task. (Efim Sandler collection)

especially by aircraft and helicopters – which were certain to detect the launch of multiple missiles.[11] The Soviets never found a solution to this problem, which eventually led to their decision to stop further construction of this class: indeed, to cease considering it a 'first line SSGN'. Of course, they still had a major opportunity to successfully take part in a theoretical conflict, but the lack of speed eventually resulted in the decision to discontinue the program after the construction of only 11 units. Even then, the successor suffered from exactly the same problem – and experienced a similar fate. That said, a submerged submarine equipped with powerful anti-ship missiles could still play an important role in a potential conflict: for example, the Project 670-class was perfectly equipped to intercept convoys expected to cross the Atlantic Ocean. It was a very versatile platform, with high potential even against well-equipped escorts, and thus the Soviet Navy was not going to abandon and discard it entirely.

The transfer of single shaft Project 670-class submarines from Murmansk to the Pacific remained a highly dangerous task – even more so if undertaken along the route under the North Pole. In 1978, two submarines of this class (K-87 and K-325) managed this feat, earning their skippers the prestigious Hero of the Soviet Union decoration. Captain 1st Class Egor Topko was the commander of this mission. (Efim Sandler collection)

Transfer to the Pacific

All the units of the Project 670-class were initially deployed with the Northern Fleet of the Soviet Navy. Based in Zapadnaya Litsa, they were assigned to the 1st Flotilla of the 11th Division. As the successors became available, the decision was taken to transfer them to the Pacific Fleet, though.

The first Project 670 unit sent to the Far East was K-201, between January and May 1974. This vessel conducted only one patrol with the Northern Fleet before being reassigned to Vilyuchinsk. It travelled via the Indian Ocean, escorted by the Project 671-class K-314. Remarkably, as soon as reaching its new home port, it was sent on a patrol in the Bering Sea. From 1974, the transfer of the remaining units to the Pacific Fleet was conducted via the northern route across the Arctic region. In 1974, the passage was completed by the K-429, which thus became the first single shaft Soviet submarine to use this route: its skipper was decorated the Hero of the Soviet Union for this achievement. A year later, K-212 (the former K-87, redesignated in January 1978) and K-325 followed but did so along a route via the North Pole: unsurprisingly, their commanders were decorated in similar fashion. All such transfers were undertaken in the company of another submarine, and mostly during the months of August and September, when weather conditions were better. For example, in August 1980, K-43 was accompanied by the Project 667BDR-class SSBN (ASCC/NATO codename 'Delta-III'), K-223. Eventually, all the remaining units followed in similar fashion by 1988, always along the same route. In Vilyuchinsk, they were assigned to the 10th Division, 2nd Flotilla.[12]

Captain 1st Class Aleksey Lushin, commander of K-212 during the mission from the Murmansk area to the North Pole and then the Bering Sea and Kamchatka in 1978. (Efim Sandler collection)

Charlie Patrols

The first operational patrol by the Project 670-class was undertaken in 1968; the first in the Pacific in 1975. Its busiest year was 1971, when 11 patrols were undertaken – all with the Northern Fleet, and all in the Atlantic. Submarines of this class had several remarkable achievements. Two units took part in Exercise Okean 75, and three in the Exercise Sever 77: others took part in exercises Zastava 79 and 81, Skitz 79 and Okean Ohota 79. For many years, they led during all missile-firing exercises, and every single submarine of the class won some form of related prize.

Another exercise very commonly carried out was the launching of missiles from multiple submarines, which was the basis of the Soviet doctrine. Such exercises were undertaken on several occasions by Charlie I-class submarines and other SSGN units. Particularly interesting were the exercises carried out after the fall of the Soviet Union: in April 1991, K-320 and K-201 launched five

Captain 1st Class Vladimir Lushin, commander of the K-325 during the same mission. (Efim Sandler collection)

A Project 670-class boat seen on arrival in the Pacific, following successful transfer via the Arctic Circle. (Efim Sandler collection)

including simulated torpedo attack and reconnaissance photography from the periscope. Both exercises were assessed as having been carried out excellently. In March 1984, K-201 was able to locate and track for two days the aircraft carrier USS *Kitty Hawk* (CV-63) – a tremendous achievement for this submarine, testing its actual mission objectives.

By 1987, the Project 670-class had carried out a total of 80 patrols. Of these, 51 in the Atlantic, 22 in the Pacific, five in the Mediterranean (all by submarines from the Northern Fleet), and two in the Indian Ocean (both in 1982, by submarines from the Pacific Fleet). However, the average number of patrols per individual vessel of the Project 670-class was lower than that of the Project 675: 7.2. This low number implied that the class was essentially obsolete by the time it reached the Pacific theatre and was in the process of being overtaken by more modern units now entering service.

missiles against the air defence systems installed in Kamchatka to test the capacities of this system.

One unit made a very special patrol. K-429, the 10th unit of the class, was assigned a mission to carry out a lengthy deployment to the Indian Ocean, lasting from July 1982 until March 1983. While en route to the operation area, sailing in the Philippine Sea in September and October 1982, it undertook an exercise under the direct command of Admiral Gorshkov, Commander-in-Chief of the Soviet Navy, installed for the exercise in Vladivostok. Together with two Project 641 conventionally powered submarines, it searched for, located and tracked a surface task force composed of seven units. Later, in January 1983 while in the Arabian Sea, K-429 was assigned the task of locating a surface task group centred on the aircraft carrier *Minsk*, escorted by three ASW units. K-429 fulfilled the mission,

Charlie Accidents

The Project 670-class proved a much safer platform than the earlier Project 650 and 675, but still suffered several unfortunate accidents, some of them related to their nuclear powerplants. Indeed, the class had the doubtful honour of one of its submarines sinking twice during its operational life. Accidents that led to the loss of crewmembers are summarised in Table 13; other notable cases were as follows.

The keel for the seventh unit of the Project 670-class, K-320 was laid in April 1968. On 18 January 1970, around 09.30 hours,

The transfer of Project 670-class submarines from the Northern Fleet to the Pacific Fleet offered the opportunity to test and train for operations under the polar icecap. This boat is seen after surfacing through the ice near the North Pole. (Efim Sandler collection)

a hydraulic test was carried out in the primary circuit of the cooling system, while the reactor core was loaded with fuel rods. Unfortunately, the pressure from the test caused the displacement of the provisional control rod, previously installed to avoid this kind of accident. Without the control rod in position, the reactor reached its critical point and began melting down: it started emitting radioactivity to the surrounding buildings and other submarines under construction. As far as is known, four workers died from radiation, while around 150 others received a hazardous dose.[13] Moreover, the sixth unit of the class, K-308, and the eighth, K-302, both required complete decontamination, as did their construction hall and most of the shipyard's installations and machinery. This work was completed only through February 1970, by when the tactical numbers were exchanged between the sixth and the eight unit of the class.

Still, the damage to K-320's reactor was extensive enough to prompt the Soviets to replace the entire system: the submarine was thus completed only in September 1971.[14] Only a year later, in September 1972, the K-320 then collided with the Project 675-class K-131, in Motovsky Bay, as described above. Both skippers were dismissed from their positions for this accident. The boat remained in service but remained unlucky. In June 1973, leaks were detected in the pipping of the reactor cooling: although repairs were applied, the submarine was subsequently limited to operating no more than 1,000 nautical miles from base, and no more than for 30 days in succession.

Another serious accident took place on 13 April 1978, when K-308 collided with K-490 – an SSBN of the Project 667BDR-class – while returning from a patrol in the Atlantic. Subsequent investigation revealed that during the entire cruise, K-308's skipper had not been involved in calculations related to the actual position of the vessel, and the navigator was using references from a radio-beacon, that indicated an error in his position of 12nm. Therefore, he attempted to reduce the error to 4.5nm. The captain then decided that the error was 'within a range of 3–5nm' to the east of the designated course and continued the exercise with the K-490, until the two vessels collided – causing structural damage to their external hulls – because their sonars failed to detect each other.

Suvorov's Ordeal

The most terrible accident involving any operational vessel of the Project 670-class was experienced by K-429, while it was deployed with the Pacific Fleet. It was a classic example of incompetence, mismanagement and faulty operational procedures of the Soviet Navy. As of 23 June 1983, the vessel was fresh back from a patrol and undergoing overhauls, with the crew on leave. Its skipper, Captain Nikolai M. Suvorov, was away and busy moving his family to the new base. At that point in time, the Commander-in-Chief of the Pacific Fleet, Admiral Oleg Yerofeyev, ordered the K-429 to leave the port as soon as possible and head for a designated training area. The Commander of the Division, Alkayev, simply forwarded and confirmed the order without complaint: of course, Suvorov did complain, but the two senior officers exercised immense pressure upon him, threatening his expulsion from the Communist Party.[15]

Left with no choice, Suvorov arranged the necessary personnel from other submarines from the base (and the base itself), to create a makeshift crew. He organised them in five groups and took 120 on board, instead of the usual 86. This was a violation of contemporary regulations under which a submarine with more than 30 percent of the crew replaced or new, could not join the fleet until all new personnel were trained and qualified to operate the vessel.

Captain Nikolai Suvorov, unfairly blamed for the sad fate that befell the once proud K-429. (Efim Sandler collection)

Unhappy about the situation, and while protesting Yerofeyev's and Alkayev's orders, Suvorov put the K-429 to sea. As soon as it was underway, Yerofeyev ordered the submarine to the training area and to commence the exercise according to plan. At that point in time, Suvorov became fed up and refused to follow orders, citing Navy regulations that demanded test-dives following any kind of work in port. Only now did the HQ back down and permitted him to proceed as usual.

That evening, Suvorov conned the K-429 into Sarannaya Bay: concerned about the safety of his makeshift crew, he wanted to conduct the test-dive within an area about 50m deep, instead of 2,000 metres within the designated training area. The test was initiated with the skipper ordering his boat to periscope depth. As could have been expected, at that point in time, a series of fatal errors resulted in malfunctions that doomed the submarine. Unknown to the crew, the depth gauges of the rear ballast tanks were not functioning. As a result, they showed zero, while actually taking 400 tons of water on board. Not realising what was happening, Suvorov ordered the flooding of the mid-section ballast tanks. With the submarine over-ballasted and starting to dive out of control, the next problem became painfully obvious: the ventilation system was undergoing maintenance and remained open in compartments one, two, three and four. Furthermore, the equalising valves between compartments four and five were open. Rapid flooding thus trapped and killed 14 crewmembers in compartments four and five, and water entered compartments one and two. The order was given to blow the tanks with high-pressure air, but another malfunction resulted in this being expelled directly into the sea. K-429 sank to the bottom. At that point in time, the survivors realised that in the rush to get to the sea, all the survival kit had been left behind. Worse yet: the emergency buoy had been welded to the hull and thus the crew was unable to activate it. Desperate, Suvorov went to the torpedo room asking for volunteers to exit through the torpedo tubes, following the emergency procedure, and try to contact the supply vessel MPK-122, known to have been in the area. Two petty officers accepted the mission and got out, eventually managing to contact the headquarters and advise of the situation – after which a rescue operation was initiated.[16]

On 26 August, around 1915 hours, the stricken submarine was located by the rescue party including salvage vessels SS-38, SS-83 and the MPK-122. While divers were preparing, the crew developed a plan to exit the vessel via the torpedo tubes and the emergency

A collage with photographs of all the victims of the sinking of K-429 on 23 June 1983. (Efim Sandler collection)

The sail the unlucky K-429, seen during the final salvage attempt, on 9 August 1984, between two pontoons. (Efim Sandler collection)

The sail and the bow of the same submarine, seen a few minutes later. (Efim Sandler collection)

hatch in compartment seven. Supported by divers, the evacuation commenced at 2236 hours, and was completed by 2300 hours: 104 were saved, but two crewmembers died in the process.[17]

The problem now was that a nuclear submarine had sunk in shallow waters. The reactors were supposed to have been disconnected by the engine room personnel, but the Soviet Navy realised it faced a potential imminent nuclear accident. The salvage operation was initiated on 29 August: soon after entering the submarine, divers discovered that the procedure of shuting down the reactor was incomplete, and the control bars were still some 70mm short of the fully down position: the reactor was still working, even if at a very low output (below one percent of its capacity) and was shut down only seven days later. The K-429 was raised from the bottom a full year later, on 9 August 1984. Four days later, it was transferred to a floating dock and then brought to the SRZ-49 shipyard in Seldevaya Bay for repairs.

Of course, the Pacific Fleet assigned full responsibility to Captain Suvorov and the Chief of compartment five, Likhovozoy. They were put on trial and sentenced to 10 and eight years jail, respectively – though granted amnesty after 2.5 years. However, the officer actually responsible for this tragedy, including the loss of 15 crewmembers, recovery and repairs costing 300 million Soviet Rubles – the Commander-in-Chief of the Pacific Fleet, Admiral Oleg Yerofeyev – assumed no responsibility at all. Perhaps unsurprisingly, after this injustice, K-429 resisted being returned to service: on 12 September 1985, short of being recommissioned to service after all the repairs, it sank at the pier due to depressurisation of the hull. Once again, the submarine was salvaged, but this time it was the government in Moscow that had enough. The ill-fated submarine was converted into a training vessel, redesignated the US-130 and decommissioned from service.

A Dangerous Retiree

The last serious accident of the Project 670-class occurred on a submarine that had been decommissioned from the Soviet Navy. K-313 had been out of service since July 1992. Around 2245 hours on 29 May 1997, it sank at its pier. The core of the nuclear reactor had been unloaded some years previously, and the submarine had no crew, so the accident posed no risk for humans or the environment.

The reason for the sinking appears to be that ice that had formed on the submarine during the winter started to melt, and the trim of the vessel subsequently changed. The ventilation flaps in the hull were open, and with the trim changed, water started flooding inside the submarine, ending with K-313 sinking at the pier of the shipyard at a depth of 18–21 metres. The Russian Navy started an operation to raise the submarine with ship-lifting pontoons between June and September 1997, during this time the vessel remained flooded with seawater, mud and debris.

The first attempt to raise K-313 took place on 5 September but failed because insufficient lift was applied in the bow area, and only the stern raised to the surface. During a second attempt, on 1 October, the forward pontoons broke their slings due to the excessive load. A third attempt was made five days later, which led to a practically fully raised submarine, but unfortunately the weather worsened, and for safety reasons, the order was given to make a controlled sinking. The fourth attempt was initiated on 10 October 1997: this time, the vessel was raised too quickly, and it was impossible to control the trim in time. As a consequence, the hulk of K-313 developed a list to the port side, capsized and sank again. Finally, three days later, the submarine was raised and transferred to shallow water before being pumped out. It was taken to the SRZ-49 shipyard in Seldevaya Bay, never again to return to active service with the Russian Navy, being manned by a civilian crew until 2006, when it was scrapped.

Modernisation of the Project 670 Class

The Charlie Is never received a general modernisation like other classes of Soviet submarines. Only four units of the class (K-313, K-308, K-320 and K-302) received an upgrade through the installation of the new MGK-400 Rubicon sonar, in place of the original Kerch.

One submarine received a major retrofit – not strictly a modernisation – so that it could be leased to the Indian Navy. The lead unit of the class, K-43, was retrofitted to the ad-hoc Project

A Project 670-class boat (left side), with a Project 675-class (foreground), and a supply ship – during an exercise in the Bering Sea – being overflown by a US Navy P-3C Orion anti-submarine warfare aircraft. (Efim Sandler collection)

Table 13: Notable Accidents of the Project 670-Class

Date	Unit	Place	Type of Accident	Description
08/08/1971	K-313	Zapadnaya Litsa	Flood	While in base, water partially flooded compartment 2
01/06/1972	K-302	Motovsky Bay	Collision	Hit the bottom while sailing
01/03/1973	K-429	Zapadnaya Litsa	Flood	Uncontrolled access of seawater to the reactor compartment
22/12/1973	K-325		Fire	Fire in the cable routes in the turbine compartment
01/02/1974	K-302		Collision	Hit the bottom
01/05/1974	K-25		Missile incident	A missile launched from K-25 hit nearby tugs assisting an exercise
1975	K-429			Water Ballast Tank no. 13 suffered heavy structural damage when blown
01/05/1976	K-320		Reactor system	Reactor suffered a depressurisation
08/10/1977	K-201		Collision	Hit Japanese fishing nets
19/12/1978	K-313		Collision	Struck auxiliary vessel MPK-90
01/04/1979	K-302		Fire	Minor fire on board
01/03/1987	K-121		Collision	Hit the bottom

6709 designed specifically to reach the levels expected by the Indian Navy. This retrofit included the new MGK-400 Rubicon sonar system, new MG-519 Arfa anti-mine sonar, new air conditioning for operation in the Indian Ocean and improvements to the cabins for both officers and crew. Secret equipment was also removed from the vessel due to it not being included in the agreement for leasing the submarine. All the relevant jobs were carried out in the SRZ-49 shipyard in Vilyuchinsk between August 1983 and December 1984.

The contract between the two governments included the training of an Indian crew in Vladivostok, at onshore installations and on board the vessel. More than 150 members of the Indian Navy were trained under the contract, after which, on 5 January 1988, the Indian Navy's flag was raised on the submarine to begin a lease period of three years. The submarine was renamed S-71 *Chakra* in the Indian Navy.

During the lease period, Soviet instructors were on board the vessel full time, supporting the Indian crew. Experts from specialised branches, such as weapons or nuclear reactors, were also assigned to support the Indians. Under the Indian flag, Indian Navy Ship (INS) *Chakra* (S-71) sailed 72,000nm, fired five missiles and 42 torpedoes, and its reactor was in operation for more than 400 days. The contract to lease the Soviet vessel provided invaluable knowledge for the Indians to help them continue with their own programme of nuclear submarines: for the first time ever a nuclear-powered submarine was leased to another country. The submarine returned to the Soviet Navy in 1991, as per the lease contract, and was decommissioned from the then Russian Federation Navy in 1992.[18] By that time, all the other Project 670-class submarines had been scrapped – several of them in Japan under an internationally funded program.

8
CONTROVERSIAL UPGRADE

The evolution of weapons systems led to the design of a new SSGN based on the Project 670. In the late 1960s, V.P. Vorobyov of TsKB-112 Lazhurit started working on two design lines for modernising the Project 670-class; one of them, designated Project 670M-1, could maintain an operational depth of 300 metres and had the OK-350 propulsion steam turbine, while the second option, Project 670M-2, increased the operational depth to 400 metres and the steam turbine propulsion was replaced by a new model, the OK-650. The second option was eventually cancelled as it implied more investment and production time in a class of submarines whose performance the Soviet Navy was not happy with. When Vorobyov passed away, the Chief Designer position for the Project 670M was assigned to his Deputy Designer, A.G. Leshchev.

The new design was focused upon a new missile and combat system, the P-120 (ASCC/NATO codename 'SS-N-9 Siren') – which, originally, was actually planned for the Project 670, but was not ready in time. Essentially, the P-120 was a submerged-launch missile with a range extended to 120–150km, fixing the shortfalls of the P-70. The combat systems for this missile required more space inside the vessel, resulting in the total length of the submarine increasing by 8.9 metres, and the displacement by around 800 tons.

All the main structural elements remained exactly the same, but with improvements in the combat systems and electronic and sonar systems. The launching procedure was automated with a digital computer for checking the missiles prior to launching and putting them into standby mode to allow the launching. This was the Danube system and saved time over the P-70's analogue launch procedure. Another system, known as Cube, automatically corrected the required water ballast in specific tanks after launching to maintain the trim and list of the vessel. Due to the increased range of the missile, the Project 670M-class was outfitted with the Molniya system that allowed it to receive targeting information from satellites. Furthermore, it received the Paravan floating antenna, with which it could receive radio messages while underway at a depth of 150 metres.

Production

The decision to construct the Project 670M in series was a controversial one. The first keel of the lead unit was laid down in 1972, while that of the bigger and better Project 949-class (ASCC/NATO codename 'Oscar/Oscar I'; see the following chapter) was laid in 1975. Unsurprisingly, there was much pressure for the work

Outwardly, the Project 670M-class differed relatively little from the Project 670 except for its extended forward hull: this contained improved electronics, sonar system and combat systems. (Efim Sandler collection)

to be carried out at the Krasnoye Sormovo shipyard because the project for the next submarine due to be built there – the Project 956 Barrakuda-class (ASCC/NATO codename 'Sierra I') – had been delayed. Furthermore, while the Project 670-class had a poor maximum speed, the Project 670M was even worse: the increase in length and displacement slowed it down by two knots. The hydrodynamics of the Project 670M were also poorer, especially along the seam between the sail and the outer hull – which also created much noise. It was only later that this issue was solved through the installation of a new shape in that area, known in the West as 'the collar'.

Eventually, construction of the full class of six units took place in the same shipyard as its predecessor, Krasnoye Sormovo, and they were built over a period of seven years, starting in December 1972 and ending in 1980. Although lower than that of the Project 670-class, this was still a high production rate of less than one unit per year (actually just 0.85 submarines per year). Technically, both projects were the same, and there was never any clear explanation for the reduction in the production efficiency of the shipyard. Probably the main cause could be found in the fact that the Soviet Navy's interest in this class was low. In addition, there was little confidence in the ability of the low-speed platform to fulfil its mission. All this created a situation where the Project 670M-class was not given sufficient priority, allowing resources to be redirected to other platforms. However, it was necessary to keep the shipyard busy and deploy the P-120 on additional platforms.[1]

The average construction time of the class was 599 days, with a minimum of 365 days (for the first unit), and a maximum of 750 days. It is curious that the most quickly built vessel was the lead unit, which was constructed in exactly a year, while the last one was finished in 376 days. This implies that the yard was probably able to produce vessels more quickly but was working below its best efficiency in order to remain busy.

Project 670- and Project 670M-class SSGNs were not only based in ports close to the Arctic Circle, but regularly operated in waters with some of the harshest weather conditions. These two boats were photographed during a break between patrols. (Efim Sandler collection)

A Project 670-class boat seen next to a Project 1134A Berkut A-class during an exercise. This was a 'large anti-submarine warfare ship' under the Soviet classification system, referred to as the 'Kresta II-class' cruiser by the ASCC/NATO. (Efim Sandler collection)

Table 14: Project 670M-Class (Skat-M)	
Propulsion	1 x PWR WM-4 of 89.2MW 1 x Steam Turbine OK-350 1 x Shaft, 18,800hp 2 x Turbogenerators TM-88, 2,000kW each 1 x Auxiliary Generator DG-500, 500kW 2 banks of battery cells, 152 lead-acid cells per bank
Length (m)	104.9
Beam (m)	9.9
Draught (m)	7.5
Displacement (surfaced/ submerged, tons)	4,372/5,570
Operational Depth (m)	240/300
Speed (knots)	12/24
Crew	98 (47 officers)
Endurance (days)	60
Weapons	8 x P-120 missiles in 8 CT-84 launchers 4 x mm torpedo tubes forward (14 reloads, model SET-65, SAET-60M & RPK-2 Vyuga ASW missiles)

The P-120 Malakhit

The Soviet Naval Staff had decided, after carrying out numerous studies, that a missile attack by submarines from less than 100km away was very risky for the launching platform. This was the new objective of the missile designers, and in 1962 Chelomey's OKB-52 offered the Navy a multiplatform design

A Project 670M-class submarine seen tied to pier while reloading P-120 missiles, prior to the next patrol. (Efim Sandler collection)

for a universal missile than could be launched from both surface vessels and submerged submarines.

A Ministerial Decree of 28 February 1963 assigned Chelomey the main mission of providing this new missile to the fleet, and other tasks related to naval missiles.[2] The initial OKB-52 proposal was approved in September 1963, with the definitive design drawings passed in February 1964.

The same missile was to be used in surface vessels and submarines by the Soviet Navy, entering service with the surface fleet in March 1972 and with the submarine fleet in November 1977.[3] The rocket booster kit for use during the launch phase was the same for both versions and expended after the missile had reached the minimum velocity to start its own engine. Two rockets were installed, instead of the usual four: this enabled them to launch from a depth of 50 metres.

Advances in electronic warfare by the United States had jeopardised the combat effectiveness of the anti-ship missiles. For this reason, from the P-120 forward, all the missiles designed in the Soviet Union, and in general around the world, looked for improved capacities under a heavy electronic environment. The P-120 was equipped with an INS for the mid-course flight phase and an active-radar seeker for the terminal phase: it could receive corrections in flight from both the launching platform and an external platform (if the latter was within range). Additionally, Chelomey decided to install a second seeker option in the missile to back up the radar. A ventral pod was installed with an infrared seeker that could help the missile to select the correct target if the radar was jammed by the enemy's electronic defences.[4]

As mentioned before, the Danube system prepared the missiles for launching and allowed the eight missiles to be launched in two salvos of four. Two of the most renowned institutes of the USSR undertook developing it. Under the orders of the academic L.I. Sedov, the Central Institute of Aerodynamics and the Scientific Mechanic Research Institute of Moscow led the launch testing of dummy missiles from submerged static platforms to develop the basic scientific parameters and engineering solutions.

The warhead available for the P-120 was a conventional high-explosive one of 840kg. It appears that a nuclear warhead of 200kT was developed for the missile, but it is unclear if any submarines made patrols with this version embarked. The intention was for Project 670M missions to be of a conventional warfare role, and to occupy some of the launchers with nuclear missiles that could not be used from the beginning of a conflict did not match with Gorshkov's doctrine of the 'battle of the first salvo'.

Test launchings were carried out between 1963 and 1968, followed by missile integration in specific launching platforms. The first actual launch was made on 25 September 1968,[5] with one fired from a static silo 50 metres underwater in 1969. These early missiles were labelled P-50 by the Soviets and were the version to be used by the surface units of the fleet. Production of the P-50 was eventually cancelled in favour of the more versatile multiplatform version, the P-120.

Missile Testing

The Project 1234-class corvette (ASCC/NATO codename Nanuchka) was the platform selected for the initial trial launchings of the P-120, conducted in 1970–1972. Between April and December 1974, K-452, lead unit of the Project 670M-class, carried out official certification of the missiles from series production. Of the eight salvos launched, four were catalogued as satisfactory while the other four were said to be substandard due to a series of minor errors that were later detected and solved. The whole system was classified as operational with the Soviet fleet by a Ministerial Decree of 21 November 1977.

The procedure for launching the missile forced the submarine to maintain a constant course and speed throughout the process until the last missile had left the launcher. Compared with the previous procedures for launching missiles from submarines, this was a minor handicap. Some of the vessels were later modernised with a new sonar system, the MGK-400 Rubicon, that was linked to the Danube-670M combat system, allowing targeting information from the sonar to be used as initial guidance information for the missile launching. In addition, the Danube system made the interlink with the Uspekh and Legenda systems through the Molniya buoy. The Paravan submerged very low frequency (VLF) antenna helped with communications.[6]

Some 500 missiles are estimated to have been produced, for both versions, the P-50 and P-120, in conventional and nuclear versions. By the beginning of the 1990s, at least the half of the total production had been consumed by the fleet. All the missiles were constructed in Machinery Building Plant no.47 at Oremburg.

The extent of the success of these missiles can only be see when the full spectrum of naval platforms deploying it is taken into account: this included Project 661 and Project 670M submarines, Project 1234 and Project 1241 corvettes (ASCC/NATO codenames 'Nanuchka' and 'Tarantul', respectively), and test hydrofoils of the Project 1240-class (ASCC/NATO codename 'Sarancha').

9
THE LAST AND THE BEST

After decades of study and development, in both the technical world and that of operational arts, the Soviet Union was ready to provide to the world the best exponent, the state-of-the-art version, of the Soviet concept of the SSGN. A revolution in naval warfare came about with the introduction of a type of submarine that had not existed previously. The Western world was shocked when the first anti-ship missiles were introduced in submarine platforms, making the Soviet Navy pioneers in a field never before explored.

The final performance achievements of the latest SSGNs, such as the Project 675-class, were still not enough for the Soviet Navy and the GenStab's theorists. They knew that all the complexities of the SSGN could be improved by investing in different aspects of the system. Consequently, the Soviet Navy continued pressing for better results, specifically looking for a missile with real long-range capabilities and a platform able to deal with the high cruising speed of a carrier battlegroup.

The Soviet Union's shipbuilding industry, together with the Naval Staff, were now ready to enter into a new epoch of gigantic designs, with capabilities far beyond the previous classes and able to achieve its objective with only one submarine. The Oscar class and their missiles, still in active service in the early 2020s, were in theory able to attack and disable an escorted US Navy aircraft carrier with a complete salvo of embarked missiles.

Not only were the missiles impressive, but the size of the submarine and the structural resistance and unlimited range of the vessel jeopardised the safety of the carriers inside their umbrella of escorts. Furthermore, it should always be remembered that the Soviet Union developed the attack against carriers as an integrated assault from various and different sources, with an attack from the resulting, future SSGN-class expected to be coordinated with the fabulous capacities that the Soviet Union's naval aviation and surface fleet units could put together in the sea at the required moment.

Design

The new vessel was developed as what was subsequently named the third generation of Soviet nuclear-powered submarines. Initial studies were launched in 1967, and the technical specification requested in 1969: both aimed at obtaining a 'heavy submarine missile cruiser'.

Eventually, the new design was fixed as Project 949 Granit. Its Chief Designer became P.P. Pustinsev, who had plentiful experience with earlier SSG projects.[1]

The principal problem with the Project 949-class was the dimensions of the missiles embarked on it. These were the P-700 Granit (ASCC/NATO codename 'SS-N-19 Shipwreck'), designed by OKB-52 Mashinostroyeniya of Chelomey. The range of the missiles was requested to be greater than 270nm (500km), which implied the body of the missiles to be a size incomparable with previous anti-ship missiles embarked on submarines: they were 10 metres long, had a wingspan of 2.6 metres, and weighed 7,000kg. Because of studies carried out by the GenStab regarding improved defence capabilities of CVBGs, the submarine was required to carry no fewer than 24 of these enormous weapons. This was an astonishing number of embarked missiles compared with previous classes of Soviet SSGNs, being three times the normal salvo of missiles on board a submarine. This was the defining concept of the full design of the new submarine. The designers needed to think in huge proportions for the new vessel. Initially, they tried to fit the new missiles in the Project 675-class, but after preliminary studies were carried out it was discovered that this was impossible due to the size of the missiles and the lack of space available in the submarine.

Many arrangements and improvements developed for the Project 661-class were applied in the new Project 949-class. The Rubin Design Bureau initially estimated the vessel would have an underwater displacement of over 15,000 tons, which was the size of some Second World War aircraft carriers. With this displacement,

The Project 649-class submarine K-150 *Tomsk* seen short of completion. This photograph provides an excellent view of the hull design of this class – including the widened centre section necessary to carry the battery of 24 launchers for P-700 Granit anti-ship missiles. (Efim Sandler collection)

Another view of the K-150 *Tomsk*, seen in the 1990s, this time with the covers for the torpedo tubes in their position. Visible in the upper right corner are the open hatches for the P-700 Granit missiles launchers. By this time, crests began appearing on the Soviet/Russian SSGNs: this one depicts Poseidon, the ancient Greek god of the sea. (Efim Sandler collection)

3.5 metres. The beam of the submarine was also increased to unusual proportions in this project.

The missiles were fitted in pairs, with one hatch flush with the external hull covering each pair. The missile launchers had a fixed angle of 45° to the main plain of the submarine, due to the inability of the Soviets to develop a vertical launcher system for this huge missile. The hatches, and all the external surfaces including the sail, were designed to operate in Arctic scenarios, with the capacity to avoid chunks of ice, thereby avoiding the danger of them blocking hatches or launch operations.

The conventional weapons on board the Oscars were not forgotten. Indeed, their principal anti-submarine weapons were torpedoes, 28 of which could be taken on board – in two distinct calibres: there were four 533mm tubes and two of 605mm.

The sonar system was the most advanced available from Soviet industry, the MGK-540 Skat 3,[3] a passive VLF TAS fully digital system integrated with a passive VLF/LF flank array sonar. The sonar was integrated with different subsystems of the submarine that could measure the depth of water below and above the submarine. The last version of the sonar system was also capable of tracking and classifying targets in a fully automated loop.[4] The information from the sonar system could be directly used by the targeting system of the missile complex. It also received targeting information from another targeting system, through external antennas. The navigation system was a modern one known as Medevitsa.

After the design had been approved by the Navy, construction started in Severodvinsk shipyard. The keel of the first unit, K-525, was laid down on 25 July 1975. The shipbuilding company Sevmash was at the time handling the biggest projects of the Soviet Navy and the largest submarine project in the world.[5] Construction of the Oscar took five years, after which it was commissioned by the Soviet Navy. The lead unit, K-525 – also known as *Arkhangelsk* – then underwent extensive testing of its new weapons system. The second unit, K-206 *Murmansk*, was laid down in April 1977, entering service with the Soviet Navy in 1983. These two units composed the first batch of this series, known in the West as 'Oscar I'. Sometime later, after the third unit of the class was launched, its existence was discovered by Western intelligence agencies. The new submarine was a variant with an increased length; it was named the Oscar II class.

Another important new feature was the installation of two newly designed propellers with seven blades, equipped with control pitch blades, increasing the stealth of the platform, and offering better performance against enemy ASW forces.[6]

According to the internal schedules of the Soviet Navy, the Project 949 Oscars were expected to be a class of 20 units: a formidable force of SSGNs to be shared between the Northern and Pacific Fleets. The

and the associated main dimensions and expected high underwater speed, the power plant needed would be huge. Two nuclear reactors were duly installed, the sections of which were designed to be as common as possible with the reactor installed on board the Project 941-class SSBNs, looking for economies in the whole shipbuilding programme.

The nuclear reactors were OK-650Bs, each of 190MW,[2] and there were also two GTZA-OK-9 steam turbines providing 98,000bhp of power to the shafts and two DG-190 turbogenerators, each of 3,200kw. The design of the whole rear section of the submarine was fully based on that of the sole Project 661-class vessel but adapted to improve the propulsion power and increase the efficiency of the propellers.

Concept

'The quest for speed', as it was called, was the objective of the second generation of Soviet submarines. The focus in the development of the third generation was their quietening, in order to make them able to confront the superior sonar technologies in the hands of NATO countries. Despite the size of the Project 949, it was optimised for working at so-called 'silent' speeds. The cooling system of the reactors was designed to operate under natural circulation, using 30 percent of the power output, through an optimised design of the main condensers. In this way, the reactor did not need to operate the circulating pumps and could avoid the emission of machinery noise. The size of the rudders, meanwhile, helped the platform to manoeuvre efficiently in underwater operations.

The length of the submarine was an impressive 143 metres, divided into nine compartments. The missiles were located in the sides of the main hull, between it and the external hull. The double-hull configuration, very typical of Soviet designs, allowed the platform more buoyancy and high resistance against underwater blasts from enemy weapons, the space between the hulls being

Table 15: Project 949 & Project 949A-Class		
Propulsion	2 x PWR OK-650B of 190MW 2 x Steam Turbines GTZA-OK-9, 98,000hp 2 x Turbogenerators DG-9, 3,200kW	2 x PWR OK-650B of 190MW 2 x Steam Turbines GTZA-OK-9, 98,000hp 2 x Turbogenerators DG-9, 3,200kW
Length (m)	143	154
Beam (m)	18.2	18.2
Draught (m)	9	9
Displacement (surfaced/ submerged, tons)	12,500/17,000	13,400/18,000
Operational Depth	/	/
Speed (knots)	/30	/28
Crew	130	130
Endurance (days)		
Weapons	24 x P-700 missiles in SM-255A launchers 4 x 533mm torpedo tubes 4 x 605mm torpedo tubes	24 x P-700 missiles in SM-255A launchers 4 x 533mm torpedo tubes 4 x 605mm torpedo tubes

One of the earliest photographs of a Project 649-class submarine. Note the number of missing anechoic tiles around the bow and the side of the boat. (USN)

Oscar I platform was found to be in need of some redesigning for a better internal arrangement of its equipment and systems. For this reason, a new compartment, numbered 10, was created. The length of the new version was increased to 154 metres, with an underwater displacement to 18,000 tons.

The construction of this class was badly affected by the fall of the Soviet Union, but was one of the few naval projects that the Russian Federation continued after 1991. Up to 20 units were planned, with 14 vessels starting construction in the Severodvinsk shipyard, not including the two Oscar I units. Of the 14 Oscar IIs, 11 were delivered to the Russian Navy up to 1996, while the work on the 12th unit was halted when more than 75 percent completed. This latter unit was known as *Belgorod*, which this book will return to later, despite it will not being completed as a Project 949A.

The 13th unit, known as *Volgograd*, had its keel laid down in September 1993, but after its construction was cancelled, the vessel was scrapped in 2012. The 14th unit was never officially laid down but was started in the yard workshop under the name of *Barnaul*. The latter was scrapped in 2012. Both units had been around 40 percent complete when they were axed.

The average construction time of the class was more than four years, but it is important to note that the major part of the work was done after 1991, and was affected in varying degrees by a lack of financial resources. Some units were finished in three-and-a-half years, while the longest time required was more than five years, with the later units continually increasing their time under construction.[7]

Operational Service

The introduction of the Project 949 and 949A-class to the Soviet fleet was an important factor in the Soviet anti-carrier strategy, which was also affected by other matters such as anti-SLOC warfare and NATO ASW forces. Since the commissioning into the Soviet Navy of the first SSGs, 68 platforms were deployed in various oceans, equipped with a total of 442 missiles on board, proving a real menace to the carrier battlegroups. With the overall improvement of the Soviet Navy in the commissioning of the Oscar classes, 13 units were introduced, with 312 more missiles, representing 70 percent of the total previous SSM capability of the fleet.

This increasing threat to the Western carriers created great concern in NATO and the US Navy. The Soviet submarine fleet could now return to its original idea of attacking carrier battlegroups through a combined arms strategy, and also increase its capabilities in anti-SLOC warfare. The Oscars could be exclusively focused on anti-carrier warfare (ACW), while a great part of the rest of the SSG/ SSGN fleet, with lesser capacities, could look to attack merchant vessels.[9] If these units started a heavy campaign against NATO SLOCs, the merchantmen would have to be organised into convoys escorted by anti-submarine- and anti-air-warfare vessels, sailing on a more southerly route. The immediate effect of this reaction was

PROJECT ANDROMEDA

During the 1960s, Chelomey developed the idea of creating a strategic cruise-missile for the Soviet Navy, following a concept similar to the one developed by the US Navy, and most famous for the RGM/UGM-109 Tomahawk Land-Attack Missile (TLAM). Always keen to increase the punch packed by the Soviet Navy in a strategic role, Admiral Gorshkov became one of the most influential godfathers of this idea and applied all the necessary pressure within the corridors of power in Moscow – against the interests of the air- and strategic forces. This went so far that on 9 December 1976, the Council of Ministers issued a decree authorising the research and development of a cruise missile with a range of 5,000 kilometres (2,700nm), under the designation P-750 Meteorit.

The range was defined by the necessity for the submarine to be able to open fire as far away from enemy defences as possible. However, together with the requested cruise speed of the weapon – between March 2 and 3, at an altitude of 20,000m (65617ft) – it dictated its future, too. The weapon was to receive the Soviet version of the terrain contour matching (TERCOM) guidance: essentially, a radar coupled to a computer that compared the radar picture with a pre-recorded contour map of the terrain over which the missile was flying.

Eventually, the P-750 was developed in two variants. One was expected to be deployed by Tupolev Tu-95 strategic bombers. The other was planned for deployment from submarines. In this regard, Gorshkov wanted to have the weapon adapted to the Project 949A-class, using the control system for P-700 missiles. However, early testing of the P-750 proved this to be impossible: the sheer size of the new missile and its support equipment, demanded much more space inside the submarine. When asked to design something bigger than the Project 949, even the most enthusiastic and ambitious naval architects refused, because of immense costs this would require.

The alternative would have been to install the P-750 into one of the numerous Project 675-class vessels: however, closer studies showed that the weapon was much too big. On the other hand, the Strategic Arms Limitation Talks Agreement I, from 26 May 1972, froze the number of submarines equipped with strategic ballistic missile launchers in the Soviet Navy at 62. This resulted in the USSR finding itself in possession of surplus SSBNs, which, in turn offered enough space for the installation of the P-750. Therefore, the decision was taken to install the weapon on the Project 667A-class (ASCC/NATO codename 'Yankee I') submarine K-420. In November and December 1978, workers at the Severdvinsk shipyard removed the missile section from this boat and between June 1980 and October 1982, installed a new section comprising 12 launchers, installed in two rows of six and inclined at 45 degrees towards either side. Unsurprisingly, this construction resulted in the increase of the K-420's length from 132 to 150m, and the beam from 11.6 to 15 metres.

The modified boat carried out two series of sea trials: between November 1982 and August 1983, and in November 1983, and was certified for service – but without any missiles on board.

The development of the missile was lagging behind the plan. The technical design was completed by 1979 and the research and development proceeded with the construction of the first prototype. The first test-launch took place on 20 May 1980 but was unsuccessful: the missile exploded while still inside its launcher, destroying it partially. The next three tests ended in similar failures: all missiles detonated either inside their launcher, or shortly after exiting it. It was only the fifth firing that resulted in a flight of 50 kilometres before the missile malfunctioned and crashed. Following additional refinement, a new series of 30 flight tests were conducted between 1982 and 1987: a few P-750s were even test installed on the K-420 in 1984. However, the integration of the weapons system proved so troublesome that it was only in 1988 that the submarine conducted the first test firing while at sea. Considering the troublesome nature of the project, it is unsurprising that this ended unsuccessfully.

Project P-750 was cancelled in 1989, as a complete and costly failure.[8] The sole submarine modified to carry this weapon – K-420 – was then converted back to the SSN configuration and recommissioned with the Soviet Navy in December 1990. By then, it was considered obsolete and, thus decommissioned in 1994.

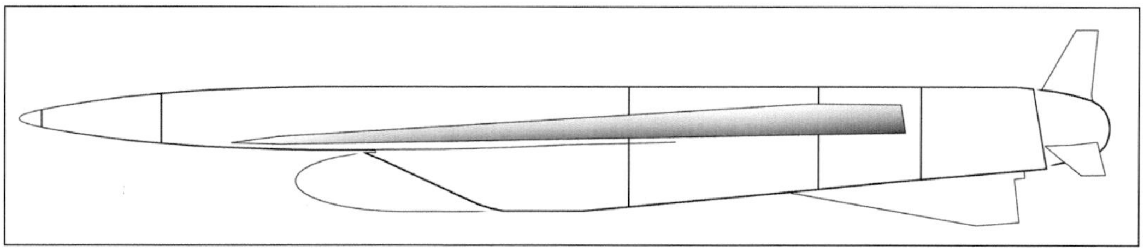

A line-drawing of the P-750 Meteorit (3M-25) – a giant and powerful cruise missile developed in the 1970s and up to 1980, with the aim of reaching targets as far as 5,000km away, at speeds between Mach 2 and Mach 3. Notably, the intake was covered by a cap that – along with the rear end with fins – was jettisoned as soon as the missile reached the surface. (Artwork by Tom Cooper)

a reduction in the number of units available to confront Soviet submarines in other areas, and an increase in the time required to supply material and consumables to Europe. Meanwhile, the Soviet ACW could continue.

At this stage, ACW was based on a combination of the SSGN Oscars available plus bombers from the naval aviation, such as the Tu-22M Backfire. Targeting information needed to come from satellite systems or a third platform that was able to send the information to a command post ashore that shared the information with the attacking platforms. In this way, they would be able to launch a coordinated attack that would overwhelm the air defence capacity of the CVBGs. According to some Soviet studies, if the situation required that only submarines execute the attack, then at least three to five SSGN Oscars would be needed to coordinate the attack and caused major destruction to the enemy formation.

P-700 Granit

Unlike any other SSGNs, the Project 949 and 949A-class were designed around the weapon that was fitted in their silos. In this particular case, the main reason for the vessel was the missile: a missile that brought together all the requirements of the Soviet Navy so that, finally, it would be able to effectively confront the menace of the CVBGs. The previous missiles commissioned for the Soviet fleet had performed far from satisfactorily; they were either long-range missiles that needed to be surface launched or could be launched submerged but had a short range. The Soviet Navy required a missile with both positive characteristics; a long range and the ability to be launched submerged.

The development of such a missile started in 1969 and was assigned to OKB-52 under Chief Designer V.P. Chelomey. The long range and submerged capacity of the new missiles had been achieved previously in other series, but there had been problems with the detection and tracking of the target.

The P-5s had worked with a third platform and retro feedback of the target from the launching platform, but Chelomey was looking for an innovative solution based on satellite systems that allowed the missiles to fly to the target autonomously. As the project expanded beyond the technical characteristics of the missile, Chelomey worked closely with academic M.V. Keldysh.[10] What both scientists developed were the technical requirements for a constellations of satellites, including their orbits, to provide the Soviet Navy with full coverage of areas where carrier battlegroups were expected to operate.

The satellites used were of two different types: RORSAT, which carried an oceanic radar to locate naval task forces in the open ocean, and EORSAT, which had equipment for electronic reconnaissance of large areas of ocean, looking for emissions from task forces. This network was able to send target information to stations ashore, the command post of the Navy or directly to the launching platform. The investment in this system was, understandably, huge, providing a good idea of the priority of ACW in the minds of Soviet defence chiefs.[11] Together with the investment in the Oscars and their missiles, they represented an important percentage of the total Soviet defence budget.

The P-700 Granit was also able to receive target data from other platforms, such as helicopters, airborne reconnaissance units and through the sonar system of the submarine. The P-700 was thus a multichannel receiver for targeting data. This idea came from the original concept of the missile as a standard SSM to be launched from submarines and surface units, but of course with the required displacement to allow the missiles to be fitted on board.[12]

The missile needed to be very fast, being expected to reach a minimum speed of Mach 1.5 in any scenario, including the sea-skimming phase, while the normal cruising speed was established at Mach 2.5. For this reason, the greater part of the launch weight of 7 tons was fuel. For the launch, the P-700 still had a strapped RATO booster, while for the cruise phase it had ramjet propulsion with an air intake in an annular arrangement, like older MiG fighter jets.

The missile used titanium alloys extensively in its structure. Not only did they provide armoured capacity against CIWS, increasing its survivability against enemy defences, but in the penetration phase against a target, the titanium alloy helped to cut through the ship's structure and thereby increase the damage caused.

More than a dozen different arrangements and designs were studied before a final design was officially presented to the Soviet Navy in 1970. One of the biggest improvements in these missiles was the electronics and associated systems. The P-700 was the first Soviet system equipped with a full digital system for targeting and navigation control. Three computers managed all these elements and were protected against interference and jamming from enemy targets. The digital computers were also programmed to help the missiles in selecting the targets and during the flight phase, minimising the risk of detection and countermeasures to the full salvo. To allow this, the missiles were programmed in a very innovative way. One missile would be selected as the leader and would climb above the rest of the salvo. It would intermittently use its active radar to locate the enemy formation and select targets, assigning a different target to each missile and avoiding the danger of multiple missiles attacking the same target. However, at least 50 percent of the salvo would be assigned to attack the main target, the carrier, inside the formation.[13] In the event that the lead missile was shot down, the following one in the hierarchy would climb and take its position. With this flight configuration, only one missile and one radar was at risk of being detected and attacked by enemy defences at one time, while a maximum of 23 other missiles flew below, with the parameters of the targets in their digital brains. Mid-course guidance updates were enabled due to the long range of the missiles.

The electronic head of the missile had three ways of locating the target. It could do so actively, based on a J-band radar for the flight phase, then there was another K-band radar for the terminal phase plus target allocation. These were combined with a passive receiver for detecting and tracking enemy emissions from long distance.

The warhead of the missile had a tactical nuclear option, of 200–350kT, and a conventional model, with 750kg of HE. Another warhead was developed for a land-attack missile, with hundreds of HE, incendiary and penetrating bomblets, the latter also useful against naval targets. There are unconfirmed reports about a fourth variant with a fuel-air warhead, exclusively developed to attack seagoing vessels, but no more information is available about such an option.

Flight Testing

Test flights of the missiles began in November 1975, under the direction of the OKB-52 design bureau and lasted until 1980. The fleet test programme started in December 1980 from the lead unit, K-525. This was not only centred on the submarines as the launching platform, for as already mentioned, the missiles would also be called on to equip surface units, creating a standardisation in the Soviet SSM arsenal, or at least trying to do so.[14] The four units of the impressive Kirov-class BCGN (Guided-Missile Battle Cruiser)

Table 16: 4M45/P-700 Granit Missile	
Warhead	Conventional: 750kg of HE Tactical Nuclear: 350kT
Propulsion	Booster with solid fuel for underwater launch from the silo, and KR-93 Turbojet cruise engine
Range (nm)	300
Speed (Mach)	2.5
Length (m)	10
Diameter (m)	0.85
Weight at launch (tons)	7
Guidance Systems	Inertial Navigation System with capability to receive corrections from external platforms, and terminal homing radar and IR seeker.

A view into two silos with P-700 Granit missiles, while undergoing maintenance. (Efim Sandler collection)

Another view of four of silos/launchers for P-700 Granit anti-ship missiles on a Project 949-class submarine, together with their individual covers and outer hatches (right side of the photograph). (US DoD)

A typical practice target used for testing P-700s and training crews of the Project 949 class. (Efim Sandler collection)

and the *Admiral Kuznetsov* CV were thus also fitted with the P-700, providing powerful anti-ship capabilities to these vessels.[15]

Eventually, in March 1983, by Ministerial Decree, the P-700 was commissioned with the Soviet Navy and entered service with the submarine units, followed sometime later by their commission with the surface units. The total production series of the P-700 was estimated at over 300 units. Taking into account that a total of 404 launchers were available in the Soviet fleet, this appears to be a rather low number. Yet it should be understood that in the middle of the production series of the missile, and the commissioning of the launching platforms, the USSR dissolved, with the subsequent economic chaos preventing the new Russian Federation from building more examples of this expensive and state-of-the-art missile.[16]

The P-700 was detected and catalogued by Western intelligence agencies during the Cold War, but the Soviets never displayed them in public parades or exhibitions, the same policy being maintained by the Russian Federation. The actual appearance of the missile remained a secret after the Cold War, with no pictures of it available. Indeed, until the tragedy of the Oscar II SSGN *Kursk* in 2000 and its salvage from the sea bottom, no pictures of these missiles had entered the public domain.

The Russian Federation has kept up maintenance programmes for the P-700 due to it being the only real means available to counterattack a CVBG. Although it is unknown how many missiles remain available, it was still in service with the Navy in the early 2020s, with training launches carried out from Oscar IIs in September 2021. The P-700 project is thus still alive and ready to serve the Russian Federation.[17]

Under the Soviet Navy, as many as 18 units were expected to be built, making a total of 20 units including the two Project 949-class boats. The Project 949M faced great internal resistance from the Navy due to their high cost. Each unit had an estimated cost of around $200 million, which represented 10 percent of the cost of a US nuclear carrier. The balance in this equation thus appeared to be positive from the Soviet side. The problem was that the full class of 20 units represented a huge part of the budget assigned to the whole new construction programme for the Russian Navy. Moreover, at the same time, construction of the fantastically expensive SSBNs of the Project 941-class were also underway in the Sevmash shipyard, creating a financial struggle for the whole Navy and a bottleneck in the shipbuilding industry, especially in submarine affairs. Others in the Soviet Navy, carrier advocates, pressed for a greater budget to be set aside for such ships, arguing that the costs of Project 949 were delaying the full Soviet carrier programme, despite the *Kuznetsov*, *Varyag* and *Ul'yanovsk* all being under construction at the time.[18]

Assessment

Submarines of what the ASCC/NATO codenamed the Oscar I and Oscar II classes, cannot be considered as 'just another Soviet SSGN', for despite their fantastic design and capabilities, there were major problems in getting them conceived and constructed – especially so during the final years of the USSR: the economic struggle the country was going through at the time was perfectly reflected not only in their emergence, but that of all of other contemporary Soviet submarine programs. Originally, the Project 949-class was constructed with the expectation of a service life similar to that of proceeding SSGN classes, with continuous patrols and deployments around the world's oceans. However, the time required to construct them, and then train their crews was so protracted that the USSR collapsed before they could actually enter operational service, and the funding necessary for them and their operations disappeared, almost overnight. Consequently, any examination of the Oscar class needs to be split between their operational life during the Soviet period until 1991, and that under the Russian Federation Navy flag thereafter.

Operational Deployment

The Oscar-class units were split between the Northern and Pacific Fleets for their main operational areas. Initially, the units would be charged with the task of ACW, while the other older SSGNs were assigned to supporting roles in ACW or to other missions. Only the huge expanses of the Atlantic and Pacific met the requirements that would allow the Oscars to reach their maximum military potential.

The third unit of the class, K-132, was the first unit transferred to the Pacific Fleet via the northern route, with 12 full days of navigation under the ice. In all, six units were transferred to the Pacific Fleet through this route, with the crews undergoing training during the voyage for attacks against aircraft carriers and methods to emerge through the ice, launching a torpedo against the ice and opening a hole if necessary.[19]

Project 949-class vessels made three combat patrols each between 1982 and 1986. After that they suffered decay between maintenance and modernisations, passing out of commission with the fleet in 1996 and 1998 respectively after they had only been commissioned with the Navy for 16 years. The decision was then made to invest resources in finishing the planned Project 949A-class and maintaining those already built.

Although the Project 949A-class units were less efficient, they still presented a good overall result in the circumstances. Prior to 1991, they made six combat patrols, with four in the Atlantic, one in the Mediterranean and another in the Pacific. After 1991, the class fulfilled 40 patrols for the Russian Federation until 2015, and there are some active units that made patrols as recently as 2021. The operational areas have been mainly in the Pacific Ocean, with more than 50 percent of the total patrols, with the rest largely in the Atlantic, along with some deployments in the Mediterranean and Caribbean.

This semi-elevated view of the K-150 *Tomsk* shows the wide beam of this class, the sail (with the bulge on the top under which the rescue capsule was located) and covers for the port battery of P-700 Granit launchers. (US Navy)

NEW OPPONENTS

By the time the Oscar-class submarines entered operational service, the threat from them and their predecessors had forced the US Navy to significantly improve the equipment of its CVBGs. Most important was the installation of an information exchange network, capable of connecting all the ships and AEW aircraft of the battle group in real time. By the 1980s, the centrepiece of the defence network were guided-missile cruisers of the Ticonderoga class, equipped with the Aegis air defence system, capable of detecting and tracking hundreds of contacts up to hundreds of miles away. Aegis-equipped cruisers could thus control the work of E-2C Hawkeyes and F-14 Tomcats, as well as coordinate the deployment of all anti-aircraft systems installed on surface vessels of the CVBG. This combination was necessary to combat the combined attacks of Soviet bombers and SSGNs and enabled the US Navy's aircraft to start engaging incoming threats at distances beyond 750km (405nm) – and thus outside the range of the best Soviet-made anti-ship missiles. Such a range was of particular importance because the Soviet Union was incapable of providing top cover for its missile-armed bombers, leaving them defenceless against Tomcats (bar self-defence through electronic countermeasures, of course). Unsurprisingly, this drove the GenStab and the Soviet Navy to the conclusion that the SSGN had become the best platform for anti-CVBG operations, while bombers assumed a supporting role to their operations.[21]

A Tu-95RT (background), trailed by an F-14A from the US Navy squadron VF-102 (usually embarked aboard the aircraft carrier USS *America*, CV-60, in the 1980s), seen during NATO exercise Ocean Safari, off the coast of Norway, in 1984. (US Navy)

The final picture is not too bad for the operational records of the class. If one unit without any recorded combat patrols, K-132, is removed, along with the ill-fated K-141 *Kursk* (which only made one patrol in the Mediterranean), the average combat patrols per unit is over five: a very good number in the records of the Soviet/Russian Federation Navy.

Inter-Arms Attack

The operational art of introducing the Project 949/949A-class was to the Soviet fleet was a return to the original roots of the Soviet ACW doctrine: the inter-arms attack. As the air defence systems of the CVBGs had been improving during the past decade, the Soviet Navy now estimated that the minimum salvo required to penetrate these defences and be able to neutralise the carrier at the centre of the formation would be around 70 missiles.[20] This corresponded to the number of missiles carried in three units of the Oscar class. Consequently, the Soviet Navy, due to the difficult operational situation in coordinating an attack from three Oscars – with only six present in each of the Atlantic and Pacific Fleets – returned to inter-arms attack tactics.

The Soviet Navy also increased the number and quality of bombers assigned to its squadrons, together with long-range reconnaissance units. The Tupolev Tu-22M supersonic bomber (ASCC/NATO codename 'Backfire') was the main weapon developed to attack enemy vessels, far away from Soviet coasts, as the SSGN fleet had been designed. The most desirable situation for attacking a CVBG was the conjunction of both weapons systems: the SSGN and the Tu-22M. Both platforms could share target information from the same early warning units, deployed close to the target formation. The main problem facing this operational solution was the difficult task of the correct timing of the attack for the different branches and the characteristics of each missile used. For this reason, the detection of the target – expected to be made by Tupolev Tu-95RT aircraft equipped with the MTsRS-1 Uspekh-1A maritime search and targeting radar system (ASCC/NATO codename 'Big Bulge'), would support all of the attacks, followed by the launching of missiles from bombers, submarines and, if available, surface units of the Soviet fleet. The attacking missiles needed to converge simultaneously over the target formation from different bearings in a bid to overwhelm the defensive system of the CVBG. This inter-arms operation of submarines and bombers created perfect conditions of forces brought together against a target, at least from the Soviet point of view, for resolving the operational problem of attacking a Western CVBG.

A view of the control centre of the K-150 *Tomsk*. (Efim Sandler collection)

Modernisation

As usual for major Soviet weapons projects, discerning their development over the year is difficult due to the lack of information, and because they are frequently surrounded by reports about stillborn upgrade projects. One of the most curious such cases was the idea to rebuild the Project 949/949A-submarines into SSBNs. During the 1980s, in reaction to the US President Ronald Reagan announcing his Strategic Defense Initiative (commonly known as 'Star Wars'), the USSR looked for the quickest and cheapest option to increase the number of intercontinental ballistic missiles deployed on its submarines. Combined with their massive dimensions, this led to the idea to reequip all Project 949/949A-class boats with 12 R-29RM missiles (ASCC/NATO codename 'SS-N-23 Skiff'). This project was discarded quite soon though.[22]

With the USSR dissolving only a few years after the class became operational, and the Russian Navy being severely underfunded, the question of their upgrades was merely an academic issue for at least a decade. One idea resulted in the Project 949AM, which focused on replacement of the huge P-700 missiles, and replacement of their launchers with smaller, yet more advanced weapons, such as the 3M54 Kalibr (ASCC/NATO codename 'SS-N-30A Sizzler') for land attack, and P-800 Oniks ('SS-N-26 Strobile') for anti-ship purposes. In 2020, an entirely new weapon – the hypersonic-capable 3M22 Zyrkon – was under development, too. Theoretically, the hull of every submarine of this design provided enough space to install 72 of them. However, due to the lack of funding, only one submarine – K-266 Orel – was ever modified to the Project 949AM standard. Therefore, the majority of the class is still serving armed with old P-700s, indicating that they are likely to be retired before long.

Accidents

For at least a decade, the formidable Project 949/9494A class vessels formed the backbone of the Soviet submarine fleet. They were the only ones still under construction when the USSR dissolved and remained impressive to the level where they continued providing the status of a 'naval power' to the Russian Federation. Generally, they proved much safer to operate than their predecessors of the first and second generation: accidents due to failures in design or lack of security were not common, although incidents caused by their operation did happen, as with any other navy in the world. The best-known case involved the K-141 *Kursk*, which had deep implications for the Russian Navy.

The K-456, while still named *Vilyuchinsk*, seen at a pier at the base with the same name: the boat was subsequently rechristened *Tver*. (Efim Sandler collection)

On 26 January 1998, the most modern unit of the Oscar class, the K-150 *Tomsk*, was at its base in Zapadnaya Litsa undergoing a hydraulic pressure test when one of its pipes exploded under pressure and leaked ammonia and nitrogen into a compartment. The accident was not immediately recognised by naval authorities due to the fact that the leak of gases led to the hospitalisation of only five crew members. Two days later, however, on the evening of the 28th, Captain 3rd Rank Sergey Solovjov died in hospital.

Another incident occurred the following year near the Strait of Gibraltar. On 2 September 1999, the Spanish trawler *Jose Maria Pastor* was carrying out its normal fishing operations when the crew noticed that the vessel started to move on its own: the vessel was towed in an aft direction for several minutes until a submarine – a big one, according to the trawler's crewmembers – surfaced and, after freeing itself from the Spanish vessel's nets, submerged and continued on its way. The identity of the submarine is not known for sure, but the only Russian Navy vessel in the area at the time was the K-141 *Kursk*, carrying out a combat patrol in the Mediterranean.

The *Kursk* Tragedy

The following year, 2000, the *Kursk* became known worldwide due to an accident that ended in tragedy.[23] During August of that year, the Russian Northern Fleet had scheduled one of its main exercises to be carried out in the Barents Sea: it included the Kirov-class nuclear cruiser *Pyotr Velikiy*, and simulated and live-firings of missiles and torpedoes. On 12 August, the *Kursk* conducted a simulated attack against the ASW units protecting *Pyotr Velikiy*, or at least this was what the sonar operators of the ships supposed. At 1132 hours Moscow time, seismograph stations in the United States, Norway and Russia detected a chain of explosions located in the exercise area, lasting for the next 13 minutes. Surprisingly, the sonar operators of the Russian Navy failed to detect these explosions – which is unbelievable due to their nearness to the suspected origin of them. That said, the exercise continued for the rest of the day, even though the *Kursk* failed to communicate with the fleet on schedule. It was only once the commander of the exercise identified this lack of communication that somebody realised that something had happened. When, at 1645 hours Moscow time, the submarine failed to report, the Northern Fleet finally started to act, believing an accident had happened, and at 1720 hours ordered its submarine salvage vessel, *Mikhail Rudnitsky*, to sea. The rest of the fleet concluded the exercise and then was ordered back to its bases.

One hour later, the Northern Fleet headquarters ordered the *Pyotr Velikiy* and the rescue submarine SB-323 to return to the exercise area and start a search operation for the *Kursk*. At 1852 hours, an Ilyushin Il-38 anti-submarine aircraft took off to support the search operation. Initially, no one on board the Kirov-class cruiser or in the fleet headquarters was worried that a serious accident or tragedy had occurred, preferring to believe they were dealing with a minor incident or a problem in the *Kursk*'s communication systems. The *Pyotr Velikiy* sailed slowly and carefully to avoid any possible collision with a surfacing submarine. Then the crew of the cruiser began throwing hand grenades into the water as an emergency communication method. By 2300 hours, the *Kursk* failed to respond and now the HQ Northern Fleet was finally concerned enough to consider a more serious accident and appropriate contingencies. It advised the naval hospital in Severomorsk to prepare to receive a crew suffering from shock and, probably, injured sailors. At 2330 hours, the duty officer in the Northern Fleet HQ officially declared the *Kursk* as missing and launched a full search and rescue operation, mobilising all the available resources of the fleet.[24]

With the submarine disappearing within a well-known and limited geographic area, the search operation progressed reasonably fast. On 13 August 2000, at 0400 hours, the sonar team of *Pyotr Velikiy* detected a huge structure at the bottom of the sea. The *Kursk* had been located.

With the events surrounding the disappearance of the *Kursk* gaining worldwide media attention, it was discovered that some of the survivors were isolated in the stricken vessel's last compartment and were safe. However, efforts by the Russian Navy to attach a submersible to the evacuation hatch and open it were unsuccessful. Norway and other Western nations offered immediate help, but initially were refused by the government in Moscow. Unfortunately, it was then found that all the crewmembers in the compartment had died from lack of oxygen.[25]

Salvage Operation

The Russian Federation eventually decided to try to re-float the sunken *Kursk*: it was down in shallow water, accessible to specialised companies – such as the Dutch Smits International and Mamoet, which were eventually selected for the task. On 7 October 2001, they successfully raised most of the vessel, and on 15 October, the *Kursk* was positioned in a floating dock at Roslyakovo. By this point in time, it became clear that the bow of the submarine – the part that suffered most of the damage – remained on the sea bottom, still in international waters. This was subsequently destroyed by explosives to prevent any intelligence operations by foreign powers.

On 26 July 2002, the official report from the investigators of the General Prosecutor of the Russian Federation was made public and determined that the submarine sank due to the explosion of one of its own torpedoes inside the fourth tube. According to the report, the sequence of events that led to the explosion was as follows. A Type 65-76A torpedo was prepared to be launched during the exercise. This type was powered by a Walter-type closed engine, which used a highly explosive mixture as fuel: 1,500kg of hydrogen peroxide, 200kg of kerosene, and air compressed at 14kg/cm^2. The benefit of such a system was high speed over a long range, but the main problem was that the torpedoes required a lot of maintenance and careful handling to avoid accidents. The personnel of the Navy were not happy to have such weapons on board due to these being extremely hazardous. The last time the crew of the *Kursk* had operated such torpedo was in 1998, and at least one of the rounds loaded as of 2000 was between six and seven years past its maintenance revision date. The lieutenant in charge of the weapons department had no practical experience with this kind of torpedo, and thus a Captain 3rd Rank was specifically assigned to the *Kursk* for this exercise, to support the crew with the necessary knowledge in this subject.

The investigation concluded that the torpedo exploded inside tube number four, with both the inner and outer doors closed. The explosion destroyed the inner doors and also caused the explosion of other torpedoes stowed in the torpedo room, causing major destruction, including of the watertight transverse bulkheads, killing all the crew except those located in the aft room. The reactor compartment was found to be safe, and no radioactive leaks or emergency were declared. From a general point of view, it is obvious that such a poor level of maintenance and readiness in the fleet were affected by a lack of funding and interest in these matters. In other words: the problem was not the submarine, its design or construction, but of more general and endemic nature, one impacting the entire Russian Navy.

The main question remaining surrounded the cause of the explosion. The principal theory is based on a leak of hydrogen peroxide from the torpedo that came into contact with non-ferrous materials and created an exothermic reaction, generating oxygen and water temperatures higher than 3,000°C inside the confinement of a torpedo tube, which further amplified the resulting detonation.

Table 17: Project 949/949A-Class as of 2022			
ID	**Name**	**Fleet**	**Status**
K-148	*Krasnodar*	North	Scrapped
K-173	*Krasnoyarsk*	Pacific	Scrapped
K-132	*Irkutsk*	Pacific	in reserve since 1997; modernisation to Project 949AM started in 2001; expected to be completed in 2024
K-119	*Voronezh*	North	overhauled 2006–2011; in reserve as of 2022; expected to be withdrawn pending commission of the Project 8851 submarine (eighth unit to be given the same name)
K-410	*Smolensk*	North	overhauled 2011–13; active
K-442	*Chelyabinsk*	Pacific	in reserve as of 2012; modernisation to Project 949AM started in 2014, expected to be completed after 2022
K-456	*Tver*	Pacific	overhauled 1996–2001; active (ex-*Vilyuchinsk*)
K-266	*Orel*	North	overhauled 2014–16; active (ex-*Severodvinsk*)
K-186	*Omsk*	Pacific	overhauled 2007–08; active
K-150	*Tomsk*	Pacific	overhauled 2013–14; active

Once the external hull had been breached, the reloads in the torpedo room began exploding, causing catastrophic damage: the crew never had a chance to save the boat. Indeed, the investigation discovered that most of the crew died while trying to reach emergency stations. Still, the radio mast was raised, indicating that there might have been an attempt to send an emergency signal. This led to the suggestion that the commander might have been informed that something was wrong with one of the torpedo tubes before the first explosion. On 28 February 2002, on direct order from the Ministry of Defence, all Type 65-76A torpedoes were retired from service.

With 118 officers and sailors on the *Kursk* dying in this tragedy, there was great criticism of how the government of President Vladimir Putin had reacted. Whatever the case, after the *Kursk* incident, the whole Russian Navy was completely refurbished, with many high-ranking officers dismissed or retired. The maintenance budget of the naval service was also increased, and more serious attention was paid by the government to the future of the Russian Navy. Historically, it can be seen that this was the moment that the Soviet Navy disappeared, and the Russian Federation Navy took over.

The *Belgorod* Affair

Work on the 12th unit of the class, known as the *Belgorod*, was stopped in 1997 due to a lack of funds to continue its construction when 75 percent complete. The vessel was mothballed and stored in the shipyard, awaiting future work. Rumours and comments abounded about the possibility of finishing the unit and including it in the Soviet fleet as an SSGN. In July 2002, the Minister of Defence of the Russian Federation, Sergey Ivanov, stated that various options were under consideration to finish the vessel. There was mention of an Indian purchase of the unit, or the possibility of modifying the ship to carry out other functions.

In 2012, it was confirmed that the *Belgorod* would be finished under another project and for a new project purpose. The Russian Federation had been developing a new strategic weapon, the Canyon/Status-6/Poseidon strategic nuclear torpedo. Much controversy surrounds this new kind of weapon, developed as an underwater autonomous torpedo, with nuclear propulsion and intercontinental range, able to detonate a strategic warhead underwater to destroy a port, naval base or section of coastline in enemy territory.

The Poseidon is supposed to be able to dive up to 1,000 metres and to have a warhead of around 100Mt. Its diameter is around 2 metres and length 24 metres. The *Belgorod*, as an Oscar II-class submarine, is a very big platform, one of the rare units able to accommodate such a huge weapon. The Project 09852 was completely different from the original Project 949A, but much about this submarine remains secret, with little information available in open sources.

A shipyard worker disassembling an Oscar-class submarine at the Zvezdochka shipyard in Severodvinsk. (USN/Todd P Ciczonowitz)

The *Belgorod* is the largest submarine in service, with a length estimated between 174 and 185 metres, according to various sources. It is also narrower than the original Oscar IIs. Its size means it will be able to carry six Poseidons on board, according to Western analysis. It will also be able to serve as mothership for the special operation submarine *Losharik*.

In 2021, the *Belgorod* was undergoing sea trials and it is expected to be delivered to the Russian Navy in the near future, but it is unknown exactly when it might receive the Poseidon

THE RUSSIAN NAVY'S SSGN CONCEPT

The Russian Navy received from the Soviet Union a vast submarine and surface fleet. Although the major part of the units were old and obsolete, some of them were modern and innovative, and of course the Russian Federation also inherited a huge and vast quantity of research and development programmes, either finished or in hand, that could open new concepts for naval operations.

The SSGN concept, per se, was a Soviet vision developed to confront a weapon that the Soviet Union was unable to face in any other way: the aircraft carriers. Unfortunately for the designers of the USSR, the state suddenly ran out of money and needed to reform all its naval and shipbuilding industry structure, along with that of associated businesses.

This led to a focus in the following projects on economic needs and considerations. The East now started to study and look into Western ways of managing naval fleets and the shipbuilding industry, in a bid to build cheaper vessels. In this sense, the SSGN platforms and their missiles were considered a luxury. Despite their technologic marvels, they were expensive and unable to be afforded by a new country that was trying to follow quasi-democratic ways of management with its naval forces.

The pure design of the SSGN was thus abandoned. The new lines of design, extending over many years, were focused on a multitask platform, able to deal simultaneously with land-attack and surface-attack roles. The Project 0885 Severodvinsk/Yasen is the ideological successor of the SSGN of the USSR. This new class is not strictly an SSGN; it is more versatile than a pure SSGN.

The main question with them was the attack system to be employed. The P-700 Granit is a massive missile specifically designed to destroy bigger vessels, such as aircraft carriers. Nowadays, the new missiles fitted on the Yasens are smaller and can be launched in higher numbers, looking to disable the carriers and their escorts rather than to physically destroy them.

The Oscars are still in service with the Russian Navy with the P-700, and while the budget can afford it, they will continue to operate. The new Yasens, based on the Western concept of the vertical launch system, will be the future shield against carriers, but will also have a myriad of other objectives. While the Russian Navy has thus gained in versatility, it has lost an important special capacity in ACW, abandoning the Soviet way of design.

torpedoes. This has been an unexpected and surprise finale for the Oscar II class, providing the Russian Navy with a completely new platform for developing new technologies and tactics.

Conclusions

The Project 949 and Project 949A–class submarines represented the zenith of the Soviet SSGN operational concept. They were developed around a missile designed only to reach and destroy the principal target in a CVBG, the aircraft carrier. In the Soviet-era project, money was, at least initially, not a problem, but the entire design was compromised to reach the objective with maximum efficiency. As such, both Oscar classes were excellent platforms, providing the Soviet Navy with the option of shadowing CVBGs and disabling their centrepieces at the onset of hostilities. Nevertheless, they proved excessively expensive to construct, maintain and operate – a true 'poisoned gift' for the Russian Navy: while excellent in their original function, their cost hampered numerous subsequent projects. Ultimately, together with bottlenecks in the shipbuilding industry, the heavy burden placed on their crew and the high cost of their operations, they proved unsustainable.

The K-150 *Tomsk*, a Project 949A-class SSGN, seen prior to its overhaul in 2018–19. (Author's collection)

The K-410 *Smolensk*, seen while preparing for a sortie. (Efim Sandler collection)

Resume

In peacetime, the best indicator of the effectiveness of a naval vessel is the number of combat patrols: it enables measurement of the ability of the unit – and the entire fleet – to be maintained in operational condition and deployed when and where necessary. When it comes to the Soviet fleet of SSGs and SSGNs, between 1962 and 1991, it is known to have put a total of 90 submarines equipped with guided missiles into service, which undertook a total of 450 combat patrols. This is likely to appear little, but it should be kept in mind that the Soviet Navy's SSGN fleet was officially established as a branch in 1966, and operated intensively until 1989, when budgets stopped further deployments. During this period, it undertook an average of 18.25 patrols per year. Obviously, this was still not an impressive number, even more so considering these operations were of only tactical importance: however, here it should be kept in mind that every patrol by a Soviet SSGN was a matter of concern for Western navies, and that the Soviet Navy's system prioritised the number of newly-constructed vessels based on their maintenance, and thus most newly-constructed submarines conducted a higher number of patrols early during their operational service, and ever fewer the older they would get. Indeed, by the mid-1980s, many of the older boats were effectively immobilised in their homebases or in shipyards, either for lack of maintenance, or the lack of funding necessary for their overhauls.

Out of these 490 patrols, most – 193, or 43 percent – were undertaken in the Atlantic Ocean; 121 (27 percent) in the Pacific Ocean, while another 101 (22 percent) took place in the Mediterranean Sea. The balance of patrols was conducted in the Indian Ocean, the Philippines Sea, the Caribbean and Baltic, though the presence of the Soviet SSGNs was traditionally lower in these areas.[26]

After 1990, due to the lack of funding and continuous internal crises, no submarines other than those of the Project 949/949A-class made any operational patrols: although proudly declaring itself a successor to the USSR, the Russian Federation was unable to afford maintaining a large fleet of nuclear submarines. Even once Moscow decided to continue with the construction of SSGNs, it did little else but adopt the Project 885/885M Yasen/Yasen-M-

A splendid study of a Project 949A-class submarine, showing details of the entire port side of this imposing design. (Efim Sandler collection)

A view from a helicopter of the US Navy of a Charlie II-class submarine underway at periscope depth in 1986. (US Navy)

class (ASCC/NATO codename 'Severodvinsk') – developed by the Malakhit bureau, created through the merger of the SKB-143 and TsKB-16 in 1977–1985. Construction of the first submarine, K-560 *Severodvinsk*, began on 21 December 1993, but financial problems delayed its completion and commissioning until 30 December 2013: that was a painfully slow, 20-year construction period. By then, two additional boats were under construction: K-561 *Kazan* and K-573 *Novosibirsk*. Both were commissioned only in 2021, though. The fourth vessel, K-571 *Krasonyarsk*, began its sea trials in June 2022. By then, five additional vessels were reported as under construction: however, considering the complete decay of the Russian Federation and its armed forces, and massive expenses of the aggression against Ukraine, launched in late February 2022, their future is presently under a huge question mark.

BIBLIOGRAPHY

Berg, John, *The Soviet Submarine Fleet: A photographic survey* (London: Jane's Publishing Company Limited, 1985)

Breemer, Jan, *Soviet Submarines. Design, Development and Tactics* (Surrey: Jane's Information Group Limited, 1989)

Central Intelligence Agency, *The Soviet Navy in the Cold War* (Florida: Red and Black Publishers, 2019)

Flynn, Ramsey, *Cry from the Deep* (New York: Harper Collins Publishers, 2004)

Gabler, Ulrich, *Submarine Design* (Bonn: Bernard & Graefe Verlag, 2000)

Garthoff, Raymond L., *Soviet Strategy in the Nuclear Age* (London: Atlantic Books, 1958)

Gorshkov, Sergei G., *The Sea Power of the State* (Malabar: Robert E. Krieguer Publishing Company Inc., 1983)

Hampshire, Edward, *Soviet Cruise Missile Submarines of the Cold War* (Oxford: Osprey Publishing, 2018)

Herrick, Robert Waring, *Soviet Naval Doctrine and Policy 1956–1986* (New York: The Edwin Mellen Press, 2003)

Herrick, Robert Waring, *Soviet Naval Theory and Policy* (Annapolis: Naval Institute Press, 1988)

Jordan, John, *Soviet Submarines: 1945 to the Present* (London: Arms & Armour Press, 1989)

MccGwire, Michael (ed.), *Soviet Naval Developments* (New York: Praeger Publishers, 1973)

Moore, John E., *The Soviet Navy Today* (New York: Stein and Day, 1976)

Morris, Eric, The *Russian Navy. Myth and Reality* (New York: Stein and Day, 1977)

Pavlov, A.S., *Warships of the USSR and Russia 1945–1995* (London: Chatham Publishing, 1997)

Podvig, Pavel (ed.), *Russian Strategic Nuclear Forces* (Cambridge: The MIT Press, 2001)

Polmar, Norman, *Soviet Naval Power: Challenge for the 1970s* (New York: Crane, Russak & Company, Inc., 1972)

Polmar, Norman, *Guide to the Soviet Navy, Fifth Edition* (Annapolis: Naval Institute Press, 1991)

Polmar, Norman & Moore, K.J., *Cold War Submarines: The Design and Construction of U.S. and Soviet Submarines* (Dulles: Brassey's International, 2004)

Polmar, Norman & Noot, Jurrien, *Submarines of the Russian and Soviet navies, 1718–1990* (Annapolis: Naval Institute Press, 1991)

Polmar, Norman & O'Connell, John, *Strike from the Sea* (Annapolis: Naval Institute Press, 2020)

Ranft, Bryan & Till, Geoffrey, *The Sea in Soviet Strategy* (Annapolis: Naval Institute Press, 1989)

Spassky, Nikolai (ed.), *Strategic Nuclear Forces: The XXI Century Encyclopedia of Russia's Arms and Technologies* (Moscow: Arms and Technologies, 2000)

Vilches, Alejandro, *Los SSGN de la URSS* (Seville: Punto Rojo Libros, 2012)(in Spanish).

Watson, Bruce W., *Red Navy at Sea: Soviet Naval Operations in the High Sea, 1956–1980* (Colorado: Westview Press, 1982)

Watson, Bruce W. & Susan, M., *The Soviet Navy: Strengths and Liabilities* (Colorado: Westview Press, 1986)

Wegener, Edward, *The Soviet Naval Offensive* (Annapolis: Naval Institute Press, 1975)

Winkler, David F., *Cold War at Sea* (Annapolis: Naval Institute Press, 2000)

Zaloga, Steven J., *The Kremlin's Nuclear Sword: The Rise and Fall of Russia's Strategic Nuclear Forces, 1945–2000* (Washington: Smithsonian Institution Press, 2002)

NOTES

Chapter 1

1 During exercise FallEx-60 in 1960, more than 200 nuclear attacks in less than 21 hours were simulated from aviation embarked on Western carriers, principally from the Norwegian Sea.

2 During the Potsdam Conference of Allied leaders in 1945, the USSR was assigned four completed Type XXI submarines (U-2529, U-3041, U-3035 and U-3515). Additionally, an undetermined number of completed assemblies and sub-assemblies, technical specifications, drawings and production equipment was captured and sent to the USSR, followed by several hundred German engineers and skilled workers. Overall, the Soviet Union thus acquired a total of 14 Type XXI units in different states of completion.

3 Established in 1948, the ASCC was a body including representatives from the USA, Australia, Canada, Great Britain and New Zealand, responsible for assigning codenames or reporting names to enemy weapons systems, the designations of which were unknown in the West. Over time, reporting names developed by it and several other bodies established by the North Atlantic Treaty Organisation (NATO) and its allies became known, erroneously, as 'NATO reporting names' or 'NATO codenames'. This is why throughout this book, codenames for Soviet submarines are given as 'ASCC/NATO codenames'.

4 V.N. Peregrudov was one of the most renowned submarine designers of the USSR. In this project he replaced Y.Y. Yergrafov and was relieved by Zosima D. Dyeribin when he was assigned to other projects.

Chapter 2

1 K-5, third unit of the Project 627/November class SSN, was partially built with all the blocks and elements from Project 627A.

2 During the war years, Chelomey, who was then a reputed mathematician and scientist, worked on the idea of pulse-jet engines, the same type that powered the German V1 missiles. He contacted Minister Malenkov, a close associate of Stalin and member of the State Defence Commission, to offer the possibility of building a Soviet version of the V1. Malenkov supported the young engineer and provided the resources of the Polikarpov design bureau, known as OKB-51, in 1944. The Soviet version,

codenamed 10X, was ready in 1945. The next cruise missile was the 10XN, which was to be installed in submarines; when the associated platform (Project 628) was cancelled, the missile entered service with the Soviet Air Force in 1953.

The last attempt of these years was the 15X with the Rolls-Royce Nene turbine, provided by the British Government for civilian use. This missile was to be carried inside a container on the deck or towed by the submarine. Due to political infighting and purges, one of the lasts decrees signed by Stalin, in December 1952, was for the removal of Chelomey and the assigning of OKB-51 to aircraft designer Artyem I. Mikoyan. Chelomey was assigned to the Bauman Institute of Moscow Technical University, where he continued working on cruise missiles. In 1954, he developed the idea of folding wings to fit the missile inside a container and improved the aerodynamics of the missile to allow the launch from directly inside the container; this was the 20X missile, which with time and improvements developed into the P-5.

With the support of the new Soviet leader, Khrushchev, in August 1955 a new design bureau, OKB-52, was assigned to Chelomey, with the main aim of developing submarine-launched cruise missiles. The same year saw the final competition between the P-5 and P-10, and the improvements applied by Chelomey made sure the P-5 missile was selected.

3 The shipyard at Gorkiy produced 113 units and at Nikolayev 72 units, while Baltic shipyards finished 19 and Komsomolsk delivered 11 units to the Soviet Navy.

4 As in other submarine accidents, inside the S-80 some crewmembers were able to survive the initial catastrophe. Some of them survived for six hours before dying due to the lack of oxygen. In another strange situation, the post-mortem analysis clearly showed that all the officers were away from the command post for a special meeting. This could be one of the reasons for the loss of the vessel.

5 The missile staff was estimated to comprise 15 members of the crew.

6 Where two different values are shown separated by a slash, the first represents that while the submarine is surfaced, the second when submerged.

Chapter 3

1 In the overhauls during its operational life, the third units equipped with these new cells were reequipped with lead-acid cells. It is commonly cited that another reason for abandoning these cells was that the supply of silver came from China, and after 1960 deteriorating relations between the countries meant this supply was cut.

2 There is controversy over information about a modification of the project called Project 651T that included the last six units built in the shipyard of Krasnoye Sormovo. According to this information, the submarines were modified to carry between four and six more 533mm torpedoes stored in the second compartment amongst the bunks of the crew and could be loaded into the forward torpedo room through four hatches installed in the bulkhead.

3 Regardless of this handicap, the Juliett was still more difficult to detect than the Echo I and II nuclear classes.

4 During the operational life of the Project 651 Julietts, the transfer and movement of units between fleets was very high; while new nuclear units were commissioned in the Northern and Pacific Fleets, the older and less capable Project 651s were sent to the peripheral fleets in the Baltic and Black Sea.

5 We must take into account that during these years it was very common in the Soviet naval industry that vessels were delivered to the Navy with many defects and unsound equipment in order to fill the assigned quotas, and in the followings months the vessels were finished under the command of the Navy.

6 In recent years, the Russian Federation has shown a different configuration for the installation of mini nuclear reactors below the Arctic to provide energy to various systems. The idea of mini nuclear reactors had its naval origin in the VAU-6.

7 This percentage is calculated from the division between the net days operational with the fleet (days from commission until retirement from the Navy, less the days expended in shipyards and for repairs and overhauls) and the total days from commission until retirement.

8 According to available information, only in 1967, 1977 and 1982 were there no Project 651 Julietts patrolling in the Mediterranean Sea.

Chapter 4

1 HEN is the acronym for the first three classes of Soviet nuclear submarines: Hotel SSBN, Echo SSGN and November SSN.

2 In 1969, Pustintsev was assigned to Project 675 submarines and Klimov was appointed the chief designer for the Echo Is, with two assistants, Margolyn and Stankievich.

3 The launchers were erected in pairs through a hydraulic system installed near to each launcher, with a power pack dedicated to each pair of launchers.

4 The Improved-Learning Coefficient, which involved improvements in the management and workforce in a shipyard in a series of vessels, provided a reduction of time between units of 23.5 percent to the second unit, 39 percent to the third one, 41 percent to the fourth and 56.2 percent to the fifth and last unit. The percentage always referred to the lead unit of the class.

5 During the test, K-45 launched a total of 13 missiles, with seven of them classified as unsatisfactory and having problems.

6 Twenty 533mm torpedoes plus six of 406mm.

7 K-122 never made an official strategic patrol as an SSGN.

8 During the repairs, shipyard workers found around 1,500kg of mud and other dirt inside the structure of the sonar dome. Nevertheless, during the exercise, K-122 conducted a successful simulated torpedo attack (with SAET-65s) against the cruiser *Varyag*.

9 According to some sources, another crewmember died of a heart attack after the accident.

10 There was damage to the sonar transducer, as well as structural damage in the bow area.

Chapter 5

1 It is curious to note that the new pair of missiles and the installation of anechoic protection on the external hull were approved at a later stage. During a revision of the project in June 1959, it was decided to install the anechoic protection plus a more modern sonar system, and in September 1960 it was decided to include the new missiles and associated equipment.

2 An endemic problem would be the glue used to fit these tiles to the steel hull. It was, and still is, very common that after some time sailing, this glue would lose its chemical properties and the tiles would start to fall from the hull, leaving surfaces bare and without this rubber coating.

3 The propulsion plant could reach a maximum of 29 knots. Unfortunately, this created problems in all the elements of the propulsion equipment and in the nuclear reactor.

4 Eight Project 658 Hotel SSBN units, 13 Project 627 November SSNs, five Project 659 Echo I SSGNs and 29 Project 675s.

5 The ability of a missile to reach its target far beyond the horizon line of its launching platform.
6 High Frequency/Direction Finder.
7 It should be remembered that in the 1950s and 1960s, GPS or GLONASS technology had not yet been developed. Determining the exact position of the submarine, the target or the reconnaissance aircraft was a very difficult task, with errors of several nautical miles common. Such errors later affected the precision of the missile attack.
8 The political position of Admiral Serguei G. Gorshkov within the Kremlin was very strong. He was the only commander-in-chief of any branch of the Soviet armed forces who maintained his position for many decades. His management of politics and of the Navy was always oriented to increase the budget and his own political power inside the Kremlin.
9 The shipyards involved were Severodinsk and SPR-10 (Polyarny) in the Northern Fleet area, and Bolshoy Kamen and Vilyuchinsk in the Pacific Fleet area.
10 Some modernisation projects could be much more expensive than the cost of the original platform. We must take into account that this class was of the first generation and probably was not worth the millions invested in it. However, these new missiles and submarines provided Gorshkov with a large number of new missile launchers for the strategy of the 'battle of the first salvo', where the survival of the launching platform was not a priority in the global strategy.
11 29 Brigade still exists in the Russian Federation Navy and continues operating some of the most secret submarine projects, such as *Losharik* or *Belgorod*. In recent years the Russian Government has invested more in these units and their operations, but information about them is scarce.
12 Decree from the Council of Ministers of the USSR No. 250-89 of 28 February 1963.
13 K-116 was the 12th unit built in Severodvinsk and initially assigned to the Northern Fleet, being transferred to the Pacific Fleet some months after its commission and serving with the Pacific Fleet during its whole operational life.
14 Northern shipyards had bigger and better resources of all kinds due to their involvement in strategic projects and those not directly related to submarines, having better know-how among their engineers, technicians and other workers.
15 The Mediterranean Eskadra comprised units mainly from the Black Sea Fleet and was composed at this time of 40 surface units and 10 conventional submarines. The supply vessels of the formation, from other fleets and not knowing the capacities of the nuclear submarines, offered to fill K-131's tanks with fresh water and fuel, two things that nuclear submarines did not usually need from external sources.
16 The Project 659/Echo I K-45 was also sent on this patrol to support North Vietnam.
17 USS *Tautog* communicated with the Pacific Fleet about the incident, believing that the Soviet submarine had been sunk due to the collision. *Tautog* reached Hawaii directly, avoiding other ports and vessels, immediately entering a covered dry dock and protecting the sail to avoid any witnesses seeing the damage. President Nixon was informed about the sinking of the vessel and decided to take no action in order to avoid a worsening in US–Soviet relations. After the fall of the USSR, it was realised that K-108 was not lost during the collision and fortunately all the crew members had survived.
18 None of the crewmembers was an official casualty, although eight of them were later sent to a specialist radiation hospital in the Leningrad area.
19 The meltdown of a fuel element inside a nuclear reactor makes impossible the procedure of removing from the core metallic elements or any adjacent elements. During the decommissioning process of this kind of reactor, all work must be specific due to any internal damage.
20 Captain Moskalenko was the commander of the second crew of K-184 and was in command during this exercise. Some Echo IIs had second crews, as with American submarines, but not all.
21 Some authors have labelled this unknown submarine as Chinese. This was because some years later, a press release was published in China with the obituaries of Chinese engineers who died during submarine trials, which has been linked with this accident. It is probable that the submarine was Chinese, but this has never been officially confirmed.
22 Two shipyards were selected, one on each main coast: Severodinsk for Northern Fleet units (K-1, K-22 and K-35) and Bolshoy Kamen for Pacific Fleet units (K-34 and K-10).
23 The first refuelling was done between 1974 and 1975.
24 Due to the accident taking place on a Saturday morning, fewer people than usual were in the shipyard and the number of personnel affected by the radiation was thus minimised. According to different sources, the number of people affected by radiation varied from 86 to 290, to more than 950.

Chapter 6

1 This error would continue in the Soviet submarines until at least the third generation, when top priority was finally given to noise emission due to the big improvements in Western digital technologies applied to sonar systems.
2 The LMC project was to equip a November-class SSN as a test bed, with the idea of fitting it on board a future attack submarine class with small displacement, which over the years evolved into the Project 705 Alfa/Lyra class. The installation of an LMC plant in the Project 661 Papa submarines would probably improve the performance of the platform, but knowing the problems that these plants created in the Project 705, the Papas would also have more problems and be more expensive than they were worth, creating a major headache for the naval industry.
3 Non-standard ways of thinking and new technologies developed in the Project 661 were used in future Soviet submarines. Such projects, not unique in Soviet industry and applied all over the country, were one of the main reasons for the final economic collapse of the USSR.
4 The P-70 had several different launchers, all of them designed by TsKB-34. The SM-101 launcher was for the floating test barge, the SM-107 for the test bed, the SM-97 for the Project 661 Papa and the SM-97A for the Project 670 Charlie I.
5 As a comparative example, the contemporaneous SSGN Project 675-class also had four torpedo tubes with 12 spare torpedoes on board, plus another two torpedo tubes in the stern. In this sense, the Project 661 had a limited capacity for conventional ASW.
6 Soviet society, in general, was enclosed inside a tight system that did not benefit from innovation, due mainly to all the procedures that came from the doctrine of the Communist Party. This was particularly so in the naval field and military systems in general. The Project 661's design philosophy was a disruptive way, supported by the government, to allow the engineers to proceed as they wanted. This, together with an unlimited budget, created the marvellous technology of the Project 661.

7 The MGK-300 was the later sonar system common to all Soviet Navy submarines, and the programme was not completely under the control of the Project 661 project.

8 It was not by chance that the main dates of projects were always in the month of December, as the Soviet system provided annual prizes for completed projects. It was common for industry managers to falsify information or say that projects were finished inside the year to receive their bonus. This also explains why vessels and submarines in the Soviet Union had long outfitting and testing times prior to being commissioned by the Navy.

9 Members of the State Commission included: President of the Commission, Admiral F.I. Maslov; Commander of the Submarine Brigade, Admiral V. Gorontsov; and Naval Architect of the Northern Fleet, Admiral N. Mormul. All ranks mentioned here are the highest ranks that they later reached in the Soviet Navy.

10 The Blue Ribbon was a prize granted to the quickest cruise vessel to cross the Atlantic. Nowadays the term is used for the most-speedy vessel.

11 Further damage detected after surfacing included to a fence on the wheelhouse, three hatches and the fairing of the emergency signal buoy.

12 According to some witnesses, it could compare with a commercial aircraft's aft area close to the engines (1960 commercial aircraft standards).

13 A third attempt was made in 1971, reaching 44.85 knots, but under poor conditions and not using 100 percent of the reactor. The Soviet Navy refused to accept this last test and the world record was maintained at 44.7 knots.

14 One item not so much noticed was the importance of the launchers. Another Soviet improvement in naval warfare, the launcher created optimum conditions for the missiles, including stowing, preservation, prelaunch conditions and allowing the launch of the missiles, avoiding the crew from having to carry out extra work on the missiles. The factory provided the Navy with a 'packet' ready to be used, which was a major improvement.

15 As will be seen later in this book, the Charlie I-class SSGN was also equipped with these missiles. The doctrine of use then was that they were necessary not only for the Project 661/Papa class, but for all the Soviet Navy.

16 Some warheads were built with other roles, including jamming and ARM. Apparently, this prototype was to study the capacity of the missile to act in conjunction with other missiles as a group. No sources confirm this warhead as becoming a production series.

17 Showing remarkable efficiency, the US Navy reacted to the high-speed Soviet submarine menace by developing new weapons, a solution exponentially cheaper than creating a submarine with the same capacities as that of the Soviets.

18 Admiral Gorshkov saw the high speed of the Project 661 as a strategic advantage for the Soviet submarine forces against Western units. For example, the Project 661 and the Project 705 Alfa/Lyra SSN, also equipped with a titanium hull and having a top speed over 40 knots, forced the US Navy to developed new torpedoes, such as the Mk48 ADCAP, and new tactics and operational procedures to deal with the menace of high-speed Soviet submarines. Gorshkov was also reasonable and preferred to derive the budget from other platforms, increasing their cost-effectiveness.

19 The controversy around this accident arose from the fact that the fleet did not declare any dead or injured. Nevertheless, a crewmember present during the accident, Nikolay Kaftaylovo, declared some years afterwards that at least four crew members died due to the high radiation doses to which they were exposed, hundreds of times the maximum permitted level. On 12 June 2000, Nikolay received, by Decree, the Valour Order in the category of a survivor of an accident on board. He suffered a cerebral tumour and epilepsy attacks from exposure to radiation. There are no records of this incident from shipyard personnel or staff.

Chapter 7

1 One of the most famous examples of the lack of availability of nuclear submarine forces was during the Cuban Missiles Crisis, when no nuclear units were available to send to Cuba, conventional submarines of the Foxtrot class having to support the Soviet forces instead. All the submarines sent were detected and tracked by the US Navy.

2 As mentioned before, the Soviet shipbuilding industry was under heavy pressure from the Navy and the Ministry of Defence to provide as many SSBNs as possible, together with SSNs and SSGNs. It should also be remembered that at this time the Soviet Navy also had a surface unit programme running. The civilian fleet was being reconstructed too, and although in other shipyards, this affected the supply chain of some key elements and the availability of skilled manpower.

3 Another important factor in this decision was the stress under which the Soviet nuclear industry was operating. Many reactors were requested by the Navy, the power industry and other sectors. This decision was an attempt to alleviate this stress. The first-generation plants were full of defects, caused by a lack of quality control and design, and the second generation needed time to improve the quality.

4 The mixture of materials in the hull created galvanic problems in the structure, leading the designers and builders to install specific zinc protection, in higher numbers compared to normal submarines, to avoid future problems with cracking in the hull. This was one of the main concerns of the crews and their officers, as under a combat situation the existence of a single crack could lead to a full collapse of the pressure hull.

5 Another feature minimising the detectability of the submarines was the low-magnetic steel used in the outer hull that created less of a magnetic anomaly, making it difficult to detect for the MADs embarked in Western maritime patrol aircraft such as the P-3 or S-3. The Project 670 Charlies also had their own degaussing plant on board.

6 The missile assigned was initially the SS-N-9 Siren, but due to delays in this missile project, the SS-N-7 Starbright was assigned to the Project 670 Charlie Is instead.

7 Another common option was to install a bigger single hydraulic system for when all of the systems of the vessel needed hydraulic power. A single problem in this system could create a critical situation for a warship. The Project 670-class submarines thus had three different hydraulic systems installed to provide power to missile covers, general services and to rudders.

8 In general, the automation of the vessel allowed a reduction in the crew to around 100 people and also improved the habitation quality for the crew, with one bunk per crew member.

9 As the Soviet government was not worried about the possibility of unemployment in one shipyard, this was not a leading factor in the decision, but the Ministry of Shipbuilding, with its own interests in mind, wanted the shipyard running on military projects and helped as much as possible to allow this conversion. The shipyard was ready to enter into the nuclear programme because the Project 683 was also assigned to the same plant.

10 Also considered for its construction were the Black Sea shipyards, but this idea was dismissed due to the political implications of crossing the Bosporus and the Montreux Convention that regulated the warships crossing the straits.

11 The lack of sufficient speed to abandon the launching area made the Charlie I missions practically suicidal, which went against the theory and doctrine of the Soviet armed forces.

12 Further awards were granted to other officers of the Soviet Navy for these voyages, of lesser degree but still important for the status of the Navy.

13 According to some reports, seven people were overexposed and treated in a special clinic.

14 The average time on the slipway of the class, excluding K-320, was 761 days; K-320 required 1,061 days, being commissioned as the eighth unit of the class while having been the seventh keel laid down.

15 Being a member of the Communist Party was important in the USSR, and in the case of the captain of a vessel it was compulsory be a member. Anyone losing membership of the Party would never again be allowed to hold a command appointment.

16 Some sources claim that the support vessel MPK-122 recovered the sailors from the sea, while others report that the sailors were alone on the surface and were forced to swim to the coast, where frontier guards found them and advised the Navy Headquarters of the situation.

17 One sailor died of a heart attack while inside the torpedo tube and the other due to being trapped by cables.

18 It is important to mention that this nuclear submarine leasing programme continues to this day. During the leasing period of the K-43, the Indian Government continued to ask for more submarines to be leased from the USSR. The political situation caused by the fall of the USSR halted these contracts. In 2012, the Indian Navy received the Akula SSN K-152 from the Russian Federation Navy, renamed as INS *Chakra II*, for a lease period of 10 years, with the option of another three, for US$1 billion. In 2019 the Indian government signed a new contract for another Akula SSN for 10 years, starting in 2025, for US$3 billion. The purpose of these contracts is to provide India with sufficient trained crews for its own nuclear submarine programme.

Chapter 8

1 With the historical rates of production at Gorkiy, it is clear that this shipyard would have been able to construct this class quicker, but they needed to hold off from some tasks until the following project, the Sierra SSN, was in its full production stage.

2 In other platforms, namely surface vessels of both large and small displacement, Chelomey was ordered to try to improve and modernise the SS-N-2c Styx missile, also from his design.

3 The more complex sea trials for a submarine-launched version created this delay in the initial operational capability.

4 An Il-4 aircraft was modified to check the correct running of this equipment, installing it on board and carrying out test flights to confirm the expected performance.

5 The ventral pod for the IR seeker was not included in this test due to it affecting the aerodynamic performance of the missiles, the designers preferring to test it as a 'naked' missile.

6 Submarines K-209 and K-508 were modernised with this sonar, and named Project 670M-1V, after 1978.

Chapter 9

1 P.P. Pustinsev died in 1977 and was replaced by I.L. Baranov. For the Navy, the main overseer of the project from the beginning was V.N. Ivanov.

2 It is interesting to note that in 1952, the output of the VM-A first generation reactors was 90MW, while by this stage more than double that output was obtained by a naval reactor. This is an indication of how much Soviet industry was improving.

3 NATO codename Shark Gill. This was a member of a wider family of sonars denominated the MGK-500 series Skat.

4 Between 10 and 12 units could be simultaneously tracked; this was the expected number of vessels in a CVBG. The information from this system was provided to the combat management system of the submarine, known as BIUS, and through this to the P-700 missile flight system.

5 The SSBN Project 941 Typhoon class, the world's biggest submarine to this day, was also constructed at the same time in the same shipyard. The resources invested in both programmes, together with the rest of the submarines in building halls and maintenance and repair programmes, were a massive burden on the budget of the Soviet Union. One can only suppose the incredible stress and pressure this placed on the yard personnel and staff.

6 Interestingly, the Project 949 Oscar Is were also fitted from the initial design with fixed pitch blades. In the following years, after being commissioned by the Soviet fleet, both units were retrofitted with the same kind of propellers as the Oscar II class.

7 After the fall of the Soviet Union, it was impossible to achieve a minimum pace in the construction rates of any class of submarine, or indeed for any military programme in the Russian Federation. It was even more so the case in bigger projects like this one.

8 The full programme of P-750 Meteorit-Ms included 50 launchings: this figure included the airborne variant, designated Kh-80 Meteorit-A.

9 In the 1980s, new studies led to the opinion that a conflict in Europe between NATO and the Warsaw Pact would last for weeks or months, and that resupply lines from the United States would again be necessary and essential for maintaining capacities at the front. For NATO, this implied a convoy system being established, deducting FFGs (Guided-Missile Frigates) and DDGs (Guided-Missile Destroyers) from other areas.

10 M.V. Keldysh (1911–1978) was one of the brightest Soviet scientists and was involved in the first artificial satellite programme (Sputnik) and nuclear developments in the USSR. He was also President of the Science Academy of the USSR.

11 This network was not exclusively used by the Oscar SSGNs. Other branches of the Soviet armed forces also benefited from this important operational information, such as the Soviet naval aviation's bombers.

12 Some sources, both Russian and Western, have mentioned the Victor III SSN as a platform that could have received the P-700. However, these sources were wrong, due to the large space required for these missiles to be fitted on board.

13 In the event that a target was sunk, and other missiles had been assigned to target it, the rest of these missiles had orders to try to locate and attack other untargeted vessels inside the formation.

14 The first stage of design was the submarine platforms, and after that they were adapted to surface units. As a curious detail, to avoid delays in adaptation to the surface vessels, the silos in these units needed to be flooded, as in the submarines, to allow a smooth launch. They thus avoided having to greatly modify the launching procedure.

15 The philosophy of designing a warship was, and is, very different between the USSR/Russia and Western countries. While aircraft carriers in Western countries are looked upon as a specialised

vessel for airborne operations, maximising the volume available for this purpose, in the Soviet Union carriers were seen as needing to be armed to attack other targets, sacrificing volume and space for this idea. The four units of the Kirov-class were fitted with 20 launchers each, while the carrier *Admiral Kuznetsov* was fitted with 12 launchers.

16 With the retirement from the fleet of older and uneconomic units, the original number of launchers finally decreased below the 300 units built.

17 The Russian Federation has always invested heavily in new missile development, but scarce financial resources have not allowed the fleet to introduce new missiles until now. The author suggests that in the decade following the publication of this work that the P-700 will be effectively removed from the inventory of the Russian Fleet.

18 The fight for a greater budget between the different branches of the Soviet armed forces was a longstanding situation, but the main problem in the last decade of the USSR was the financial struggle the country faced due to the Navy's many new and expensive programmes: the Typhoon and Delta IV SSBNs, Oscar I and II SSGNs, and Mike, Sierra and Akula SSNs. There were also the many surface units, such as the Kuznetsov-class CVs, Kirov BCGNs and various cruisers and destroyers. The total budget assigned to their construction, maintenance and modernisation was strongly attacked by other branches of the armed forces and politicians.

19 The majority of these voyages were carried out under the Russian Federation flag, but followed the original Soviet strategic deployment, which never changed in this sense.

20 It is important to differentiate between neutralising a carrier, which implies sufficient damage to its systems and structure to prevent it from continuing with air operations, and sinking a carrier. To sink a carrier was much more difficult to achieved, requiring many more missiles to be fired.

21 Tu-142 reconnaissance aircraft were also menaced by F-14 Tomcat fighters, further reducing their capacity to fulfil their mission.

22 This project made no sense because at this time the Soviet Union had two different classes of new SSBNs in production: the expensive but superlative Project 941 Typhoon and the more economic and versatile Project 667BDRM Delta IV. If this project had been approved, the Soviet Navy would have lost its best attack submarines and nowadays the Russian Navy probably would not have any Oscars operating with the fleet.

23 The accident involving the K-141 *Kursk* has attracted much speculation and many conspiracy theories. This author has studied and read practically all available theories, and his personal conclusion is that the official investigation carried out by Russian Federation authorities is correct. Nevertheless, 22 years later, much discussion and polemic still surround the incident. An extensive bibliography, including dozens of books, is available on the subject, but this author will try to summarise the incident, inviting the interested reader to check with other sources and reach their own conclusions.

24 The resources available, and the status of those resources, were in poor condition, due to the lack of funding for proper maintenance. This was one of the most embarrassing aspects of the *Kursk* disaster.

25 As mentioned earlier, a lot of detailed information is available about the *Kursk*, so only a brief description is offered here.

26 Not included in this number are nine operational patrols carried out by the Project 659-class ('Echo I') in the Pacific during 1962–1970, where they served as gap-fillers until enough SSBNs were available.

ABOUT THE AUTHOR

Alejandro A. Vilches Alarcón was born in Seville in 1980 and has a Naval Engineering degree in propulsion systems from the University of Cadiz. During the last 20 years he has worked in Spanish, French and UK shipyards, on both civilian and military projects. He has published articles in specialist magazines in Spain, France, the UK and US, and is the author of four books in the Spanish language about naval history, focused on Soviet submarines and Second World War naval operations. He currently works in Gibraltar's shipyards.